INTERNET OFFENSIVE

OFFENSIVE

YEARS OF SMEARS

GEOFFREY WHEEN

Wasteland Press
www.wastelandpress.net
Shelbyville, KY USA

Internet Offensive:
Years of Smears
by Geoffrey Wheen

First Printing – March 2011
ISBN: 978-1-60047-559-7

Printed in the U.S.A.

0   1

To Spent Forces

TABLE OF CONTENTS

INTRODUCTION

In the closing section of my first book, *Ill A Fraud*, is a fleeting and deliberately imprecise reference to how the internet can be used as a retaliatory and abusive weapon. Without saying so I had in mind a particular item about me which had come to my notice in 2010 thanks to a tip-off. Its malicious and vindictive purpose was obvious, and its source more than probable, since it was exactly the type of scurvy device which the U.K. Government [including its judiciary, which both like to pretend, mendaciously and fraudulently, is "Independent"] is in the habit of manufacturing. Its content concerned civil proceedings brought against me by the U.K.'s "New Labour" Government [a counterfeit label stuck on a dirty old box of tricks] in the name of its venerable Attorney-General, who at the time was the oft-lauded Lord Goldsmith, alias Mr. Flip-Flop of Iraq War fame, about whom more later. Clearly somebody thought that my case had some legal significance not only among the clique of busy deadbodies inhabiting the Inns of Court and taverns of Tabernacle Street [wherein can be found much the same bleating sheep] but also in the widest possible community beyond, which only the tentacles of the internet could reach. Either that, or it was just some low-level piece of offal who had nothing else to do with his or her time and public money.

Given that the case in question and its appearance on the internet spanned more than a decade you might think that it was about something of legal and social significance. It was, but not in the way The Establishment ever intended. Quite the opposite. Its intention – which just happened to coincide with dirty Labour's political agenda of handing ill-qualified women and minorities jobs at the expense of better-qualified applicants, who just happen to be men – was to make me, or anyone else who saw through and challenged this politically-inspired propagandist discrimination look stupid. Anyone who believes that this strategy was not politically inspired and activated should ask themselves whether it is and was consistent with other examples of social engineering foisted on the general populace against its will by the same gang of jerks who along their trodden path chucked in a couple of wars for good measure. Why have policies, practices and legislation promoting and encouraging a shattering and divisive influx of aliens if they can't get jobs? Answer – supply them, at the expense of the natives. Consider these damning findings from a review entitled "Immigration – Labour's enduring legacy to Britain" conducted by the think-tank Migrationwatch [1].

- Up to 5.5 million non-UK born people arrived in the country as long-term immigrants between 1997 and 2010 – equivalent to almost one a minute
- The scale of the movement [which is changing Britain fundamentally and irrevocably in ways the majority of the population didn't request nor want and were not consulted about – shades of the Iraq debacle] is the largest in the U.K. since the Saxon invasion over 1,000 years ago
- According to the chairman of Migrationwatch it isn't clear whether gross incompetence or politically motivated desire to change the whole nature of society is to blame. How about both, and much more besides?
- A former adviser to the three musketeers, Blair, Straw and Blunkett, claimed that the flood of migrants over the previous decade was due partly to a politically motivated attempt by ministers to radically change the

country and "rub the Right's nose in diversity".

The object may indeed have been as stated, but the effect was to rub the faces of many – Right, Left and Centre - in the dung-heap created by the Blairite brigade whose modus-operandi included threatening and intimidating those who, like me, took a stand against them and what they were up to. Having laid the country to rest and waste nowadays while his spouse has the gall and audacity to make shed-loads of loot advocating human rights the great ham actor Blair himself gallivants globally flogging his counterfeit charm and pretensions to literary talent. Fair enough, for morons and Appeal Court judges with political cronies and ideologies matching those of "New Labour's" old-hat, vote-bribing windbags. But 10 years later? A decade spreading the same tired shit on the internet? Could it be because I was still around, confounding their fondest desire – that critics of these rat-bags should be silenced by authoritarian muggers? Or, to use the terminology of the QC [which has a number of definitions] who acted for the Attorney-General, that the object of the exercise was to render me a "spent force", a disgusting, dismissive expression which [like his name, Jay] has stayed with me ever since, as it must have done with other victims of schadenfreuders.

No, to me the significance of these actions is not the doomed attempt to silence me, a lifetime loather and latter-day denigrator of the British Establishment, hypocritical and corrupt political and judicial systems included, but the fact that these events took place at all. What are they intended to achieve in the public interest, directed as they are against an old man in the twilight of his life? What else do they prove, other than what I've been saying about this dross is spot-on? How appropriate that Lord Goldsmith should be the political appointee charged with squashing the little men – the pests who count for nought in his circles, wherein reside other Lords of The Realm, Rings and Flies. Who knows, maybe my contemporaries, the "spent armed forces" in Iraq will live to see the day when Blair, Goldsmith and their co-conspirators get their come-uppance and become forces even more shot than their reputations and integrity.

In the meantime, whatever these squirts were up to and why in The Hole I had better things to do with my life, culminating in the publication of my second book, *Mortar Boarding*. But I kept tabs on the internet slur, which by now was infiltrating entries about my books. The impetus to turn it to my advantage came when I hit on the idea of writing another book about morality, which according to senior judges – of all people – was indistinguishable from the law. Such nauseating cant and hypocrisy could hardly go unanswered. Here was an opportunity to put my side of the case, and what British justice meant in practice, "miscarriages" and all. So along with other material, more well-earned and deserved swipes at the pathetic English judiciary and feminists/feminism and my response to the original judgment and Court of Appeal Order, I inserted these pearls of judicial wisdom and independence into my third book *Moral Beaks and Claws*. There the matter might have ended, as it should have done. But never under- estimate the petty-minded, malicious eagerness of half-wits to spend other people's money on pointless causes. After all, isn't that a fair summary of the Iraq War debacle? In my case the weapon of choice was the internet, which increasing numbers of Institutions and individuals have come to realize is both a blessing and a curse, a vehicle for creating and organizing revolutionary forces. And for vindictive crackpots and dunderheads to vent their spleen and spray their waste-products far and wide. And they're just the good guys.

Accounts of my often-bewildering and inexplicable experiences with various Universities with which I tried to enroll for a PhD in Criminology, are contained in my book *Mortar Boarding* [2].   Latterly other peculiar events had occurred. Classic symptoms of phone-tapping and computer-hacking, about which U.K. Government agencies produced strange or no answers. References to documents which meant nothing to me, followed by referrals to the U.K. Information Commissioner, whose ability to string out the simplest problems was formidable even by the standards of the foremost exponents of the art – lawyers. All of which amounted to stone-walling and if not conspiracy, its bed-mate, collusion. For some reason it took me longer than it should have done to join the dots, to discern the pattern on the paper. In retrospect I could have saved myself a heap of work and thought about just what was going on. How easy to say with hindsight. Blindingly obvious even, provided one knew about the internet smear, about which I was sublimely oblivious for a decade or so, and then only when I was tipped off. Word would have gone round these Universities and other bodies like wildfire, as bad news always does. Hence the lies, deception and covers-up. Just as was always intended by dint of the smear, the pre-arranged justifications for it and the eternal insertion on the internet. All to achieve one objective – the creation of a "spent force", to use the eloquent and equally crude expression of the hatchet-man employed by the U.K. Government to serve up porridge and mush, and a generous helping of tripe, before and at my appeal hearing.

But another, seemingly bizarre, possibility existed. That my e-mail correspondence had been intercepted, legally or illegally. [Incidentally, not only did my contact inside the U.K. Attorney-General's office, of all places, not understand the law about this and other issues he resorted to threats to shut me up. Which, of course, increased my suspicions about the role of the U.K. Government in the 10 year-old smear campaign. More about this later]. Meanwhile other incidents pointed in the same direction. In brief [since they have already been covered in my previous books] they included my submitting an article to the Editor of "The Sunday Times", John Witherow, complaining about actions and inactions by the U.K. Government involving my own case and discrimination in the job market favouring women and minorities. Shortly afterwards the Government just happened to get off its arse and take legal action against me. So either the two events were pure coincidence or they weren't. Who had a vested interest in shutting me up? Feminists inside the newspaper, who only needed to "leak" my article to those of like [or no] mind inside feminism-addicted Government circles? The same lot who might just have come by the information and my article by unorthodox means, like communication interception?

Another mystery-cum-coincidence. The theft of the RAM [containing confidential information about my research work and book contents] from my computer while it was in transit between New Zealand and Thailand, which the thief had had the time, opportunity and desire to cover-up, actions wholly inconsistent with those of a random. petty thief. Then a strange reference to me and bemusing litigation in documents obtained from the Ministry of Justice, and again [in documents received from the Information Commissioner], an entirely unfounded allegation and veiled threat about me made by another employee of the U.K. Government. The second two stemmed from the same Employment Appeal Tribunal case published on the internet. Increasingly the smell of rotten eggs and dregs was beginning to permeate my environment.

Talking of which, knowing something about the leaders and methods of the previous discredited, disreputable and tarnished "New Labour" Government if it were still in power I might well have concluded that these events were just business as usual for that crowd of clodhopping clowns, and taken a different tack. But it wasn't, thank goodness. Fresh management was running the store, which could hardly be blamed for what the egregious Blair, Brown and assorted wreckers had succeeded in achieving. And at least the LibDem element had opposed the vile and monstrous Iraq invasion, so its hands were comparatively clean. On balance it should be worth trying to find out what was going on. The outcome was more surprising and alarming than ever. But after all's said and done, a Hole is still a Hole. So what else can anyone expect from an empty shell?

CHAPTER ONE

Legal Treacle

We're told that England is now a classless society. That's for sure, in the sense that whatever class it once possessed has long gone. But no, its class divisions are as strong and protected as ever, and, barring the solutions adopted by the Sans-Culottes and Bolsheviks always will be, since the existing state of affairs – the status quo, or status quo vadis – suits the privileged minority very nicely, thank you very much. Who, after all, doesn't prefer to be wringing the neck of the chicken rather than ringing the changes? So to preserve their relative superiority it's in the interests of the oppressors to con the victims into believing us and them are now we. Thus "we're all in it together" deludes "The Sun" bather/stroker into believing his worth is as great as that of the Old-Etonian, toffee-nosed, upper-class twit who exhorts the put-upon to work, toil, labour [but never New Labour] while he "works" in the more refined, leisurely way to which he has become accustomed and earned by dint of his birthright. Not that Dave is the only, or indeed the best, example of the snob-ridden, elitist tier which takes care of itself and the decaying, decrepit institutions it created and doggedly upholds come what may. I could be talking about the clowns in Westminster, but for once I'm not. No finer example of the classless society in practice and operation exists than in the renowned English judiciary. If in doubt, take a look at the potted biographies of the Lords on High published on the internet. As might be expected they share a few common advantages over the rest of humanity arising from their positions of privilege in classless England, such as Oxbridge educations, knighthoods and/or peerages and fancy archaic titles designed to impress the masses. Among their notable number and accomplishments I detected the following:-

- The Right Honourable Sir Nicholas Wall, President of the Family Division, Head of the Family Justice system. Previously a judge in the Employment Appeal Tribunal until 2003 [about which more later]. In his spare time – of which he must enjoy more than his fair share – he attends the opera [for which a ticket for someone of his status, if he needs one, runs to roughly the equivalent of a season ticket to watch The Reds at Old Trafford] and composes clerihews, which until I consulted the dictionary I was under the impression was an anal infection. Now I know better. Apparently its inventor, the English scribe Edmund Clerihew Bentley, penned short comic or nonsensical rhyming verses ridiculing famous people. How very apt for a senior judge and prominent member of The English Establishment to engage in such activity. And what a rich vein of talent to mine and mimic. At whom could his jibes be directed? Surely not his pitcher-colleagues warming up in the Bull Pen, ever ready, able and willing to deliver another curve-ball travesty of justice? Impossible, as is the very idea that a judge of all people could and would have a sense of humour. Such rumours of humour, which have been circulating on the internet, obviously to bring the law into disrepute, must be scotched-and-iced immediately

- Lady Justice Arden, Head of International Judicial Relations, who has travelled extensively to help promote the rule of law. [Instead of lecturing to others maybe her time and our money would have been better spent sorting out the shit in her own back-yard]. Still, she did play her part in producing "the longest statute ever passed by the British Parliament". Is that something to brag about, any more than having the world's largest tape-worm dining off your guts?

- Lord Justice Goldring, Senior Presiding Judge, who "oversees the work of the Presiding Judges in each circuit in England and Wales". Forgive my ignorance, but whenever I've had the temerity to record a complaint about English judges two things have always happened. Firstly I'm told there's nothing to complain about [presumably because judges can do no wrong, even when they supervise, overrule and participate in trials constituting rank perversions of justice] and secondly they are "independent", which in my book equates to being autonomous. So if they are truly independent – which they are patently not – how can their work be overseen by another judge or anybody else on a daily basis? And if Lord Justice Goldring is sitting back and letting them loose to do their worst – at which they are very good – why does he and his job exist at public expense? The rest of this book provides numerous concrete examples of how the shabby English judicial system operates in practice.

- On a lighter note, purely coincidental though it may be – as are so many other events in English history – if ever an individual were destined for the apex of the judicial triangle it must have been the current Lord Chief Justice of England and Wales, otherwise known as The Right Honourable Lord Judge and/or Baron Judge of Draycote in the County of Warwickshire. [26]. No problem when one of his lackeys rings the maitre d' of a chic Soho restaurant to reserve the best table for his Lordship and his party of twenty – on the taxpayer, naturally.

Listed below are what seem to be the principal characteristics enjoyed by lawyers, judges and the quixotic system they uphold. In each case I illustrate my contentions with excerpts from the book *Plausible Denial* [1], whose author, the prominent lawyer Mark Lane, had earlier virtually single-handedly dismantled and discredited the notorious Warren Commission's report-cum-whitewash on the assassination of the U.S. President John Fitzgerald Kennedy. Incomprehensible as it seems now, we need reminding that at the time Earl Warren held the highest judicial office in America, so might be expected to possess and abide by the highest possible standards of legal knowledge, principles, morality and integrity. Anything less, on any score, was unacceptable, given the prevailing circumstances.

Although the chosen extracts necessarily relate to the U.S. system of justice and its participants they apply equally well, if not more so, to their counterparts in the U.K. and other countries which subscribe to the ludicrous, corrupt and fraudulent mantra The Rule of Law, otherwise known as Rule by Lawyers for Lawyers. Just how alike in blinkered thought and ruthless deed are these masters of our destinies can be judged from the following gems:-

"He explained that his friend Earl Warren had a greater responsibility than we would ever know or begin to appreciate. And that the reputation, *even the life of one man* was of little consequence when compared to the enormous stakes that were involved" [page 52]. [My italics]. Need I add, the "one man" sacrificial pig was Lee Harvey Oswald, who according to the Warren Commission was the lone assassin, both of which contentions seem increasingly unlikely. True to form, following the lead of such luminaries as Stalin and Hitler the criminal organization masquerading as the assessor of virtue, the saintly, sanctimonious CIA tried to counter mounting public skepticism by urging fellow-propagandists to stress that the members of the Warren Commission were chosen for "their integrity, experience and prominence". The CIA then suggested that efforts to impugn the rectitude and wisdom of those members cast doubt on the leadership of American society [page 72]. Simultaneously in their eyes no doubt the reverse would apply when it came to their dishing the dirt about foreign regimes such as in Libya [24]. But to their credit they were spot on about any hierarchy. Once you realize that some judges are as rotten and corrupt as the people they condemn you're entitled to ask who appointed them and why.

With the benefit of hindsight, it does seem anachronistic that the CIA of all bodies could be portrayed as an upholder of American values and justice. You might just as well assert that the Cosa Nostra is actually a benevolent society run by nuns. Maybe the lawyer, Mr. Snyder, was yet another fantasist who knew nothing of its activities, even though Kennedy himself swore to smash it into a thousand pieces after the Bay of Pigs debacle. Thanks to Mark Lane's authorship, what else is or was known about an organization which would never stoop so low as to cover up the facts? [Before I go any further, the thrust of his book is that far from being a goody-two-shoes outfit the CIA was heavily implicated in, if not responsible for, Kennedy's death]. For a start, the CIA fingered Oswald as an individual who'd been photographed visiting a "suspect" embassy [firstly Cuban, then Soviet] in Mexico City. Warren swallowed the story. Later the FBI confirmed it wasn't Oswald [pages 61, 62 and 64]. Its first report also said the CIA's director, deputy director for plans and boss for the western hemisphere had conspired to lie to the Commission about Oswald's supposed presence at the Soviet Embassy [page 63]. Small beer, you might think, in an organization rewarding slimy liars for counterfeit information [24] and employing persuasive techniques like torture, water boarding, false imprisonment, deceit, perjury, crude violence and other forms of "hostile interrogation" [pages 313-5]. Not that standards were allowed to slip. Like its British counterparts entrance to the CIA was restricted to those of impeccable breeding, background and education, as befits a "fraternity or secret society" [page 218].

So how is it possible for transparently superior, upper-crust English and American aristocrats to be hoodwinked by social and intellectual pipsqueaks, let alone an artisan who had suffered the same indignity at the hands of the Austrian corporal Hitler? Here I turn for ideas to another reliable and invaluable source [2]. Well, for a start it does help if one of your negotiating adversaries is pissed if not the entire time, at least most of it. In the words of one observer "Everyone knew that Churchill started every morning by drinking a big portion of whisky....It wasn't a secret to anyone that he had a weakness for drinking" [page 180]. Personally speaking, as one who has been known to engage in the odd bender or hundred, the very idea of reaching for the bottle at breakfast and then continuously until the following morning makes me wretch, so Churchill's habitual and compulsive "weakness" for booze was not only akin to that of a drug-addict he was no more fit – mentally or physically - for purpose than the sad souls roaming public parks swigging Benzedrine and cadging hand-outs from passing pedestrians "for a coffee, guv". Or as Churchill's companion-at-arms, Roosevelt, put it more politely on hearing that the cigar-chomping alcoholic had become Prime Minister "Churchill was the best man that England had, even if he was drunk half of the time" [page 104]. Coming from the mouth of a man who scarcely knew Churchill personally at the time that was probably an understatement, unless he meant that the P.M. was sleeping it off the other half of the day, so wasn't actually bending his elbow. If so, even that excuse won't wash, since alcoholics remain inebriated day and night, 24/7.

Invariably they are also fantasists who genuinely believe they don't have a problem or weakness, and just to prove the point act as no rational person does. For instance, during one visit to see Stalin Churchill's behavior was recorded as "eccentric" and "childish" [page 161]. But Churchill was superman, so defied reality. His reality was the bottle, the controller of his thoughts and actions. In short, Churchill was incapable of, and wholly unsuited to, conducting any negotiations or making any decisions, never mind momentous ones. Undoubtedly his enemies knew that, so why not his allies, assuming he had any?

If, as popular myth requires us to do, we believe that Roosevelt and Churchill were arm-in-arm the facts prove otherwise. Churchill, senses and common-sense permanently afflicted by the demon drink, may well have believed that the Yank would not yank him around and play footsie with the Georgian ruffian. After all, Churchill, the aristocrat born and bred in palatial surroundings had much in common with Roosevelt, the suave, sleek and moneyed sophisticate, whereas Stalin was but an uncouth interloper, wholly out of his class in their company. Their gifts, talents, worldly experience and political nous would surely outgun and outmaneuver his every time. Except and except.

The first negative factor in the equation - Churchill's chronic dipsomania - has already been addressed. The second was just as obvious and alarming. Roosevelt had been an ailing cripple since childhood, but now the Grim Reaper was knocking, loudly and incessantly, on his door. Like Churchill, but for entirely different reasons, he was in no fit state to get out of bed, never mind conduct tough negotiations with even a passably competent operator. Which Stalin, warts and all, was certainly not. In fact, among those who saw him in action he appeared to be the opposite. Hardly surprising, given the company he kept and eliminated. Put together, they were no match for the wily, cunning and canny old fox Stalin.

As if their physical and mental frailties – who still believes that alcoholism is simply a physical disease? - were not enough, both Western leaders suffered from another common handicap. Each possessed, and were cursed with, overpowering, overweening and often insufferable egotism [page 105], as befitted their snob-ridden, privileged upbringing, station and destiny in life. Why else would Churchill, a political has-been who never was, persist when other pensioners would have been content to prune their rose-bushes? He embodied the English class system – the born to lead system – imbued in childhood, where attending Harrow and Oxford, Eton and Cambridge, was not just expected it was conventional, almost a right and route to rule [page 187]. [Anybody who swallows the guff about Britain being a "classless" society should ask themselves a couple of questions. Firstly, which schools did the present leaders of the two major political parties attend? Secondly, in what way do they represent the interests or aspirations of the people they purport to act for, otherwise known as nobodies?].

So the delusions – alcohol and gritty optimism fuelled - continued. Neither Churchill nor Roosevelt lost any opportunity to reassure themselves that they would prevail, as they had in the "moral" cause and fight against the vile and evil Nazi regime. While Roosevelt convinced himself that he could "handle" anyone, Stalin included, the English, Churchillian strategy of belittling and denigrating Uncle Joe – surely he knew what was going on? – held sway, compatible with homegrown snobbery, innate superiority and intrinsic racism, about which Stalin was hardly inviolable. Thus various crude and abusive epithets were trotted out, such as an observation by some colonel named Jacob that "It was extraordinary to see this *little peasant* [my italics], who would not have looked at all out of place in a country lane with a pickaxe over his shoulder, calmly sitting down to a banquet in these magnificent halls" [page 158].

There are several things to say about the comments of this unutterably stupid snob. The implication that Stalin, or as he preferred to call him, the "little peasant" somehow did not belong, and had no right to be, in surroundings worthy only of, say, English royalty. And him, or is it Him? of course. And where was the place in question? Why, in Moscow, which when I last checked, was in a country apparently run and ruled exclusively by serfs. And the banquet was not only being paid for by the peasantry it was being held in honour of the classy piss-artist himself, permitting him to while away the night spending other people's money. Would the great man and his minions object if Uncle Joe [otherwise known as the leader of the country] slipped in with his hammer and sickle for a tipple or two? Let's ask the masters of the universe what they think. As if anybody cares. Others opined that Stalin was "not quite a gentleman" [page 158], that unlike Churchill the Soviet people were "straight from the plough or the lathe. They were rough and inexperienced" [page 159], that Stalin himself was "a peasant who didn't know any better" [page 160] and that his occasional breaches of good taste were occasioned by his "bad manners and lack of 'class'" [page 233].

After Stalin inevitably got up his nose – down which he was accustomed to view the hoi-polloi - another ultra-snob, Churchill's Foreign Secretary and effeminate lackey Anthony Eden – another deadbeat loser responsible for the Suez debacle - displayed his brand of insufferable English hauteur. Stalin's boorish, peasant origins were apparent during "diplomatic" talks, justifying feelings of superiority on the part of his English detractors [page 121]. What he may not have realized, if he cared, which I rather doubt, is that these creeps feel the same way about everybody but them, and more to the point are more often wrong than right, just as they were in concluding that Stalin was a mere puppet, being controlled and manipulated by other unseen hands [page 352].

Nevertheless, the English always knew and know how to behave. In keeping with the ceremonial banquet to be held in his honour the sot proposed to turn up, if he could stand up, attired in an outfit which one observer described as "like a mechanic's overalls or more still like a child's rompers or crawlers". Come to think of it isn't such gear – apparently designed by Churchill to wear during air raids - entirely suitable for someone who's childish and liable to shit himself any second? [page 158]

Meanwhile during the tripartite talks Stalin looked and listened, knowing all too well that tactically the wisest strategy was to encourage the piss-artist and the near-dead to underestimate him. Far better to bear the incoherent, philosophical ramblings of the sot and the matey "handling" from the withered vine than to offer anything worth having in return. Promote their pre-conceptions. Act dumb, just as peasants are. It's hard to imagine that Stalin of all people didn't know what insufferable snobs Churchill and his ilk were and are. Why else would they have sent, in a British mission to Moscow, ostensibly to discuss an alliance with the Soviets, an upper-class receptacle with no political weight but the spectacularly extensive and absurd handle Admiral the Honourable Sir Reginald Aylmer Ranfurly Plunkett-Ernle-Erle-Drax? [page 14].

Even less endearing than the snobbery were the ingratitude and treachery – which both the Soviets and Poles suffered in full measure at the hands of the British – and the moral outrages. Not surprisingly considering its nature in Laurence Rees' book [2] appear about ten references to morality in its various guises. Strange that the eternally hypocritical and superior should be so affronted by the behavior of "peasants" who did far more, suffered and endured far more to achieve victory than any other nation. What else can you expect when a country and its population have been raped , pillaged and plundered by a bunch of barbarians led by a satanic lunatic who's out to conquer the world? Did the moralizers in England and America suffer the same fate? Yet the same bunch didn't hesitate to make and drop The Bomb on Japan. Was this morality or retaliation in action?

"It is difficult, even in retrospect, to know which is more pathetic; his [meaning Warren's]* belief that the American people could not be trusted with the truth or his reliance for the truth upon the CIA. Even if everything Warren had been told by the CIA was true, his response, endorsed by President Johnson………….was unsupportable in a democratic society. Warren's primary sin, however, was not venality. It was monumental, mind-numbing stupidity" [page 54].

* my brackets.

And since Warren relied on the ultra-reliable CIA to tell the truth, the whole truth and nothing but the truth it's worth noting that one of its operatives, the saintly and impeccable "Hunt had testified that he certainly hoped the CIA was attempting to kill Castro, and had no objection *based on morality* to the assassination of the leaders of the Soviet Union" [page 271]. [My italics]. {By the way, the next time we naively and trustingly read a book review or internet blog apparently it's best to ask yourself who wrote it and why, since the dead hand of the CIA might be controlling even those joy sticks [page 72/3]}.

Reassuringly, the attorney "Snyder told the jurors that it was unthinkable to consider that the Federal Bureau of Investigation, Chief Justice Earl Warren, the distinguished members of the commission and other prominent Americans would have made false statements about the assassination of President Kennedy. It is 'absurd', he stated, to believe that the FBI or the CIA would cover up the facts........Have faith in our American institutions, Snyder pleaded" [page 317].

To their credit, many Americans did not swallow the moonshine. "I can't believe the Warren Report. I know it's all a lie", and "When the time comes that an American can't tell the truth because the

Government doesn't, that's the time to give the country back to the Indians — if they'll take it" [page 285]. But compared to other critics of the Warren Whitewash Mark Lane's treatment, insults and all, at least didn't run to linking him to the Gestapo, courtesy of the down-and-dirty CIA, a swinish organization devoted to consuming and disgorging waste products [page 376].

The predictable, clichéd drivel uttered by one lawyer [in this case Snyder] might well have come from the mouths of many others — as it still does. Lord Denning, the distinguished but fixated doyen of English justice, possessed of unsurpassed moral insights and judgments, and latter-day dead-wrong U.K. Appeal Court judge was slavishly devoted to The System first, second and last. Likewise other judicial icons such as "Even Lord Devlin" [pages 13 and 18 in 1], as if he never put a foot wrong. Not forgetting the buffoon Lord Hailsham, who among his many daft utterances once implored us to put our trust in the judges. Many innocent patsies like Oswald did just that — guilty or not, he might, after all, have expected to be safe inside a police station for a few hours at least — and suffered the consequences.

At which point, consider below the two very different perspectives about the police, extracted from *Rush to Judgment* [3].

The [Warren] Commission believed him [the Chief of the Dallas Police] and asked others to share its trust" – page 230, my brackets.

Jack Ruby's "bartender had standing orders to serve hard liquor to all police officers who came into his nightclub – an illegal practice" – page 230. "Anyone that came in from the police department" to enjoy Ruby's free hospitality and "drinks on the house" [page 232] included "certain attorneys in town" – page 231. The gregarious and popular Ruby, who according to one of his longstanding acquaintances was "on speaking terms with about 700 out of the 1200 men on the police force" [page 233] was apparently paying off the Dallas Police Department for special favors" [page 234] and supplying off-duty paying jobs, free dinners and drinks and women – strippers and customers – to officers [page 234]. According to another source Ruby not only bragged that he was immune from criminal conviction but he could do as he pleased in Dallas thanks to what he had on the police department and judges [page 238]. "Favors and bribes were frequently exchanged over a period of many years and the police repeatedly refused to arrest Ruby for crimes committed publicly" [page 240].

Remarkably and unexpectedly, in the same publication Mark Lane asserts that "Miscarriages of justice......when they arise, generally arise not from corrupt purpose but from human error" [page 16}. About which I ask this. Does he really believe that innocent patsies end up in prison, and stay there, by mistake, or as he puts it *from human error?* Human error committed by cops who, en bloc, are transparently and irredeemably corrupt, as his other sources [quoted above] demonstrated? Before reaching this startling and inexplicable conclusion how much research did Lane conduct into such cases [of which there have been all-too-many] in England? Are its police, in many cases, any less corrupt than their U.S. counterparts? Is pointing a firearm through the grill of a police cell and threatening to use it against a defenceless, cowering prisoner scared shitless and *who just happens to be innocent* also a mistake?

Take a look at the latest example-cum-shambles, hot off the press. Along with plenty of others I well remember – how could you forget? – the case of Jeremy Bamber, convicted for the murder of no less than five members of his own family in their "castle", a remote farmhouse in Essex in 1985. The object of the exercise, as it is in all cases, was to close the file and shovel any embarrassing inconsistencies under the carpet until the patsy dies, whereupon any questions of guilt or innocence would largely become academic. To that end The Establishment has mainly succeeded, since Bamber, in the eyes of many people, was and is not only innocent for his sins he's already been behind bars for 25 years, equivalent to half his life. And to whom does he owe this recurring feature of the English judicial system? Owzabout a clutch of judges, who between them have already rejected two appeals and may have the burden of concocting reasons to repeat the process. I say "may" because to the surprise, if not astonishment, of many Bamber's attempts to appeal for a third time have been hampered by the Criminal Cases Review Commission, which [as at the time I write] has issued a provisional rejection and is now awaiting a response from Bamber's lawyers. All this, despite what the trial judge described, with typical litotes, as a "less than thorough investigation" by the police. Some understatement.

Even by police standards, which for consistency, have remained shoddy, shabby and often corrupt pieces of work throughout my lifetime, the Bamber balls-ups – described by a journalist who attended the trial as a truly awful investigation - took some beating, as has the victim. Evidence was not recorded or preserved, the police burned bloodstained bedding and a carpet, the scenes-of crime officer didn't see or examine a vital gun silencer, moved a rifle – which wasn't examined for fingerprints until weeks later without wearing gloves - a hacksaw blade lying in the garden somehow evaded detection for months and investigators who not only failed to take contemporaneous notes but only recorded official statements about their interviews with Bamber weeks later. Etc, etc, and forever etc. Not to overlook the contributions made to his well-being and protestations of innocence [which have remained consistent throughout his ordeal] by Bamber's erstwhile confidantes and family. His cousins, who discovered crucial incriminating evidence and were the beneficiaries of his estate. And his loyal girl-friend, who told the police

Bamber had confessed to her, whereupon his number was up whatever the evidence proved one way or the other. The fact that she made at least two statements, one contradicting the other, and that she'd found out Bamber had two-timed her, seemed to get lost in the rush to put the boot in [23]. All of which and more – plenty more – might amount to a "mistake" in the eyes of those who regard aberrations as normality [aka "human nature"] but still form part of a chain of corrupt judicial practices stretching back hundreds of years.

More than that, who else is and was involved in these State crimes, which Mark Lane euphemistically dubs "human error". Let me guess. After the army of dedicated and incorruptible law-enforcers [or should it be debt-enforcers?] who somehow or other selected a few score innocents [who, in many cases, again happened to be Irish], came the sifters of the "evidence" in the Crown Prosecution Service, aka State lawyers, followed by bevies of forensic experts who somehow relentlessly and expediently cocked things up. Nothing new or unique there either. Ask a few of the innocent victims of this "scientific" hogwash. Or was it witchcraft? Whatever it was it and the expert testimony of con-men certainly did the trick for the juries, lawyers and above all judges. The Maguire family – Irish, for their sins – stitched up in "one of the more celebrated and disgusting of the infamous English miscarriages of justice" [24]. Judith Ward, banged up for 18 years thanks to a "conviction by ambush" [24]. John Berry, who languished behind bars for a mere 12 years, courtesy in no small measure to the crackpot opinion – [dressed up as fact] that a device which was in fact harmless somehow transposed itself into a deadly apparatus which was only "designed and manufactured for a terrorist operation" - of a scientific expert whose scientific qualifications came to the sum total of zero. Not that this pseudo-boffin was entirely to blame. The trial judge was so moon-struck he had the mumbo-jumbo-claptrap transcribed and read it to the jury, accompanied, no doubt, with nods of approval at regular intervals just in case some half-wit failed to get the message. Their message. The State Message, stated as fact. Finally, the legendary F.B.I. and cracker of the Lockerbie bomb mystery, denounced by one of his predecessors for "systematic fabrication of evidence in criminal trials" [24].

Then more lawyers hovering around threateningly in and out of Court. Last but not least the Bench, or as I prefer to call them, the Moral Beaks. The assorted trials, the successive appeals, the ridiculous "head-in-the-sand-and-snouts-in-the-shit" judgments churned out by the top-dogs. Praise be for Mark Lane, a patently decent person and exceptional [in many ways] lawyer – which I am not – but about miscarriages of justice he is about as accurate and reliable as my golf swing. As wrong as the stooge-ridden Warren Commission was, and set out to be, from the outset.

A plane full of passengers and crew is blown up in the lowering skies over Lockerbie in Scotland. Why? For no reason? I very much doubt it. So what preceded this mass murder of innocent civilians? That rather depends on who did it. Or who didn't. No matter, so long as you can find a culprit. Which, as the police prove over and over again, is far easier to achieve than finding the perpetrator and the evidence proving it. Hence miscarriages of justice – the tip of the iceberg where crime statistics are concerned. Who keeps figures of convictions where the victim didn't do it but can do nothing about it? Who cares, except him and his family? Certainly not the real villains of the piece who fitted him up, sleep easily at nights, collect their fat pensions and have kept him inside for decades. With plenty of precedents to follow, the Lockerbie scandal, which earns the distinction – among a catalogue of worthy contenders – of claiming an "honoured place in the history of British miscarriages of justice" [24], thanks to the remarkable contributions made by a triumvirate of senior Scottish judges ["Lords" all] who judging by their garb look as if they've just awoken from their nocturnal slumbers, pyjamas and demeanours unruffled and judicial facade intact.

Before a marginally less condemnatory 3 page assessment by Dr. Hans Kochler this is what Paul Foot had to say in conclusion. Al Megrahi – who alone was convicted – was not only not guilty the judgment and verdict were "perverse". "The judges brought shame and disgrace to all those who believed in Scottish justice, and have added to Scottish law an injustice of the type which has often defaced the law in England. Their verdict was a triumph for the CIA.....". Can a more damning conclusion be reached than that the outcome not only compares with the stitches-up concocted by the English judicial system but also satisfies an outfit like the CIA? Both are reminiscent of the "chaotic, insecure conditions at Heathrow airport" [whence the bomb surely emanated] in December 1988, where "anybody" could add another bag to an unsupervised luggage container [24]. And get away with it, thanks to the connivance of a few score and ten "independent" cover-up merchants.

This Special Report authored by Paul Foot – who died some years ago – has by now inevitably been overtaken by events. The equally inevitable lies surrounding Megrahi's release on "compassionate grounds" because he had terminal cancer and would soon be dead – which, needless to say, he isn't. The sordid parts played by the usual suspects in the deception. The families of the deceased, who've been kicked from pillar to post by a bunch of conniving liars and cheats. Business as usual for dotty Britain con.

It is on record that the U.K.'s highest court [then the House of Lords] equated the law to morality, and said they were inseparable. Such a claim seemed to me to be not only preposterous but to confirm that judges have no comprehension of reality and are, therefore, unfit to judge others. Hence my book *Moral Beaks and Claws*. Below are a few extracts supporting my argument, courtesy of Mark Lane.

"[President] Johnson called upon Warren, and Warren explained that he had acceded to the demand to set aside his belief system and his sense of justice in the face of this national crisis and international emergency" [page 51]. International emergency? Really?

As for their fraudulent pretensions to independence, Magazine publisher "Hamilton also argued that the question of truth and of intent must be decided by a jury rather than a judge. Hamilton feared, he said, that a judge might be swayed by allegiance to the government" [page 233]. Whatever possessed him to imagine that, even fleetingly? Even though we might wonder why their certitude issues from vacuous assumptions and their inferred conclusions are replete with non-sequiturs we all know that we can take the independence of judges for granted. We know that – just as we can be sure that the moon is made of cheese – because they and politicians keep saying so. The "or else" is understood but unspoken. So when we hear that the legal authorities not a million miles from London suddenly "snapped to attention" and fingered two Libyans for murder, about which the case against both was, in the tone adopted by those who are sure of themselves and what they do in the name of "justice", "incontrovertible" – a highly prejudicial and defamatory term to use, especially as one of them walked free and the other was by common consent fitted up – and "the failure of the Libyan authorities to release them for trial in Scotland was an insult to international law" [24] we must disregard the obvious stink of political tampering and instead ask ourselves how many times the U.K. and U.S.A. Governments have cynically broken international laws on the grounds that blowing human beings to smithereens is, as we all know, merely enhancing their body of human and civil rights, even though the body is a dismembered corpse? The problem is that others may view such actions in an entirely different light and seek revenge. Thus violence begets violence, atrocities massacres, terrorism ditto. By and on whom? And where do "miscarriages of justice" fit into the equation?

"Supposed to be law enforcers, they tend to conceive of themselves as the law. They are more responsible than the average man, they are more infantile. They are attached umbilically to the concept of honesty, they are profoundly corrupt.....their work is authoritarian; they are cynical; and finally, if something in their heart is deeply idealistic, they are also bloated with greed". This is the condemnatory verdict of Norman Mailer, in his review of Mark Lane's expose *Rush to Judgment*, reproduced in *Plausible Denial* [page 368]. About whom was he speaking? Hard to tell, given the plausible possibilities. Actually, the police were the targets of his barbed shafts. But they might equally well have been aimed at other so-called upholders of law and order. No prizes for guessing who else fills the bill.

Defying the impossible, do lawyers actually commit mistakes? Yes and no. Deliberate mistakes certainly, and even deceit. Judge for yourself when the law is clear and unequivocal. Take defamation, for instance. In the US where a public figure is the target the appropriate standard is *actual malice*, as decided by its Supreme Court. Yet somehow or other in the first trial the plaintiff's lawyer managed to convince the jury that was not so, conveniently resulting in the award to Howard Hunt [of Watergate fame] of $100,000 in compensatory damages and $550,000 in punitive damages. In Mark Lane's words "the only explanations I can conjure up are ignorance or a deliberate effort to mislead the court to thus secure some advantage to his client and for himself" [page 180]. Could it be that the old but unspoken reliable – greed – had reared its ugly head yet again? Put more politely, "Lawyers, due to training, temperament and financial considerations, are generally not driven by concerns for judicial economy" [page 209], meaning they fart around wasting court and client time when doing so suits their pocket-book.

Why not stuff everybody, especially wealthy clients, when the legal system not only permits, but encourages, procedures like taking depositions, where say three lawyers from the same law firm spend [or is it waste?] six hours. Result? A bill for the client, if he's lucky, of a mere $4,500, plus another tab of $1,500 for their time spent discussing the procedures over lunch – for which the client also pays, naturally [page 158]. And lest we forget pseudo-"justice", how about the independent and impartial trial judge? Was he or she asleep at the time, or did he or she swallow the same guff?

If, as we are again meant to swallow, the class barriers are being broken down – which means the evolution or revolution hasn't already taken place, so them and us are not yet we – why the continuation of the weird and wonderful and the strange and archaic? Whichever description you apply it's as relevant to the individuals as the titles they fall over themselves to adopt. This ritual of title-mantling gives the lie to them and the system to which they cling. Only snobs, who essentially are those who crave the right to look down on others for no discernible reason, drool over "honours" – unique in The Hole – and especially The New Year's Honours List, wherein Fred, the local road-sweeper, has been awarded an O.B.E. for service to sweeping the road [or as the snobs prefer, "service to the community"] alongside [but beneath, naturally] the newly appointed judges in some court or other. Hard to believe, and impossible to justify except in the context of the eternal English class system to which they avidly and religiously adhere – otherwise, they would turn their backs on it, as some notables like Paul Schofield have done, while thousands of creeps who are and were not fit to be his dresser grovel for some meaningless accolade, which in their eyes attests to their perceived importance.

It's hard to resist the allure and temptation to be "respectable", the more so in the eyes of others of like mind – always assuming they have one of their own – but like everything else in life there's a price to be paid, which some might characterize as selling your soul to the devil. As the renowned historian and scholar A. J. P. Taylor put it "The Establishment draws in recruits from outside as soon as they are ready to conform to its standards and become respectable. There is nothing more agreeable in life than to make peace with the Establishment – and nothing more corrupting" [25]. I wouldn't know about the latter, because the competition is so strong it's virtually impossible to make meaningful comparisons. But I can imagine few things less desirable than being a member of their cliquish club or complying with their standards, which seem to equate to looking after them and theirs come what may. As for rubbing shoulders with the likes of Philby, Burgess, Blunt, and Maclean - all automatic, ideal entrants to the ghouls' gatherings – I can but wonder what it feels like to invest your confidences, trust and innermost beliefs in your bosom friends for decades only to be sold down the river cynically, ruthlessly and remorselessly by a bunch of duplicitous, scheming, lying and cheating two-faced bastards. Nor were or are they the only rotten apples in the pork-barrel. To me making peace with them would be an achievement I don't even begin to grasp, let alone recognize : as for life's pleasures, going down the pub for a beer or three beats mixing with that lot hands down. Could that be because I've known what The Establishment is and always will be, and I want no part of it or them?

And what, may I ask, are the Lords and Ladies, Honourables and dishonourables, Dames and Sheilas, and Sirs and serfs cluttering up the judiciary required to do to earn the right to remind the rest of us how important they are? How about get out of bed, turn up for work and do a job to their dubious standards. Once in a while, you understand, depending on the exigencies of the service they are supposedly performing on behalf of the community. And woe betide the individual who doesn't bow [and scrape] and adopt the "etiquette" of the court, such as calling His Royal Highness [or whatever] by his or her adopted title. "Case dismissed for contempt of court", meaning perceived discourtesy to his nibs. And why the daft wigs, gowns and "My Learned Friend" bullshit? Tradition, old boy, tradition. A tradition of being pretty useless to man and beast and getting away with it.

Just for doing their job, invariably to an indifferent standard and often to an inferior one, judging by the many judgments I've ploughed through over the years, these titled, pompous spongers - knocking on 4,000 of them in England and Wales alone, would you believe [see Appendix 1] – manage to scrape by on three grand or more a week [I didn't say a "working week", since it doesn't exist in judicial circles] plus a bloated pension matching their torsos and egos. All paid for by their social, intellectual and unwashed inferiors, most of whom only survive by working far harder and longer. Yes indeed, that's what the "classless society" means. Coupled with regular, systematic reminders – otherwise known as brainwashing – about how upright, moral, honourable, incorruptible and "independent" they are, while more and more of their victims scratch their heads and wonder who really deserves to be behind bars. But take heart. According to the same horse's-mouth the number of judges is swamped by the "42,000 men and women holding judicial office in England and Wales" [4]. Are they bragging about something that can't cut the mustard and doesn't earn its corn?

For a sample of more unending bureaucratic bullshit about the English judiciary one need look no further than a clutch of publications taking up space at public expense on the internet. Below are some examples:-

The lack of a written constitution – which in practice allows judges [not "courts"] to ride roughshod over the rights of the citizen and to create "case law" via their often quirky opinions and values – operates "famously and almost uniquely" rather than, say, "notoriously". Considering how long "the law" has existed in England, and we're told the only other countries which persist with this crazy anachronism are Israel and New Zealand it's high time this system was dumped, along with its proponents.

As for the so-called "reform" of the role and functions of the Lord Chancellor – another daft and childish title – it's good to see that for once the U.K. Establishment reacted so positively to the acerbic criticisms penned by the foremost authority on the subject of the English

Constitution. Hardly surprising, coming from a man who described the office as "a heap of anomalies" prone to "sinister temptations". And when were his opinions aired? Why, in 1867, a mere 144 years ago. Comparatively recently by English standards, taking into account other more pressing priorities, like fiddling expenses [5].

Throughout these documents – at least one is devoted exclusively to it [6] - one theme recurs with predictable regularity. The constant prattling on – more brainwashing - about the non-existent "independence" of the judiciary is not only boring and unconvincing it's a flat out distortion of reality. Much like its blurb about judicial appointments [7]. Despite the previous racket "in fact" [not opinion] working "rather well" apparently some astute observer of the British way of life noticed that judges were being appointed "in the image of existing judges". Shock, horror. I don't believe it, and neither will they. But there's an obvious, easy solution. To "have a judiciary that has the confidence of citizens, it must fairly reflect all sections of society that are in a position to provide candidates of the requisite ability" – to be picked by a panel who judging by the internet all come from the same middle-class, Establishment background.

According to the internet these worthies comprise:-

Chairman – vacant

Vice Chairman – Lord Justice Toulson

Mr. Justice Bean

Lady Justice Black

Judge Frances Kirkham

Judge David Pearl

District Judge Charles Newman

Jonathan Sumption – barrister

Edward Nally – solicitor

Professor Dame Hazel Genn – Dean of Law Faculty

Dame Lorna Boreland-Kelly - magistrate

Harrit Spicer – governor of L.S.E.

Sir Geoffrey Inkin – public servant

Sara Nathan – journalist

Francis Plowden – independent adviser

Hardly people of the commoners. But the idea, let's call it a "policy", is brilliant, combining New Labour feminist and minority junk with Dave's appeal to the classless society. So where will the new breed of legal-eagles with "the requisite ability" who will inspire the "confidence of citizens" – meaning everybody, featuring illiterates, deadbeats, drop-outs, spongers, drug-pushers and convicts, all of them with law degrees, preferable from Oxbridge, and at least 10 years legal practice - come from? How about fantasy-land, where politicians and other fairies reside? Otherwise, forget it and stick to what you're good at and qualified for. Thieving, lying and cheating. In other words, try politics [7].

Still, once you're in you're in for life, whatever havoc you cause along the way. All in the name of judicial independence and non-existent accountability. If you can manage to wade through the nauseating hogwash about one [8] try reading the eye-wash headed "Judicial conduct" without reaching for the sick-bag. According to the purveyors of the new, reformed system perfection is nigh, witness "official statistics" [9]. Wasn't this bullshit trotted out for decades by the police – another self-regulating bunch who repeated the same tune ad nauseam? No complaints received proves everybody's happy, everything's hunky-dory, instead of the opposite? Did only their victims know full well that after repeated, systematic abuses of their rights at the hands of the police it was not only a complete waste of time trying to persuade some head-in-the-sand zombie that his uniformed mate, or more likely, their boss in C.I.D. was corrupt if they continued to stir up hornets' nests the boys-in-blue would exact revenge, courtesy of institutionalized retaliation and fit-ups, sometimes extending to their own numbers. Needless to say, when a police surgeon gave of his time to help out after the Lockerbie disaster for his efforts and trouble he was smeared by police and lawyers. Later he was sacked, for which he received no credible explanation [24]. But there again, why should he get an apology or explanation? Nobody else does, in a land where such courtesies are infra-dig. Still, when you spend your life telling people who are in a position to judge for themselves that whatever you do and say has the confidence of just about everybody you run the risk of some of them saying you and your insistent assurances actually amount to something that looks, smells and feels distinctly iffy.

Ever wondered how and why justice works in practice? Listed below are a few clues, primarily intended to help would-be litigants in person, or people who for one reason or another [usually financial] want to act for themselves in court proceedings. On the face of it the list seems straightforward, innocuous and obvious enough. Its significance lies in who issued it, and what the "advice" – or, as I prefer to think of it, advisory warning - actually conveys. Without saying so, it discloses the factors which influence and affect judges in their motivations and attitudes prior to dispensing their wholly illogical and warped brand of "justice". Factors which have nothing whatever to do with what they assert is all that counts inside a courtroom – no, not morality, evidence or justice. Just to remind the reader, in order of importance below are the "tips on self representation" [meaning the individual is presenting and arguing his or her legal case before a judge] issued by a USA Superior Court [10] which help your case.

Generally, "you must act, dress, and speak in a way that helps you with your case". Is there any reason to believe this advice is nonsensical or peculiar to one Court? No on both counts. It resonates not only throughout the USA but in all similar judicial systems, because judges are much-of-a-muchness everywhere, more's the pity. So let's analyze what the advice tells us about judges and their system of junk justice. Surely it can have escaped no-one's notice that above all else what counts in court is superficiality. Thus item 1 implores the self-litigant to dress "professionally". Now to most people, if you happen to be a building worker the customary attire inside his "profession" may well be a filthy, ragged T-shirt, a pair of oily, grimy jeans whose arse has seen better days and steel-capped boots with dog-shit clinging underneath. Hardly what the doctor or the judge would suggest or appreciate in their domains. But elucidation is at hand. "Clothes that are neat and clean" should meet the bill. But where the law is concerned surely sporting a ridiculous, archaic uniform, complete with horse-hair wig or renting a pin-striped business suit, starched collar and matt tie, the like of which you would never be seen dead in lest your mates collapsed in a heap with mirth are more likely to win the day? After all, looking like a prick for a day or two [or a decade or four, as lawyers do] in order to incur the pleasure of a judge of like mind is a price well worth paying, even if the exercise costs you a grand or two and you'll never live it down.

Tip number 2 concerns how you act, meaning being respectful to the judge [who, as a breed, for some reason rarely reciprocate], the opposing party [usually someone you have good reason to hate and despise, such as ex-wives, boy-friends and those who transpose], witnesses ["grasses" or "rats" outside] and "people in the hallways". Not forgetting the strangers [probably FBI under-cover agents] and assorted perverts you might encounter massaging their meat in the washrooms. And, so says tip number 3, as if we didn't already know "you must be on time". Here another suspension of disbelief comes in useful. Ignore the reality that judges require you to do as they say, not as they do. To them, being "on time" means sometime now or never. While you're expected, nay required, to turn up not just on time but well before that allocated for the start of your case they pay not the slightest regard to it, your case or you.

So while you sit around twiddling your thumbs, gazing at the perambulations of assorted wig-wearing twits, shifting your cramped arse around on rock-hard furniture conveniently located in draughty rooms or corridors for hours, days or until rigor-mortis sets in the "punctual" judge [if he or she exists] is nowhere to be seen. And if you beef about this palpable contempt for you and your rights – as I did - they mark your card and ensure you pay for your temerity. Nevertheless the litigant is urged, always remember the 4 p's *Professionalism, Punctuality, Politeness, Preparedness.* Incidentally, for the benefit of those who never comply and have never encountered the word before *Punctuality* is helpfully defined as "being on time". And important though unspoken, take a bath once in a while – cleanliness and Godliness also count in a "moral" environment. Abide by the judicial codes of conduct and appearance and all should be well.

Hang on. Isn't justice supposed to be blind? If it is, why should and does it matter if a litigant turns up wearing a T-shirt bearing the slogan "Judges are [insert as necessary]"?   Why should he be penalized for telling the truth? No, in the bastions of the deluded and deluders truth bows before the whims, caprices and bigotry of pompous stuffed-shirts who demand, not deserve or earn, respect. And in turn give you none. Not even an apology for their tardiness. And where in the list of "tips" does the small matter of "evidence" crop up? Without it you lose, with enough of it you should win your case. Why should superficiality matter one way or the other? It shouldn't, but does, because judges are nothing if not conceited bullies out to prove what moralizing do-gooding zealots they are, determined, above all, to uphold, impose and perpetuate their corrupt and discreditable system on the rest of us.

What impresses these refugees from reality? Wearing a freshly-pressed tie. Wearing a dog-collar doesn't. Unless, of course, it's displayed by a member of the clergy [akin to that worn by the judge's ancestors], in which case in assessing the pros-and-cons of the case the Reverend's attire is weightier than the litigant's mere tie. Better still, wear the unmistakable M.C.C. tie, bestowing the class and integrity of all gentlemen. And betraying latent hopes and aspirations. As he slumbers during a complex fraud case the trial judge wishes he was somewhere else. Anywhere but this confounded place. "Someday" – he muses to himself, in broken Latin – "I'll be resting my amply-proportioned arse on the benches in Lords Pavilion, a fully-fledged member of the M.C.C, sometimes jostling and mingling among not just fellow judicial know-alls but celebrities like Tim Rice, politicians like John Major and even a smattering of people who used to play the game, like that working-class chappie Botham, so know what they're talking about, unlike the rest of us. Still, since when have ignorance and incompetence been hindrances in climbing the judicial ladder?" So whatever else you do, litigant, don't let on that some fraudster who'd just conned his way out of a stretch in the nick by using the old M.C.C. tie ruse had shared the tip on the internet. Just rent the tie for a few days, and let it work its irresistible magic. There's every chance you'll not only win the case but the judge will ask you to put his name forward for admission to the Lords Taverners.

Before I leave the subject adherents of the unspeakably infantile and crass televisual offerings will, no doubt, be familiar, if not enamored, with a delectation called "Judge Judy". If it weren't named after the beachfront side-show of my childhood, "Punch and Judy" it should have been, since both bear uncanny resemblances, not least the sadistic violence on view. On the show bearing her name Judge Judy adjudicated on disputes between hostile, vehement and sometimes violent adversaries. The fact that these war-games take place inside a tv studio is disguised by paneled walls, court trappings and atmosphere down to a pseudo-court flunkey whose role it is to command the assembled throng to "all rise" before Judge Hey Jude struts into her "court". There she dispenses her worldly and legal opinions about the parties and issues in question, for all the world like her counterparts down the road. Where she might well be due ten minutes hence. Realising this, and knowing her bread's buttered on both sides, after a signal from the flunky she utters before the show has hardly started "Case dismissed. I'll concoct some reasons later. Right now I've got a cab outside waiting to take me to the studio where I've got a show to do, appearing as myself". And she wouldn't be kidding.

At one time I thought the hectoring harridan who played Judge Judy and clearly modeled herself on The Awesome Thatcher was an actress, akin to Martin Shaw playing Judge John Good Deed in the ludicrously implausible t.v. series featuring a High Court judge whose integrity and morality somehow overcame the plotting and scheming of his numerous enemies inside the judicial and political hierarchies. Even if he achieved the impossible by landing the job in the first place such an individual would not last five minutes inside that jungle. Yet at no stage did its producers or distributors dub it a farce, or even a comedy. Nor did its creator, G.F. Newman, who I associate with left-wing delectations about corruption. Have I got the wrong end of the stick about him and the redoubtable Judge Judy? Was she fact or fiction? Yet lo and behold, another day there she was, being interviewed by the much-married Larry King - who since they were invented virtually single-handedly kept manufacturers of technicolour braces [or is it suspenders?] and jet-black hair-dyes for the nearly dead afloat - on his imaginatively-titled programme "Larry King Live". Which, while not exactly falsehoods, flirted with the truth on two counts. Firstly it was dubious whether The King was actually still alive, since his actions and questions frequently raised doubts and eyebrows. And with his show being taped for later transmission the suffix "Live" – meaning, in American parlance, now – was somewhat phony, as were his attempts to prove that someone who'd been broadcasting for a century or more was, like

Zsa-Squared-Gabor, still only 39. [Strange how the American Dream in all its glorious beauty happily and nonchalantly tolerates, if not encourages, disposal of human beings on the scrap heap when they reach the ripe old age of 30 yet simultaneously expect and demand their nightly fix of predictable pap from showbiz oligarchs like Larry King and Johnny Carson, whose yukky outputs began when dinosaurs like them roamed, reigned and ruled].

Not so with Judge Punch-Up and Judy. In her case life didn't imitate art. They were one and the same. The same hectoring mannerisms, the same know-all certitude, the same menacing, steely glare if and when interrupted in full flight by pesky nuisances like her interviewer or commercial breaks, the same shameless posturing. Was this crass behaviour a genetic defect or taught in law school? Who knows or cares, when the dummies who queue and sign up in droves for the privilege of being publicly humiliated in yet another orgy of inadvertent and unintended judicial and juvenile delinquency apparently consider their five minutes of fame and shame on her show to be "cool" and "exciting", along with the most boring and mundane trivia from their drug-induced fantasies?

As might be expected of those whose lives, we are led to believe, are grounded in morality – two of them being bible-punchers or proud members of the profession some like to regard as fused with that quality – the evidence implicating the three B's [not to mention other lawyer-sycophants like Jack Straw and Jeff Hoon] in infinitely more troubling and tragic events is distinctly unsettling. Despite concerted resistance to calls for publication of the relevant documents – logically and reasonably based on the doctrine that dupes don't deserve to know why and how they've been led up the garden path – some of the truth has escaped two years after the events. One minute Caesar's pressing his case and ample floppy belly where they make the most impression, the next desperately trying to fend off stabs-in-the-back. Et-tu Brute–Blair?

Recounting my own correspondence with the office of the Attorney General is instructive for several reasons. This is the U.K. Government Department in whose name civil proceedings were launched against me in the Year of Our Lord 2000, and which became the focus of my attention a mere decade later. In my case the Lord in question was no other than Goldsmith of somewhere or other [11], better known as Mister

Flip-Flop, renowned for "changing his mind" – which, of course, anyone can do, just as anyone "can make a mistake", unless you happen to be a lawyer – about the legality of invading Iraq. The problem is and was that we are not talking about matters about which the rest of us change our minds [such as which movie to watch on the box] or make a mistake about, for instance, the price of a kilo of carrots. No, by and large our transgressions are relatively minor and above all do harm to nobody else. As if we didn't already know, that's why we aren't trusted to make life-and-death decisions. They're made by – who else? – lawyers, who spend their lives convincing the masses they alone are fit for purpose.

Lord Goldsmith, the killer-Whale in the U.K.'s school of judicial marine-life, had the job of doing what he had been doing for decades while and after attending law school. He had to interpret the law. He did, to the consternation of individuals who, by all known criteria, were not fit to lick his boots in his field. They included the likes of Tony Blair and his crony, political-appointee and ass-lickin' subordinate Jack Straw. Both also lawyers. Neither in Goldsmith's class, or so we're told, including by Blair, who while giving evidence at the

Chilcot Iraq War Inquiry stressed what a classy guy and lawyer Goldsmith was. Did I forget something? Oh yes. By that time – in fact, well before then – Goldsmith had changed his mind, or more precisely his considered legal opinion, having regard to all the circumstances of the case. In short, "no" to a war became "yes" to a war. But in what way had the relevant law or circumstances changed so dramatically so as to compel such a drastic change of heart and mind? Could it be because Goldsmith had been persuaded [forced?] to pay a visit to Washington, there to be hectored and pushed around by Bush and Straw's bosom pal, the boiling Rice? Not to mention other neo-cons and Perles of Wisdom.

Thereafter Goldsmith saw the light and the error of his ways and of his opinion. So purely by coincidence the Christians Bush and Blair got their way – by a miracle, you might call it – and Goldsmith proved that yet another lawyer could look both ways and still get the answer morally and legally wrong. Like anybody else I can judge the first criterion, and count the body-bags. As for the second, I can see on the internet what Goldsmith and others said at the time, and judge whether the judges were as they claim they are and have always been. More tellingly, if Goldsmith's second opinion were right other Governments, bodies and senior lawyers would have fallen into line, instead of the opposite. For instance, in an obituary about Lord Bingham of Cornhill the "Telegraph" newspaper said:-

"In 2008, shortly after standing down as senior law lord, he [meaning Lord Bingham] said that in his opinion Lord Goldsmith's advice to the-then Prime Minister Tony Blair on Britain's invasion of Iraq was 'flawed' because 'it was not plain that Iraq had failed to comply in a manner justifying resort to force and there were no strong factual grounds or hard evidence to show that it had'; moreover, he argued, it was up to the entire Security Council to decide whether Iraq had failed to comply with the resolution" [12].

Most people would agree – some vehemently and understandably – that none of the evidence available at the time could possibly justify what Goldsmith did, said and his volte-face, particularly having regard to what was, and is, at stake. By nature and training lawyers tend to be ultra-cautious. At best at the time Goldsmith could not have been sure of his ground – indeed, most people believe he was flat-out wrong morally and legally to act as he did. The same applies to Blair and his cohorts, who resorted to invention about WMD's and their targets, and now claim he especially couldn't foresee what would happen and in any case what he did was right. Doesn't any petty despot act and say the same? In their book as time goes by it's no big deal to trot out a succession of differing, if not contradictory, arguments to muddy the waters. Firstly, Blair, Straw, Hoon and others concluded independently that invasion was justified. Secondly, so did Goldsmith, although not before his opinion had changed in line with theirs. Thirdly Goldsmith was independent [which he never was in practice] so being the Government's legal adviser his advice [once it was the "right" advice, obtained - or is it "wrung out?" - without political pressure from anybody, U.S.A included] was the only advice that mattered, and upon which the U.K. Government could rely, especially as its author was, in the legal community, the cat's whiskers who could do no wrong. And if he was, it's all down to him, because after all's said and done he's the expert, ain't he?

Anybody who still believes that Goldsmith did not cave in to the unbearable political pressure exerted on him at home and abroad – which is exactly the opposite of what being independent entails - should take a long look at what he said and did at the time. For instance, paragraph 13 of Goldsmith's memo to Blair dated 30 July 2002 says it was "clear" – translated from legalese, that means certain – that without a fresh UN Security Council resolution taking military action would be unlawful [13]. Much the same message was contained in his draft advice handed to Blair on 14 January 2003 [14] and repeated on 12 February 2003. As the onset of hostilities loomed large the Attorney-General's advice to the UK Prime Minister of 7 March 2003 [15 and 16] – which Blair saw fit to conceal from his own cabinet and the permanent secretaries of key government departments, reportedly because some of them couldn't be trusted with such papers [17] – gave no hint of what was to come. However, along with Blair other experts with little or no knowledge of what they spoke defied the growing tide of cynical disbelief. Foremost among them was Jack Straw, who disregarded the opinions of the entire legal team in his own Department, by then the Foreign Office. One of them, the deputy head, duly resigned her position, in contrast to her boss, who became Sir Michael Wood, doubtless for outstanding service to cause and country [17]. Then, on 17 March 2003, the volte-face, complete with Goldsmith's attendance and presentation to the cabinet, none of whom were allowed to ask questions – presumably because only awkward, if not unanswerable, ones would have eventuated – although the waiverers were treated to one side of a single A4 sheet, doubtless containing all the information and potted opinion that their limited mental capacities could sustain [18]. And so to war.[19 and 20]..

For a summary and critique of the sordid debacle from an Australian perspective see "How we were duped over Iraq' [21].

Never mind what these illustrious and entirely trustworthy examples of artifice in action say and do, you don't have to swallow their guff. You don't have to be a lawyer or politician [or God forbid, both] to appreciate the implications and ramifications of your own actions. From start to last Goldsmith knew a foreign government would be overthrown, a foreign country would be invaded and countless individuals, most of them innocent civilians, would be killed if he rubber-stamped a plan concocted by another foreign regime hell-bent on revenge and finding scapegoats for its own foreign policies and aggressions, many of them unlawful. Goldsmith knew all of that from the get-go. He also knew all the above would happen *even if he was absolutely certain that the law was crystal clear, could not be challenged in any meaningful way and his duty was to say exactly that*. But he didn't. He contradicted himself. Which can only mean the law was not unambiguous, that it could and probably would be challenged and therefore again he should say so. Which is more or less what he did say – first time round.

Frequently lawyers don't know the answer. It's no disgrace to say so, and get other opinions before lighting the fuse. By doing what he did subsequently some would say that Goldsmith – as the bastion of last resort – has no less blood on his hands than his political masters in the U.K. and U.S.A.

Incidentally, if, as appears to be so, Blair professes ignorance about the potential [now actual] consequences of his own role and actions he and a few thousand disciples and advisers of his must have all been out when several televised discussions warning of the perils in doing so [all of which, plus more, have eventuated] were broadcast before the invasion took place. Of that I am certain because I watched and well remember some of those programmes. Shortly before the hostilities began I happened to be in a bar in Melbourne, Australia, swilling beer with a group of Australians. In came an earnest young student, imploring us to join the protest march due to take place through the city centre the following day. "Thanks but no thanks" was our collective response. I had better things to do. But above all I knew the gesture was utterly pointless and futile. Politicians like Howard, Blair and Bush [to all of whom I say good riddance] don't give a fig about what other people think or say. So while kids are dying – thanks to this gruesome threesome and "independent" lawyers who are nothing of the kind – Blair swans round the world flogging his book, which by all accounts is as crappy as they are.

Meantime Goldsmith has landed on his feet and caught the next gravy train. Who better than a renowned lawyer and peer of the realm to impress a US [for useless?] law firm only too ready, willing and able to fork out one or two million a year for the privilege of having the Goldsmith moniker and credentials on its headed notepaper?[11]. How about Blair himself, once he's finished swanning round the world flogging his overweight book and reputation to the relentlessly gormless Yanks? Whereas Goldsmith's name would mean nothing to the average American once he was identified as the man who legally gave the green light to Britain's great and glorious invasion of Iraq out would come a veritable bevy of homilies and homages. He might even earn the ultimate accolade – being branded a Patriot by the man himself, Big Bill O'Reilly, on Fox News. Some might argue that since in Bill's eyes the world's population seems to comprise either Pinheads or Patriots – which by a remarkable coincidence just happens to be the title of his latest book, which he touts unabashedly on his "news" program – in Goldsmith's case Bill has got his piss-taking cues in a twist. But no. After all, Bill – a man of infinitely false modesty and hypocrisy, who loses no opportunity to remind us he is a "simple" man who nevertheless was smart enough to attend Harvard, as apparently did the manifestly intelligent George W. Bush – works for Fox News, which judging by its output is about as "independent" as U.K. lawyers like Lord Goldsmith.

And laud him they will, much the same as they have his erstwhile boss and commander, the Right

Honourable Tony Blair P.C. and bar. Anybody who wonders why the same individual is widely admired and respected in America yet is despised and denigrated in equal measure whence he came should ask themselves who appeals to who and why. Would an English man or woman have answered the question "Do you know where Iraq is?' with the ultimate in red-necked arrogance and crassness "Who cares? It won't exist soon, anyway". Or, as I overheard an American saying to another tourist, "Welcome to our playground". Outside the entrance to an arcade of bars. Not in the United States of America, but in the American "colony" of Thailand, which when I last checked was an independent country populated and run by Thais. With that mentality you can understand why war-mongers like Blair go down well in Dreamsville, as do the Royals and ex-Royals like Lady Sarah Ferguson, last seen trying to extort a small fortune for the privilege of her making a couple of phone calls to her ex-hubby, a dumpling last seen loafing around in some palace or other. They're welcome to her and her habits, but do Americans know more about Blair and Goldsmith and what they did than do Brits, or is it that superficiality wins every time? Or maybe it's just that anybody compares well alongside the likes of the ultra-tarnished Bush and his regicidal regime, where deceit, humbug and conspiracy [reminiscent of the Nixon era] ran the show. Par for the course, and not just in the U.S.A.

It could hardly have escaped the notice of Blair and the creeps surrounding him that in America what seems to be is what is.   Thus springs another unforgettable image, set among the sweeping landscape of Crawford, Texas. There, in a ranch fittingly owned by an inveterate cowboy-dude named Bush, an infamous "tete-a-tete" [a phrase of French derivation latterly mangled by American linguists] took place between the ranch-owner and his poodle from across the pond [22].   Amid conspiratorial asides, mutterings and meaningless drivel about "special relationships" comprising extensive and sustained arse-licking a deal was not so much thrashed out as stitched up. It concerned a foreign country and a foreign regime, the latter of which had incurred the displeasure of the gun-totin' Texan heck-son and on and by his lead his obedient and eternally-grinning pompadour, whose name Bush could not recall. No matter. Somebody or other had to be taught a lesson – at others' expense, naturally – to show the world how butch-for-butchers the conspirators were.   Their conversation, which can only be imagined, remains a top-secret, although sources close to the U.S. President suggest that it ran along the following lines, based on transcripts of previous discussions between the two.

President - "Here's my, sorry our, decision about the invasion of what's its name, oh yeah, EyeRack. What d'ya mean, Goldfinger sez it's illegal? I decide what's legal. And who the fuck is this Goldfinger, OK Goldsmith? He works for you, right? Not exactly? What the fuck does that mean? Listen, buddy. OK Tony, we're invading. You and me, together. Soon, if not sooner. No discussion, no half-measures, no more bullshit. You do whatever's necessary at your end. If this guy Goldminster's a problem, fix him. Otherwise I'll fix both of you. Haven't you got some shit on him you could use to twist his arm or break his legs? If not I'll get my boys to find some. Don't worry buddy, you can sleep easy. it's all in the bag. We'll be in and out of wherever faster than a sex-starved rabbit. Sign this, and I'll give you a guided tour of the spread. Then we'll nobble the press. What's that scrawl say? Tony who? Is that you? Are you sure? No matter, you Brits can be relied on to do as you're told, unlike those awkward

French bastards. They can't even be bothered learning English".

Then the enduring but less-than-endearing spectacle of these two purveyors of purgatory strutting their stuff towards the awaiting press corps. Tough guys personified, hands thrust in jeans' pockets, stride matching booted stride, dope in league and aspiration with dupe. The man from The Big Country meets the lickspittle from lick-your-ass.

APPENDIX ONE

Judicial Statistics

2010

Judicial statistics

			In Post
Justices of the Supreme Court[1]			11
Heads of Division	Lord Chief Justice Master of the Rolls President of the Queen's Bench Division President of Family Division The Chancellor of the High Court		5
Lords Justices of Appeal[2]			37
High Court Judges[3]	Chancery Division	18	108
	Queen's Bench Division	72	
	Family Division	18	
Judge Advocates			9
Deputy Judge Advocates			5
Masters, Registrars, Costs Judges and District Judges (PRFD)			48
Deputy Masters, Deputy Registrars, Deputy Costs Judges and Deputy District Judge (PRFD)			80

		South Eastern & RCJ	Midland	North Eastern	Western	Northern	Wales	Total in Post
Circuit Judges	Total	307	93	80	61	103	36	680
Recorder	Total	549	202	131	140	155	56	1233
District Judges (County Courts)	Total	164	68	65	50	76	25	448
Deputy District Judges (County Courts)	Total	209	114	90	83	110	34	640
District Judges (Magistrates' Court)	Total							143
Deputy District Judges (Magistrates' Court)	Total							151
								Total: 3598

[1] The twelfth Justice of Supreme Court, Sir John Dyson, was subsequently apointed on 13 April 2010.
[2] This figure includes Lord Justice Carnwath, Senior President of Tribunals

http://www.judiciary.gov.uk/publications-and-reports/statistics/judges/judicial-statistics/?wb...   1/3/2011

CHAPTER TWO

Vexed Haters

Like all good men and true vexatious litigants were born and flourished amid the dirty green pastures of England, home of football, tepid beer, fish and chips and tripe served up by morality personified, common-as-muck law and its agents, judges. Only fitting, therefore, that The Vexatious Actions Bill of 1896 should be introduced in the House of Lords by the Lord Chancellor to protect one of his cronies, the Archbishop of Canterbury, no less [1]. Could it be that even then some far-sighted beak foresaw the day when The Pope himself would be sued because the lives and posteriors of inconsequential little people had been buggered-up by an errant, deranged priest? The prospect was as unthinkable and untenable as branding the police corrupt simply because the Everest of evidence accumulated throughout what apologists euphemistically dub "miscarriages of justice" cases pointed in the same direction. Still, even though the look, taste and smell of shit usually means one thing Lord Denning and his disciples could only detect the aroma of roses while ill-educated, naïve and trusting Irish patsies rotted away or died at their and Her Majesty's pleasure.

The fact that the offspring of the ermined stoats stifled and often smothered basic legal principles and human rights "via the subterfuge of vexatious litigant legislation" [1] didn't seem to bother the seeders of destruction, who then and since have never stopped reminding the rest of the world that theirs is the standard we should try to emulate, forlorn though the aspiration must be. Not everybody fell for the scam. Perhaps because they saw through the guff and realized the implications and flat-out contradictions involved in giving people something with one hand and then taking it away with the other – courtesy of some judge, honest or not – in many countries vexatious litigants don't exist. But why, after all's said and done, should such dilemmas bother the tiny minds of those who already know all the answers and much, much more besides? As if we could ever forget, in living-in-the-past backwaters such as England [which coincidentally has no written Constitution preserving basic rights and protecting the vulnerable against tyrants dressed-up as Santa Claus] they were and will always be the Supreme beings [some of whose arses occupy the comfortable seating – or is it thrones? – in the aptly named Supreme Court] and, praise be, our eternal intellectual, spiritual and moral superiors, who by dint of birth, privilege, stodgy grey matter and unceasing and single-minded ruthlessness have managed to wangle themselves into a position where they can do and say more or less what they want, regardless of the consequences, because where they are concerned [and nobody else counts] there are no consequences.

Of course, once you've devised a system depriving them, the common people, of their rights it can't be allowed to fall into disuse. That's why it exists. To turn the screw, rack the back, twist the knife, to do what bullies were born to do – bully. Victims have to be found, denigrated, humiliated and subjugated in the public interest [nowadays the public internet], under the Rule of Law. Let's see. The relevant law, the Vexatious Actions Act, was enacted in 1896. To justify its passing into law vexatious litigants need to be found - or fitted up. No problem about the latter. Few "democratic" countries can compete with the U.K. when it comes to fingering and framing scapegoats. Being curious about the numbers and identities of my fellow miscreants [and with a good bit of help from the Freedom of Information Act, U.K. Government and the irreplaceable internet] I downloaded lists of vexatious litigants [see Appendices 1 and 2]. Although they were downloaded the same day [19 October 2010] for some reason they don't coincide, even though their source is the same. That seems to me to be of less significance than the sheer bloody-mindedness of the clowns who stuck this drivel on the internet and left it there. Of what possible interest or concern to anybody [perverts excepted] is the fact [if it is a fact] that old, sick, infirm, ailing and often deceased victims of a sordid and callous justice system were branded vexatious litigants in the U.K. in the year dot? Does it really benefit a billion Chinese to know this, because some half-witted bureaucrat has stuck it on the internet at public expense? Even such idiots must know that the objects of their cowardly scorn are no more, and may well have expired decades ago. So are they likely to be suing anybody, anywhere, in the foreseeable future? No matter say the single-minded [if they possess a mind] smear-mongers. Let's use our latest device, the internet, to spread the shit as far and wide, and for as long, as possible. Our motive, Alice, is malice, the driving force behind the inventors of all grind-downers.

Naïve ignoramuses like yours truly might ask a simple but fundamental question. Why bother having laws at all when these deeply flawed and often immoral [by their standards] browbeaters exercise their own laws involving kicking the rest of us in the teeth? Ipso facto, why bother having another group of subservient, obsequious, pliant, bloated, self-serving and opinionated deviants, spiced with the inevitable pottage of puke-inducing lawyers, spending countless hours and mountains of our taxes mulling and nit-picking over legislative minutiae? Followed, in due course, by the wigged ones repeating the process once, twice, thrice, maybe more. All because according to them we occupy their fantasy-land called The Rule of Law. Given their collective record and achievements, what's law got to do with it? As for the not-so-odd and sod criminal and traitor, what happened to positive vetting and snooping when John Stonehouse somehow slipped through the gaping, elephantine hole in the spycatchers' net and ended up not doing porridge for a lengthy stretch but telling the rest of us how to behave, while this product of Old Labour swanned around in his official chauffeur-driven limo, enjoyed his many other trappings of office and milked the taxpayer and the Ministerial dupes who trusted and confided in him whenever and however he could? A sordid little con-man, a less honourable individual than this "Right-Honourable Gentleman" would be well nigh impossible to find among his seediest constituents and other fraudsters residing behind and propping up bars throughout the hammer and sceptred septic-tank called England. [For those with short memories about established Establishment corruption, see footnote 2].

Among Appendices 1 and 2 scandal-mongers will search in vain for my name. The explanation is simple. Not for me your average overlooked entry among the Smiths and Jones of this world. No, I was the first of a new breed with a list of our own [Appendix 3], and above all, dozens [probably thousands over the period involved] of internet entries carrying my own heading and individual branding and insults. What a pity I didn't know. All that effort and money for nothing. There I was, sublimely oblivious to the goodies about me accumulating in store on the internet. Don't let on, but I didn't even have a PC, and when I occasionally needed a document somebody else did it for me –

for a fee, of course. To me, computers were pointless. As for the internet, just kids' stuff. Give me books every time. Imagine my disbelief when the truth gradually dawned, thanks to a tip-off from an acquaintance. Even then I had no idea what to do about it. The general consensus was very little to nothing. To me the internet was the preserve of nerds and anoraks. Even when I found out, what can an individual do when he is up against a Government juggernaut with unlimited resources and bottomless grindability? In the U.K., with its laws and judicial system and attitudes, forget it. But I was in Thailand, which was very different. For a start, it had a Constitution protecting Thais and foreigners alike. Together, as in my case, one had extra rights benefitting families. So the situation was not hopeless. Just problematical and potentially ruinous, what with the dreaded legal buzzards forever circling and cawing overhead, ever ready, willing and able to make a killing, to feast on my flesh and bones.

Before dealing in more detail with my case I now address what this system of public intimidation and humiliation is and amounts to. First, some statistics produced from internet entries [Appendices 1 and 2].

Numbers and Years of Brandings

One branding – 1950, 1955, 1958, 1959, 1961, 1970, 1971, 1973, 1975, 1976, 1979, 1989, 2007, 2010

Two – 1956, 1964, 1965, 1966, 1980, 1982, 1990, 1991, 1993,

Three – 1981, 1985, 2002

Four – 1983, 1988, 1994, 2006, 2008

Five – 1962, 1969, 1992, 1995, 1999

Seven – 1986, 1987, 2005

Eight – 1984

Nine – 1998, 2003, 2004

Ten - 2001

Twelve – 1996, 2000

Fourteen - 1997

Notes

- According to the U.K. Government's published figures between 1950 and 2010 some 190 individuals were branded by High Court judges as vexatious litigants. Yet more – such as myself – received the same treatment in 2000 onwards at the hands of the Employment Appeal Tribunal [which contains at least two laymen] and in my case the Court of Appeal.

- Of the 190 mentioned above [spread over a period of 60 years] no less than 91 were condemned between 1996 and 2005. In other words this purge of the dissidents – comprising nearly half of the total – took place in just a decade. Purely coincidentally Blair and New Labour took office in 1997, concocted some fairy-tale about WMD's to justify a fraudulent war and invasion, and were finally ousted in mid-2010, although we all know that this would have had no effect on the judiciary, which according to rumour-humour is entirely independent and untainted by political influence, corruption and arm-twisting

- In 3 years [1996, 1997 and 2000 [and almost in 2001] vexatious litigant orders were being dished out by the High Court at an average rate of one or more a month. So if this task was not given priority what else were our lords and masters doing during this period, apart from completing and presenting their expense claims for rubber-stamping?
- Analysing the data as best I could [and disregarding the sole Company listed] I calculated that the proportion of men to women vexatious litigants was 3 to 1 respectively
- Two people are described as "deceased" – one since March 1992, nudging 20 years ago. So in naming them for public consumption and ridicule does the U.K. Government know something nobody else is aware of? Are they concerned that aggrieved spirits from the after-life will suddenly rise in protest and re-open unfinished business in the hallowed U.K. Courts? We can't have that, not without obtaining our permission first. Otherwise The System - our System, not to mention us – will look stupid. Naw, forget it. The

identities of the dead are only on the list and the internet because we employ idiots who don't care one way or the other. And/or can't speak, write or understand English.

- And what about others who may or may not still be with us, and if so barely? Take the case of Ida Matthews, who according to the Black List on the internet was given the treatment on 30 October 1950. Can Ida ever be forgiven for offending some pompous bully-boy of a judge who by now should be long gone? Certainly not. She [if it is a "she"] could start abusing our court system again, by suing some asshole who's been pissing through her letter-box. No, equality before the law is our maxim, whether or not the yob urinating in her hallway was released on probation only yesterday. But Ida was a hundred only last week. She had a birthday card from The Queen. She won't re-offend. Surely you could make an exception in her case. I implore you, your deity, take her name off the Black List before she passes away. Certainly not. Next you'll be asking us to remove the names of all the miscreants who transgressed up to say 1970 – a mere 40 years ago. Before we know it there'll be no list left. Don't you know why it exists and we use the internet as a soil pipe? It's to hold people up to public ridicule – the thing people most dread, at least according to Mel Gibson. And he should know. Apart from pandering to the lowest common denominator and sadistic tastes we have to consider the public interest. That's the overriding consideration. That's the point of publishing worldwide the names of common-or-garden nonentities who crossed swords with some pompous haranguer before most people living on the planet were even born. Name and shame is the name of the game. Provided we're not on the receiving end, naturally.

- Crazy people produce crazy results. Poor Ida Matthews is as nothing compared to other gems. Don't forget, Appendices 1 and 2 were downloaded from the internet as recently as 19 October 2010. Believe it or not, for our delectation and thigh-slapping enjoyment the following vexatious litigants were [and for all I know still are] exhibited, along with the years of their relatively recent [compared to the age of the Universe] brandings:-

1888 – Maria Annie Davies

1889 – Caroline Rawlins. Also Elizabeth Torkington and John Torkington

1892 – Giovanni Milissich

1894 – Millie Marcuson

1899 – Robert Henry Potter

1911 – Jane Cormack

1914 – Bernard Boaler. Also Louisa Robinson

1918 – Samuel Abraham Pitchforth. Also Robert Thompson and Marie Washington

1927 – Emily Dalton

1928 – Robert Loftus

1929 – Isabella Hutchinson

1932 – Alfred Thomas Newman and Annie Newman

1936 – Annie Jane Beck and William Winterburn Beck. Also Fanny Franks

1938 – Frank Charles King and Louisa Elizabeth King

Could it be that somebody realized just how ridiculous and offensive this exercise was and is to many people? Hard to say one way or the other. Judge for yourself. What is the significance and meaning behind the bracketed exclamation mark concluding the entry "MOSS [aka MOFFAT], Gerald Deceased [!]."   Did somebody finally ask the obvious question – why are we including the name of somebody who is with us no more? Or maybe he or she wondered if "Deceased" was/is the middle name of Gerald Moss-cum-Moffat? Hence the exclamation mark, as if to say "What a weird name that is!" But other mysteries remain. Why no date, when it's supplied alongside two other "deceased" entries? Not to mention that several dozen other individuals will by now have met their maker.   Maybe the anonymous list-compiler [whose "update" apparently ended on 14 December 2004] didn't know that apparently Oliver Alfred Sydney Cutts had also passed on, we know not when.   Still, one of two – or is it actually nearer thirty-two? – is the most respect our elders and betters will get from smear-mongers.

Even a glance at the list above should demonstrate that vexatious litigants often seem to prefer a pincer movement in their tactics, presumably because two heads are supposedly better than one. Just how successful this ploy is in practice is, of course, virtually impossible to gauge, since to the best of my knowledge no information exists regarding individuals, couples or any other combination who faced but somehow avoided branding. Thus we are saddled with the disappointed dual losers, who at least have the consolation of knowing they neither fought the good fight nor lost it alone. If their experience was anything like mine theirs was a losing cause from the outset, whatever the facts and law said. In alphabetical order I doff my hat to:-

Anthony and Shirley Branch

Alan David and Ann Margaret Collins

Harry Desmond and Lewis Frank Foley

Daniel and Liubov Ford

Glenford and Linbird Green

Margaret and Roston David Leicester

John Edmund and Teresa Murphy

Arthur and Frieda Alberta Robinson

Albert James and Eileen Stella Margaret Webb

Ellen Elizabeth and Francis Wood

For good measure one Appendix supplies four more pairings, viz

Annie Jane and William Winterburn Beck, Frank Charles and Louisa Elizabeth King, Alfred Thomas and Annie Newman and Elizabeth and John Torkington.

Then there's the curious case of the Gleaves, who at first sight appear to be twinned but on closer examination are apparently one and the same individual, namely Roger Charles Augustine Gleaves, who achieved the remarkable if not unique feat of having his botty smacked, judicially speaking, not once but twice in 1982 and 1985. Equally deserving of mention is "Kalibala" – pinned down as a "male"- and the splendid, impressive and confusing O'Neills, comprising Margarita O'Neill [aka John Morris] and Thomas O'Neill [aka Lord Charles Leslie Falconer of Thoronton]. Or Thornton, depending on which source takes your fancy. Speaking personally, the problem with monikers not a million miles away from Lord Falconer is that you can never be sure who and what you're dealing with, especially as the English [myself included] do enjoy a titter when it involves taking the piss out of the aristocracy. Likewise Peter Rubery Hayward [aka Sir Nicholas Walter Lyell, formerly P R Hayward]. Thus, with a wave of his wand the commoner and vexatious litigant Peter Hayward becomes a knight with a new handle and respect. And not just from the hoi-polloi. Can I emulate Sir Nicholas Lyell by changing my nomenclature to The Very Honourable Sir Boswell Newthaven? Or something resembling Dick Chitole, another vexatious litigant whose remarkable and dubious moniker surely expresses with precision and clarity how I and many others regard those who publish smears about others on the internet. Meanwhile spare a thought for the Reverend Paul Stewart Williamson, who obviously ain't exactly your average vicar. Tut, tut and more tut, Rev. Taking on The Establishment? Only mugs like me do that. What must your flock-knockers be saying behind your back, you naughty, naughty boy. Good on ya, mate?

Needless to add, the overwhelming majority of members of the august club of vexatious litigants did not enlist voluntarily. More often than not they owed the honour to some bilious, obscure High Court beak who was obviously not best pleased about activities incurring his touch-paper animosity, such as breathing in his presence. As for myself, without wishing to brag about it, I was the founder member of VexLit Part 2 [Appendix 3], whose fall from grace or rise to prominence had common roots with my distinguished ancestors but diverged when the sadly-departed New Labour Government created what might be termed a New Justice System, replete with individuals who are commonly referred to as "laymen", "lay people" or political stooges, depending on which side of fantasy one occupies [see Appendices 4 and 5]. Without being too ungenerous, we VexLits 2 became the latest progenitors of the New Experiment in social, socialist engineering, whereby the human race was divided into those entitled to work [aka women and minorities] and deadbeat losers [aka New Labour M.P.'s or men who were born and educated in England and were transparently better qualified to do the job but suffered from an incurable disability which was out of fashion with the dumb, illiterate twerps constituting the Labour Government. The disability was widespread among non-women and non-minorities. The only remedy was to visit Thailand for a gender operation, which was extremely drastic, time-consuming and embarrassingly painful in the region of the groin and the wallet. So, to my chagrin, I passed up the chance and instead broke wind. So I was forced to endure another operation, this time conducted by Industrial [now Employment, it sounds better to the masses] Tribunals and the Employment Appeal Tribunal, buttressed – naturally – by our brothers in the Court of Appeal, all harnessed to the left bandwagon wheel. Good idea, as all socialist claptrap is. We've had plenty of practice, the system's in place and the outcome's assured. Let the sadism commence.

So to whom am I and the other miserable wretches indebted for bestowing, publishing and maintaining our distinguished status as vexatious litigants, or, as I would prefer to say, dropping us in the shit and keeping us there? I must begin where the proceedings against me began and in whose name the internet smears appear, namely the U.K. Attorneys-General.

According to information obtained under freedom of information legislation the identities of the most recent Attorney-Generals are as follows:-

Sir John Morris – 1997-9

Lord Williams of Mostyn – 1999-2001

Lord Goldsmith – 2001-7

Baroness Scotland of Asthal – 2007-10

Dominic Grieve – 2010 - now

But the names of none of the above appeared on the documents I saw at the Court of Appeal. In most cases the reason was obvious – they didn't occupy the job before or in 2000, when the order was issued against me. But that doesn't mean to say they couldn't have done something about the internet smears from 2000 until now, Dominic Grieve and Ken Clarke, both Ministers in the new coalition Government included. They chose to do damn all despite my protests and complaints. As for the previous bunch of losers, the least said the better.

No, whatever information bureaucrats provide I can usually recall who my enemies are. Although at the time I didn't know why his name was on the documents authorizing the proceedings against me and I'd never heard of him – which is unusual, since most authoritarians have a habit of thrusting themselves down one's gullet – the mental note I made eventually proved to be accurate. The name of my benefactor was on another list of Solicitors General largely supplied to me under FOI legislation. It comprises:-

Sir Derek Spencer [1992 – 1997]

Lord Falconer of Thoroton [1997 – 1998] – see "Footnote" below

Ross Cranston [1998 – 2001]

Harriet Harman [2001 – 2005]

Mike O'Brien [2005 – 2007]

Vera Baird [2007 – 2010]

Edward Garnier [2010 – now]

No prizes for guessing who it was. One Ross Cranston, an Australian carpet-bagger who, having exercised his delegated powers to act as a tough-guy enforcer and thereby done his duty in the public interest, has since departed the UK political scene. Crocodile tears will I shed none.

Footnote – are my worst suspicions now confirmed that somebody out there is taking the piss? In my earlier sympathetic, if not pathetic, aside about vexatious litigants I referred to Margarita O'Neill [aka John Morris] and Thomas O'Neill [aka Lord Charles Leslie Falconer of Thoronton – or Thornton, whichever version you prefer], who according to Appendices 1 and 2 were branded vexatious litigants on the same day, namely 9 June 1998. Now I come across Lord Falconer of Thoroton, which location, according to official records, enjoys no less than three different spellings, doubtless designed to drive the Post Office mad. Can this be true, or have I missed something on my travels? One minute the U.K. Solicitor-General and, need I add, another crony of the latter-day saint and Catholic-convert Tony Blair, the next a vexatious litigant. Could he have authorized proceedings against himself? Absolutely, if the dates are any guide. His term of office was between 1997 and 1998, so he had plenty of time to rubber-stamp his own destruction in mid-1998. The mind boggles. But the doubts persist. Take another look at the pseudonym of Margarita O'Neill. Does John Morris ring any bells? It should. He was the Attorney-General from 1997-1999, more or less coinciding with Falconer's reign.

<u>Conclusion</u> – too ridiculous by half, even by New Labour standards [if there are any]

As regards the Employment Appeal Tribunal, according to information made available to me under FOI legislation its Presidents comprise:-

Sir Thomas Morrison [1996 – 1999]

Sir John Lindsay [1999 – 2002]

Sir Michael Burton [2002 – 2006]

Sir Patrick Elias [2006 – 2008]

Sir Nicholas Underhill [2009 – now]

In England and Wales the Resident EAT judges are Judge Peter Clark and Judge McMullen QC.

Since Lindsay and two laymen [Messrs. D. Chadwick and P.R.A. Jacques] issued their order against me and directly or indirectly authorized its insertion on the internet in 2000 none of their successors have put a stop to it, and Underhill has not only endorsed such action he has made it clear that in his eyes thinking and acting otherwise is infra-dig.

Two lists of lay members of the EAT are at Appendices 4 and 5. The names of Messrs. Chadwick and Jacques appear on the first list [dated November 2004] but not the second [dated December 2010]. Next to nothing is known about these two, because apparently those who condemn others to notoriety on the internet are entitled to their privacy, whereas the victims and their families are not. As for The Honourable Mr. Justice Lindsay apparently he and his employer have no qualms about displaying his credentials on the internet, although according to the same source "lay members *normally* have an equal voice in making decisions [my italics]. [Don't bother asking when and why, because such information is only for those who must be obeyed without reservation]. How reassuring, though, that in an age of austerity for people who do an honest day's labour to eke out barely enough to keep the wolf from the door and to pay the bills for a couple of wars Dave and others responsible – "we're all in this together" says he, as if butter wouldn't melt up his backside - have embarked on a major recruitment drive to enlist another 350 members of Employment Tribunals, doubtless in response to the shoals of illiterate and incompetent females and minorities – and their lawyers, naturally – who can't wait to plunder the public coffers with their discrimination claims. Presided over by a clique of sympathetic or pathetic judges struggling by on two grand a week, most ably aided and abetted by a couple of "members" [laymen to you and me], one each from the employee and employer "panels" – formed from whom and how and selected by whom and how I know not, but can imagine. But we do know – if you believe what you're told – on what basis judges get the cushy numbers in life. Funny that my own experiences coincide in few respects with the Qualities and Abilities listed in the job description at Appendix 6.

Legally speaking, Cranston authorized the vexatious litigant proceeding against me, and Lindsay, Chadwick and Jacques produced a judgment upheld by three Court of Appeal judges, about all of whom more later. Issuing an order against me was not inevitable. Nor was sticking their decisions and judgments on the internet for a minute, let alone for more than ten years. [Note the example at Appendix 1 in Chapter 4, which was downloaded on 22 January 2011. Although the smear supposedly relates to an individual named Barker it's not his name that still appears in BLOCK LETTERS in the heading. I wonder why not?   Perhaps because Underhill and his mates inside the English judiciary seem to think the victims can and must do nothing about it]. Since when were they crowned Masters of the Universe?

For an exercise in smug humbug and self-satisfied and vacuous justification for a system rejected by most countries because it clearly breaches basic human rights one need look no further than an article dated July 2010 published on the internet by the U.K. Treasury Solicitor, ironically under the banner "Human Rights", as if this insult to the intelligence actually enhanced, not diminished, such rights [3]. Below, for one's amusement, are a few extracts, with my observations.

- Limiting the right to a fair trial enshrined in Article 6 of the European Convention of [sic] Human Rights "must be done only when no other options remain". Well here's one option that's always been available, mate. Don't have the system, like most other countries, which manage to survive without it despite being looked down on by upper-class twits cluttering up the streets of Whitehall. And, as a lawyer – and therefore, somebody who reputedly knows everything, especially about the law – try checking the title of the European Convention before next rushing into print

- "This ensures that the provision is not being used arbitrarily to remove a citizen's rights". Ensures? Believe it or not, he's on about "the fact that personal consideration is given in each case by one of the Law Officers". Putting aside the two grammatical errors in this single paragraph [which I refuse to do] is this individual seriously asking us to accept that "Law Officers" safeguard human rights? If so he or she is trying it on with the wrong person and asking a few million others to disregard inconvenient, scandalous but historical abuses of power euphemistically dubbed "miscarriages of justice"

- The final paragraph of this propagandist missive contains a few more gems, like "Those who have been proclaimed vexatious……are simply required to take an additional step". Somehow "proclaimed" seems so much better than the bald truth, where words like "branded" and "smeared" might crop up. And the victims are "simply" required to do the light fantastic to regain what's been stolen from them by some officious busy-body – sorry "Law Officers, who in my case were nothing of the sort. Two of the three branders were laymen, and therefore no more qualified to pass judgment on me and my actions than the local postman, who at the time could have been no less than the latest rising star in the New Labour ranks, who has recently plummeted to earth, aided and abetted by his devoted and faithful spouse, whose daily dalliances with his [and obviously her] body guard and caresser remind us that we are all sinners at heart – except judges, need I add in haste. "Simply" it may be to The Treasury Solicitor but simply it never is to normal people, thanks to him and his increasingly avaricious and incompetent brothers-in-law. See for yourself, if you're inclined to squander your life-savings, house, car, marriage and whatever's left observing the antics of the wig-wearers.

- Best of all, the final sentence, quoted in its entirety. "It has, therefore, been held that the Section 42 and consequently, the Section 33 procedure, does [sic] not violate either the European Convention on Human Rights or the Human Rights Act 1998". Nice to see the correction from "of" to "on". But what about "therefore", "consequently" and "does", in the singular? Is the latter another grammatical error, or, more logically, does it mean whatever was decided applies to a Section 42 case and "therefore" and "consequently" were tagged on afterwards, as if the procedures and laws are identical, which they aren't? Most importantly of all, what does "been held" mean and amount to? Been held by whom, in what forum and when? If it's "been held" by a Court, why doesn't the source of this information supply the details, because to me anything less is not only worthless it raises the possibility that we, the readers, are being conned into accepting the unacceptable. Did a European or International Court make the decision? If not, who cares what the judiciary which concocted this abominable and intolerable system say and rule in its own defence? At the foot of the Treasury Solicitor's homily to U.K. justice is a list of six cases, four of them beginning A.G., meaning the Attorney-General. Another involves the Official Receiver. The list [which we are told is not exhaustive] is headed "Some useful authorities relating to vexatious litigation" [3]. My doubts are not assuaged. Nor were they about Essex University.

Following publication of three books in quick succession I decided to take a break, which in my case meant being relatively unoccupied for about a week. Physically, that is. Asking myself "What next?" I decided to have another bash at enrolling for a PhD in Criminology, researching landed property fraud, which formed the nuclei of my books *Mortar Boarding* and *Ill A Fraud*. Trawling the internet, in England the most promising prospect seemed to be Essex University, which appeared to have top-notch supervisors [the very people I most needed, and didn't get, after enrolling for a similar course, which I soon quit, at James Cook University in Australia] in the relevant Department. Being a "nothing venture, nothing gained" type of individual, at the end of August 2010 I duly applied for entry to Essex University. Curious to know how my application was progressing, soon afterwards I looked into the Essex U processing procedures, and came across a reference to "myEssex" , a portal conveying information to applicants to its courses. Sifting through the items on the webpage produced little of interest. So I tried searching under myEssex geoffrey wheen, which produced an entirely unexpected result. There, at the top of the page, in the most prominent position possible, was the bad penny, the EAT case, yet again. How could this be, and what was the point? More disturbingly, who could link myself, this particular University and a 10 year-old EAT case? And how? Thinking the outcome might be a fluke, I tried various other combinations, to no avail.

Back to square one. How could anyone link me to Essex U? I was an applicant, not a student. Apart from myself and my partner [who had told nobody else] only Essex U knew I'd contacted and applied to it. Nobody could have intercepted and opened the envelope containing my application and supporting documents because they were enclosed in a parcel in my presence in the local FedEx office, and thereafter sent via its courier service to Essex U. It was inconceivable, at least to me, that FedEx had played any part in the latest internet smear. Which left Essex U and two other logical possibilities. The first was that Essex U had contacted an outside body and/or person in order, for instance, to check my credentials. Not only was that to be expected doing so was part and parcel of the Essex U processing procedures. Nothing wrong with that, unless somebody had seized the opportunity and knowledge to stick one on me via the internet. If so, at the very least my privacy rights had been impinged. But it wasn't a fanciful or even remote possibility, because certain University-types would have relished the chance to wreck my enrolment chances and get even on the internet in one foul swoop. After all, Universities no more appreciate criticism from outsiders than do other Establishment props. [for a sample of academic quirks and jerks see my book *Mortar Boarding*]. To narrow down the contenders, I asked Essex U who, if anybody, had been contacted, and got no reply. Which could mean one of several things. Either it had been in touch with outsider[s] but refused to divulge who on grounds of confidentiality or for some other unknown reason, or it hadn't, which meant nobody else was implicated. Of the two I found the first the more likely possibility. If so, Essex U was involved in a cover-up. What's more, although it flatly denied being responsible or involved if it were innocent and had been roped into a mess it seemed peculiar to me not only that Essex U seemed unconcerned and even tried to blame Google and asserted the same result could be obtained regardless of the input [which I rapidly disproved], but also that it didn't get the entry removed pronto. Against that, it had nothing to do with the dirty tricks which had gone before our contact in August 2010. But for now at least, it stayed in the loop.

Here there are three distinct but related areas of concern. They are [a] missing documents, [b] why my application for PhD entry was rejected and [c] how and why the familiar smear about me came to be linked with Essex University on its website, which exists for the benefit of its students, which, being a mere applicant, I was not. Which in turn raises another, more disturbing and sinister possibility. If the answers don't stack up what does that amount to?   If the answers made sense independently of each other maybe yet again the unfortunate coincidence whitewashers would prevail. If, however, they didn't………? So, taken independently, do the explanations ring true, or were the reasons concocted because Essex University was not coming clean and was implicated or involved in a cover up?

So it was necessary to look at three things.

Firstly, why my application documents went missing, which is not a minor issue. To an alarming and superficially baffling degree I had already experienced this phenomenon, and chronicled it in my book *Mortar Boarding*. In a nutshell, it involved incompetence or worse by University employees – invariably female – who, on the face of it, couldn't be trusted to peel a banana. Time after time, in different countries and Universities, they somehow managed to lose or misplace important documents such as enrolment applications. Now their stupidity may have been of no concern to the dopes who employed them in the first place, but privacy, security and I.D. theft issues were involved, often about disinterested parties. For instance, I was invariably required to supply personal information about my partner, which these clowns showed little or no concern to protect. Nor did the ICO take the issue seriously, any more than it did about the legal or illegal interception of our confidential and sensitive communications, some of which exercises breached the laws of the foreign countries where we lived.

Since when has it been the business or right of the U.K. Government to record and read my communications to the Attorney-General of Thailand, or to tap my or her phone calls to Thai lawyers? Ask them, as I did, and get bullshit in return for your trouble. And just like their attempts to prove black is white the excuses I received from these Universities ranged from the dubious to the bizarre. So what did Essex University have to say when, would you believe, my PhD application, sent from Thailand to England by expensive FedEx courier for security reasons, got lost, or as one wag put it went missing, but was not lost. Try telling that one to the parents of a toddler who's disappeared without trace. "Don't panic, take it easy, he's only missing, not lost. He'll turn up sooner or later. Now can I get back to reading "The Sun"? Cor, look at those beauties".

So what did Essex U have to say about the subject? Familiar alarm bells started resonating when, after I had enquired what was happening about my application on 22 September 2010 the Executive Officer to the Vice-Chancellor told me "We do not however appear to have a record of your application which I find puzzling given our thorough admissions processes". I agreed, the more so since the procedures about registering my application weren't followed either, as I was to discover later. However, again on 22 September 2010 - 3 weeks after my application was received by the University and only after I sent a chasing e-mail – a Graduate Admissions Officer said the following:-

"I've tracked the FedEx envelope to the University. It was received in central stores on 2nd September then forwarded and signed for in the department of Sociology by Sheila Marina. Michele Hall was away from 3rd – 13tth September and it is their policy to leave all post until her return. I see no reason why Michele not to have sent it on to me when she was able to open the post, but she admits there will have been a delay in this. She is checking her office again". In a separate e-mail about this episode it was stated "it has highlighted a flaw in our procedures which we will be looking at'. Yet when I advised her on 3 September that according to FedEx the documents had arrived the previous day the supposedly absent Michele Hall replied by return, stating "This would have gone to our central mailing office, so should be with me today. I will contact you as soon as I have the documents". Does that sound like the same person who "was away from 3rd – 13th September?" And if Michele Hall was actually at work on 3rd September and not "away" – which is consistent with her answering my e-mail that day – why didn't she pursue the documents, which she told me should be with her later that day? Funny how I always seem to be at the receiving end of institutional "flaws" perpetrated invariably by females. And stories which don't make sense. Nor did it end there. It never does, especially where women are involved. Like invariably.

Issue Number Two. Essex University's explanations about the internet entry – the most obvious underlying reason for, or at least influence on, the adverse PhD decision, whatever its formal answer[s]. Understandably, prudently and logically in the final paragraph of his e-mail to his colleagues dated 16 September 2010 the Director of Information Services said "I would urge some caution and care in ensuring that we provide a single co-ordinated response". In other words, make sure our ducks are in line. [Some of the relevant correspondence is at Appendix 7]. Likewise the tactics employed by others involved in what was smelling more and more like a conspiratorial cover-up going well beyond the reaches of Essexland.

Here again, I complained to the Information Commissioner, who apart from ignoring my six straight e-mails [dated 17, 22 and 23 September

2010, 14 October, 14 and 21 November 2010 about Essex University and others, including the U.K. Government snoopers, then tried to fob me off with half-baked, feeble excuses about how busy he was. Funny how another document I obtained recorded that if I complained to the Information Commissioner he "will find there is no case to answer" – at which point he had issued no such conclusion. All he'd done was pretend I and my e-mails to him didn't exist.

Finally, the reasons given for declining my PhD application. Here the most instructive way to proceed is to compare what should have happened – per Essex University's formal internal procedures, which were of course prepared and approved long before I and my application put in an appearance – with what actually occurred. At this point I provide below a copy of my research proposal, which, along with other salient details, was only submitted because the relevant Head of Department had encouraged me to apply. Why he did so, in the light of what happened later, is another question open to different interpretations.

Below is the research proposal I submitted as part of my application.

Research Proposal

FRAUD IN LANDED PROPERTY

First, a brief and cursory reference about terminology. Whereas most people associate fraud with a breach of criminal [invariably Statute] law civil law [e.g. a tort or breach of contract] may also have been impinged. Indeed, both a criminal prosecution and a civil suit might successively be launched. However, due to their limited but onerous remits law enforcement agencies like the police and F.B.I. concern themselves solely with alleged criminal offences, so any statistics and other information gleaned from such sources are not only strictly limited they conceal and distort numerous other incidents of fraud unreported by individuals and institutions. Just how many and their impact cannot even be estimated – how can one count something which apparently hasn't happened? – but various sources, including the police, know that fraud is seriously under-reported and estimated. Consequently what we know is but the tip of a voluminous iceberg of unknown weight and dimensions.

Which brings me to what is meant by "property". Researchers and others elsewhere have a habit of using the term loosely and ambiguously, creating yet more doubt and confusion. Although the word is bandied about, including in texts and police statistics, property not only encompasses a host of assets in the context of my research property fraud and mortgage fraud are frequently interchanged, when in fact fraud in the landed property sphere is no more restricted to mortgage fraud than theft is to burglary. Yet why this is so is easy to explain. So far as current knowledge and academic research are concerned to all intents and purposes they are synonymous. Plenty is known about mortgage fraud, and next to nothing about all the rest. [I cite some examples of the great unknown in my book *Ill A Fraud*]. To a property practitioner this is baffling, not least because the scale of, and pickings from, mortgage fraud are as nothing compared to other activities, such as city centre developments and re-developments and out-of-town shopping malls. Are we to believe that property fraud begins and ends with the comparative peanuts [some peanuts] from mortgage scams? Or is the volume of the fraudberg far greater than the mortgage fraudsters, victims and investigators would lead us to believe? A size which organized crime could and would handle without much difficulty, thanks in part to the preponderance of industry insiders known to be involved in expanding mortgage rackets. Who are they? Just about any group involved in making, processing, checking and approving mortgage applications and issuing loans. Along with attorneys, appraisers, owners of businesses, builders, realtors, title agents, real estate investors, straw buyers and their recruiters, even a senior bank executive. Not just conspirators, organized criminals in the business of threatening and intimidating honest practitioners who don't play ball.

If American sources are any guide the losses incurred from mortgage fraud alone run to billions of dollars a year and climbing. By way of example, from among the 67 FBI cases which I dissected and analysed for my book about property fraud [about which more later], in a mortgage fraud allegedly perpetrated by only a handful of the officers and employees of a Money Store and their associates mortgage lenders were estimated to have been deprived of over $35 million in loans. Not only did the boss alone take $16.8 million apparently she squandered her victims' home equities on luxuries for herself and spent a cool $800,000 on a wedding for herself and a co-conspirator. But compared to the likes of Charles Ponzi, Bernie Madoff and lawyers Marc Dreier and an anonymous defence attorney [branded "a street gangster"] charged with heading a racketeering conspiracy that included murdering a witness in a drug case, the attempted hiring of a hitman in another drug case, wire fraud and money laundering her transgressions were almost petty. Nevertheless, the female contingent inevitably play no small role in real estate swindles. Not only are female realtors prevalent and highly successful in the business my analysis of the F.B.I. evidence suggested that the gender gap between real estate fraudsters was narrowing. Between the ages of 31 and 35, 41 to 45 and 51 to 55 the proportion of male to female property fraudsters dropped to about 2 to 1. Between them by my reckoning of 67 cases reported by the FBI for 2009 alone the total losses incurred by the lenders exceeded $1.013 billion. For one year, for one type of property fraud, in one country [where mortgage fraud has been likened to a "near epidemic"] and according to a single source. For what it's worth, another source estimated that in the U.S.A. annual losses from mortgage fraud ranged from $4 to 6 billion.

Although these figures are mind-boggling, what struck me above all was the disparity between the estimates, attributable, to a large extent, to the pace of acceleration in incidents of mortgage fraud. At what point do "estimates" become guesses? And are these "losses" actual ones, bearing in mind that lenders can and do attempt to recoup their outlay via, for instance, forced sale of re-possessed houses, about which even less is known? Talking of which, how big a problem is property fraud in burgeoning economies like China and India [where corruption is a staple diet] and in countries where secrecy is the watchword?

Stating that figures and statistics alone mean very little can be otherwise demonstrated. It is indisputable [see, for instance, various studies conducted by Michael Levi] that purely in financial terms a single property scam may eclipse the losses sustained by numerous victims of other frauds and crimes such as theft. So how is the damage to be counted and assessed? In numerical or financial terms? Are we to disregard the one event because it involves a sole, and above all wealthy, victim who/which can cope with the loss? If so, the argument is fallacious, because the effects of property fraud invariably ripple far beyond the point of initial entry, often affecting property values in whole districts or neighbourhoods. And sometimes well beyond. Analysts seeking explanations for the failure by the US housing market to recover despite kick-start incentives [including exceptionally low mortgage rates] have said that none of it makes much difference to demand when house-owners default because the job and income they pretended to have to get on the housing ladder didn't exist. Thousands of them, with more to come. Ten or even twenty years before the US housing market is back where it was only 2 or 3 years ago. Meanwhile houses valued at $300,000 then now fetch $120,000. Did someone suggest that real estate fraud is a victimless crime?

But hasn't the global recession at least curtailed mortgage fraud? On the contrary, is the somewhat surprising and deflating answer, at least according to informed sources. What property fraudsters lose from picking one pocket they recoup or expand by filching from another. So anyone who claims that mortgage and property fraud are one and the same is ignoring logic and what motivates fraudsters, who I've likened to entrepreneurs who prefer invention to industry to turn a profit. As

Frederick Bastiat, the 19th century French economist, author and statesman said shortly before his death "Men will resort to plunder whenever plunder is easier than work. Under these conditions neither religion nor morality can stop it". [About this, my book *Moral Beaks and Claws* refers]. Is fraud a latter-day equivalent of plunder? If not, it's a close relative. Theft not by force - re-quoting Bastiat, "Law is force......what a violent and futile effort it is to use force in the matters of morality and religion" - but through artifice and cunning, characteristics of a predatory fox, in my eyes the vulpine embodiment of a fraudster.

In the lexicon of crime fraud is a prized option for existing or potential transgressors. Again, I assessed the pros and cons in my book. The pros win hands down. Put simply, landed property fraud is relatively easy to accomplish, difficult to detect and often carries vast, if not obscene, rewards. Added to the theory is the practice. The ignorance and indifference of the police, the reluctance/refusal to complain [tantamount to complicity], the inadequacies and complexities of the relevant laws and the probability of an acquittal [in the unlikely event of the perpetrator being nabbed and prosecuted]. A depressing scenario? If in doubt, consult the record of the Serious Fraud Office, which seems to have an unerring tradition of squandering public money on botched prosecutions. However you slice it, fraud certainly beats work. Without wishing to rub salt in its scattered wounds, the UK's Serious Fraud Office [otherwise known in "Private Eye" as the "Serious Farce Office"] is a bad case in point. Seeking and obtaining information from it was like pulling teeth. Almost 15 months after I initially requested information from it – and then only after the Information Commissioner had issued a condemnatory Decision Notice did it deign to supply not what I had requested but a few crumbs which I boiled down to the following single sentence, about which even then it tried to impose restrictions on its publication under copyright laws. This hard-earned gem [or was it paste?] was "About mortgage fraud, over a 20 year period the UK SFO successfully completed just 4 prosecutions involving about 13 million pounds and resulting in the imprisonment of 10 defendants for a total of 25.5 years and their disqualification to act as company directors for a total of 29 years." Compare its performance – which was only marginally worse than those of other public bodies in the UK - with that of its counterpart in New Zealand, whose Director answered all my requests, and of the F.B.I., which [like an officer of the UK's Building Societies Association] made no attempt to conceal the magnitude of the problem and its counter-response. Nor is the problem a new one. Nearly twenty years ago I first read a book entitled *"Mortgage Fraud"* written by Michael Clarke, whose message then and now was loud and clear. But still largely ignored, at least by law enforcement agencies in England. Hardly surprising, given that the police accord fraud a low priority, resources are finite [even though the Metropolitan Police manage to cram in a mere 55,000 employees] and financial institutions – which frequently adopt policies of silence after being defrauded – can and do pass on losses to non-participant victims, namely the general public. Is this what fraudsters mean when asserting that fraud is a victimless crime?

Trust, an instinctive quality inculcated in everyone at birth until battered by experience, is our Achilles heel which the fraudster seeks, exploits and betrays. Without trust scams abort. At the risk of stating the obvious, much the same could be said about greed, the cornerstone of capitalist endeavour and initiative. Who can resist the allure, the temptation, to be better than the next man? That said, a surprising number of victims virtually beg to be swindled through their own stupidity and failure to take the most elementary precautions. Clearly the world is full of gullible people who can't wait to be gulled. No legislation, no warnings, no safeguards can or will protect those who still believe in fairies, or in property terms a sure-fire way to get rich overnight. Victims of fraudsters seem to differ from those of other criminals. Whereas most people have no qualms about admitting that their assets have been stolen by thieves or burglars and complaining to the police about it, when it comes to fraud the opposite seems to be the rule. Suffering in silence [sometimes permanently] seems to be the preferred, if not only, option. Is this because seeming to look stupid in the eyes of others is to pile insult on injury? And who wins twice over? Why, the betrayer of trust, ever ready to repeat the dose for his next "victimless" victim, some of whom are racked with unremitting guilt and remorse, endlessly asking themselves the unanswerable question "How could I have been so stupid?" No consolation to be told they aren't the first, nor will be the last, willing but unwitting dupe of an unscrupulous actor ever-ready to seek out the next prey of his victimless scam.

In one of its judgments the venerable House of Lords has it on record that because fraud/deceit is immoral it deserves singular punishment. For my part [as I argued in my latest book *Moral Beaks and Claws*] I contend that by virtue of their own arguments fraudsters are amoral and therefore beyond redemption, at least until they recognize and accept the consequences of their own actions on other people and society as a whole. Until then my sympathies reside almost entirely with the victims.

My book *Ill A Fraud* was aimed at a wide readership possessing little or no knowledge of property fraud. As such it makes no pretensions to be an academic tome written for a select, exclusive readership. On the contrary, I recognize and accept its limitations. However, before writing it I undertook research for about two years, so much of the spadework for a PhD has already been done.

Despite the lack of co-operation from many quarters – some of whom were intent on denying me access to their domains – and the hopeless inadequacy of freedom of information legislation, which by and large was used as a vehicle to stymie and delay my work some progress and enlightenment have resulted from my toil. Beforehand, with the notable exception of mortgage fraud virtually nothing was known publicly, or at least had been published, about property fraud. Michael Levi, an academic and author of various articles and leader of the group which produced an ACPO report [which said almost nothing of relevance to my work] is probably the foremost expert on fraud in the UK, yet is clearly no expert on property fraud. Nor, to the best of my knowledge, is anyone else. So, as I pointed out in my book, academic exploration into this desert of knowledge was and is warranted and necessary. By the same token some criminologists have argued that their discipline is too theoretical and being multi-faceted should be more receptive to input from non-criminologist specialists from other fields. If that is so in my case the question then becomes, how does and can what I've already done slot in with the wider picture and context and with current and future work and thinking in the Sociology Department of Essex University? To find out I scanned the research interests of the relevant staff, only to come across two specifying criminology. Disappointing, but not desperately so, since they happen to be Doctors Pam Cox [Dean of the Graduate School] and Eamonn Carrabine, the Head of Department, who suggested I apply. So hopefully suitable supervision can be made available.

In conclusion:-

- In my view my research has made, and would make, a substantial contribution to the current body of work in the field, such as it is
- Further work would probably entail empirical research
- Having already completed substantial research and a book my producing a PhD within another two years at the outside would not be an unreasonable aim and expectation
- Being retired, I can and would devote my time and energies full-time to the task, which I am confident would be completed satisfactorily and promptly

After spending my working life in real estate one of the principal reasons for my taking this initiative was to acquire fresh knowledge in a new but related field, of which criminology appealed most for various reasons. So I would need and welcome input and guidance from supervisor[s], especially about the theoretical aspects of criminology.

………………Geoffrey Arnold Wheen
…………………………………Date

According to Essex University's Graduate Admissions Handbook Issued November 2007 and Revised October 2008:-

8.5.1 – If the selector feels that the applicant does not have the potential to succeed in the chosen scheme or area of research, then the application should be rejected. This will generate a letter to the applicant, and they may request feedback if they wish.

8.5.2 – Rejections for research study in an area in which the department/centre can offer supervision, should be reviewed by a second selector if they are initially rejected

13.1.2 – Ensure that where an application is received to undertake research in an area in which the department offers supervision, two designated and trained members of staff are involved in the admissions decision.

Essex University also has a "principle" barring direct or indirect discrimination on umpteen grounds, age included.

Compare the above to what happened.

In an e-mail dated 22 September 2010 [obtained under the Data Protection Act] from a Departmental Administrator to her colleague she said, inter alia, "As Eamonn will be unable to supervise the student himself, he had been waiting to speak with Dr Pete Fussey, a newly-appointed member of staff working in the field of criminology'. ["Eamonn" is Eamonn Carrabine, the Head of the Sociology Department].

According to version Number 1 [included in the first batch of documents sent to me] on 22 September Carrabine said to Fussey "It was good to catch up earlier on today, and following on from our conversation about PhD supervision I have left in your pigeon hole an application from Geoffrey Wheen. I am forwarding on his initial email to me and I think it might be an interesting thesis to supervise".

Hours later the same individuals correspond. This time Carrabine tells Fussey "I understand that the applicant Geoffrey Wheen has been in touch with the University chasing up his application – Pete I've taken back the folder to have a closer look at his application and I'm not sure that his proposal is up to our academic standards. Plus on closer inspection I don't think it is really in your field. I have the file with me if you want to look over it, but will be passing it on to Lydia for her view as Graduate Director as she will need to assess the academic merits of the application".

[Fussey is supposedly qualified in criminology. Lydia is Lydia Morris].

This is an individual who knew my application was deposited at Essex University from 2nd September onwards – because I had told him, by e-mail – so could have had access to it from then onwards. I was also told my application, which couldn't be located, was with him. The same individual encouraged me to apply and supply confidential information – neither of which were secure –

together with a research proposal and an example of my work. Having had plenty of time to mull it all over, decide it's an interesting proposal to supervise, consult a potential supervisor [Fussey], and pass on my application for further action within the blink of an eye for no logical or apparent reason he suddenly and inexplicably decides all his previous actions and thoughts were up the creek.

Incidentally, after I applied for all the information Essex U held about me inexplicably my own application was excluded, which seemed very peculiar then and now. Why did Carrabine and the data controller not spot this glaring deficiency before sending a supposedly complete basket of documents? What did they have to say? Surprise, surprise. It had been "overlooked".

Version Number two – which surfaced after I had requested more information and had raised the issue of the internet entry involving Essex U with the Vice-Chancellor's and Registrar's Offices, originally on 15 September 2010, – ran roughly as follows. My research proposal is crap, which anybody can assert about anything when he's put up to it or told to do so. That's the value of having had a proper job, working in organizations which do just that constantly, regardless of the truth.

Finally, on 12 October 2010, the Graduate Director, Professor Lydia Morris wrote as corroborate the refusal and supply her own reasons, coupled with the comment "We do not routinely give reasons for a negative decision". About which I refer to the extracts from Essex University's Graduate Admissions Handbook, quoted earlier.

Originally, no problem. Then, weeks after my application had been received, only one concern was raised – academic standards, about which they had had the requisite information for weeks. After I continued probing and obtaining more information the reasons started changing, and involved other members of staff, one of whom [Fussey], a new-appointee, who judging by his photo on the internet looks marginally older and therefore experienced than the students to whom he preaches, had apparently been given the file, and then had it taken away the next day, so his opinion was not sought – except later, to pad out the excuses – an old dodge favoured by lawyers. Moreover, if Carrabine and Fussey had acted in unison, by rejecting my application promptly the

University's procedures say that's the end of it. [Actually, if the Handbook had been applied and Carrabine thought what he's supposed to have done before his customary flip-flop he could have rejected my application on his own]. So why didn't they do so? Why did Essex U waste weeks waiting for the opinions of the boss, which were superfluous? More beefing up, or attempts to conceal what actually happened?

None of which was known to me at the time. But smelling the same rodent as now, on 6 December I requested additional information from Essex University regarding individuals who had been offered enrolment on its PhD course in criminology.

At Appendix 8 are its answers, which do not support or sustain its original rejection about my inadequate qualifications. On the contrary, given their ages and admitted lack of work experience, most of them appeared far inferior to me, much as I expected. Although the information supplied was seriously deficient as regards Criminology in particular here was more evidence of padding and contradictions between the current story, the previous ones and the relevant Handbook. Bit late in the day, too, to tell me Essex University only runs a PhD course in sociology, not criminology. In which case, were either Carrabine or Fussey ever qualified to supervise me or my research proposal? What does it matter, when the name of the game is obfuscation and delusion. Conclusion – true and convincing? No siree.

Strange too that the Information Commissioner's Office – which has insisted that the drivel about me on the internet for over a decade does not contravene the U.K. Data Protection Act, as if that were the end of the matter legally, ethically and morally - has never responded about this and other obvious gaps in the chain of events.

·

APPENDIX ONE

List of Vexatious Litigants [1]

Vexatious litigants

A vexatious litigant is a person who has been forbidden by a High Court Judge to issue civil proceedings in any court in England and Wales without permission. Below is a list of the vexatious litigants and the date the order was made.

List of vexatious litigants

A | B | C | D | E | F | G | H | J | K | L | M | N | O | P | R | S | T | V | W | Y

A

ADAMS, Leslie James - 20 May 1966

ABIOLA, Zainab Duke - 21 March 2006

AKENA, Adoko - 20 May 2004

ALEXANDER, Anthony - 26 November 2003

ALLAN, George Harvey - 18 June 1964

ALLAN, Theophilus Vincent - 8 July 1987

ALI, Haider - 13th May 2008

AMIN, Azad - 12 July 2000

ARNOLD, Dorothy Mignon (aka Gracie) - 17 December 1956

ARORA, Krishan Kumar (for a period of 12 years only) - 23 July 2001

AUBURN, Jack (aka MORTON, Herbert) - 4 November 1976

B

BADIBANGA, Kay Etienne - 17 February 2003

BARNES, Peter Michael - 4 December 2002

BARRETT, Alan Gordon (for a period of 12 years only) - 9 October 2001

BARRETT, Stanley Arthur - 20 October 1953

BEBBINGTON, Ann Marjorie (aka EASTON, Ann Cholmondeley) - 31 January 1969

BECKER, Dorothy - 13 March 1969

BENTON, Paul - 28 July 2004

BHAMJEE, Ismail Abdulhai - 8 December 2003

BISHOP, Malcolm Frederick - 5 July 2000

BLACKSTONE, James Luke - 19 December 1994

BLANK, Maurice - 11 March 1970

BLOY, Walter - 17 June 1993

BOOTHE-CHAMBERS, Michael (known as Mike Chambers) - 14 June 2001

BRANCH, Anthony - 17 February 2005

BRANCH, Shirley - 17 February 2005

BRANTSCHEN, Anne (Marsh-Read) - 18 November 1971

BRIDGEMAN, Albert - 21 November 1980

BROOKNER, Bernice Karen - 18 November 1997

BROWNLIE, Andrea - 16 October 2007

BURGESS, Ralph - 14th July 2004

BURKE, Stanley - 8 November 1985

C

CADIGAN, Jeane Josephine - 31 January 1956

CAMERON, Sheila - 29 July 2004

CAMPBELL, John Dobson - 29 July 1997

CHITOLE, Dick Lucien - 27 July 2004

COLLINS, Alan David - 9 December 1996

COLLINS, Ann Margaret - 9 December 1996

COOPER, Barry - 15 February 1979

COOPER, Dan Colin - 23 November 1983

COUPE, Ellen - 29 November 1999

COVEY, Andy - 6 October 2000

CUTLER, Roy Edward - 2 December 1986

CUTTS, Oliver Alfred Sydney (Deceased) - 4 March 1992

D

DAISYSTAR LTD - 1 December 1997

DAUNCEY, Sandra - 4 December 1991

DAY, Leonard - 9 July 1996

DE VRIES, Juda - 7 November 1986

DENNIS, Cecilia - 3 February 1965

DOSWELL, Errol Edward - 15 February 2005

DOUGLAS, Paula May - 8 June 2006

DROZDOWSKI, Andrew Martin - 6 April 1998

E

EBERT, Gedaljahu - 7 July 2000

EDGAR, David Alan - 1 February 2002

EDWARDS, Simon Albert - 1 July 2010

EDWARDS, Ralston Peter - 20 June 2001

EWING, Terence Patrick - 12 February 1990

F

FABIAN, Michael - 18 June 1997

FIELD, Royle (aka FIELD, Roy) - 27 November 1987

FIELD-ROYSTON, Mark A - 3 November 1997

FLETCHER, Simon William Peel Vickers (aka FLETCHER, Vel William Peel) - 12 October 1983

FODEN, Veronica Beryl - 7 April 2005

FOLEY, Harry Desmond - 18 February 1997

FOLEY, Lewis Frank (aka FOLEY, Frank Lewis) - 18 February 1997

FORD, Daniel - 12 June 2008

FORD, Liubov - 12 June 2008

FOY, Toneye - 26 October 1987

FRADKINA, Raisa - 26 November 2003

G

GALLOWAY, John Murray - 27 March 1990

GILL, Thomas Patrick - 14th November 2006

GLEAVES, Roger Charles Augustine - 25 June 1982

GLEAVES, Roger Charles Augustine - 7 March 1985

GOBLE, Francis George - 20 November 1995

GOLDSTEIN, Dr Anthony Jonathan - 12 December 1995

GOLMICK (aka GOLMICK-WAHL) Greta Hedgwig Frieda Maria - 31 October 1962

GOUGH, Bernard Alfred (also B A Gough Equipment Ltd) - 20 March 1995

GREEN, Alfred Edwin Ambrose - 3 November 1983

GREEN, Glenford - 9 May 2001

GREEN, Linbird - 9 May 2001

GUSH, Thelma - 5 December 1961

H

HALE, Ronald Gerald Derek - 11 May 1981

HANNAM, Peter - 20 October 1988

HARALABIDIS, Nicholas - 24 November 1997

HAYWARD, Peter Rubery (aka Sir Nicholas Walter LYELL formerly P R Hayward) - 17 February 1994

HELLYER, Michael Marshall - 7 March 2001

HENRY, Joseph Josiah - 31 January 1969

HODGSON, Francis - 22 March 1996

J

JAMIESON, John, Reginald - 13 December 2001

JOHNSON, Harry - 26 February 1996

JOHNSON, Kenneth - 7 January 1986

JONES, David Owen - 16 December 1983

JONES, David Robert - 7 December 2000

136 | *Internet Offensive: Years of Smears*

JONES, Marcus David - 20 March 1989

K

KALIBALA (male) - 12 February 1996

KHAIRA, Asa Singh - 26 October 2000

KNIGHTLEY, Betty - 14 June 1986

KOHANZAD, Nader - 9 October 2001

L

LANDAU, Ivan Aubrey - 11 May 1992

LANDAU, Mrs Audrey - 3 March 1994

LANGTON, Philip Sidney - 10 February 1966

LAWAL, Adekunle Adejare - 11 March 2004

LEICESTER, Margaret - 28 October 2005

LEICESTER, Royston David - 28 October 2005

LEWIS, Kess Thomas - 17 November 2004

LONG, Helen May - 10 July 1969

LOWE, Nicholas John, also known as IKESON, Nicholas - 14 January 1998

LUCAS, Queenie Evelyn - 1 December 1986

M

MacCARTHY, Michael Reginald - 19 December 1962

MAHON, Kevin Dermot (for a period of 12 years only) - 8 October 2003

MARLOW, George Edwardv23 January 1962

MARSHALL, Christopher - 16 July 1998

MATHEW, Thomas - 15 February 1991

MATTHEWS, Barry - 14 November 2000

MATTHEWS, Ida - 30 October 1950

MENSAH, Esther Modukpe Dzagbley - 13 May 2004

MENZIES, Rowan Gavin Paton - 2 August 1996

MOHTASHAM, Elahe - 19 May 2005

MOORE, Barbara - 18 May 1962

MOORE, Edna May (aka SQUIRES, Dorothy) - 5 March 1987

MORRISS, Barbara Ellen Rhoda Fielding - 14 April 1997

MOSS (aka MOFFAT), Gerald - Deceased

MOTTERSHEAD, Ruth Ann - 29 March 2000

MURPHY, John Edmund - 25 October 1984

MURPHY, Teresa - 25 October 1984

N

NNADI, Alaoma Godwin - 14 December 1984

NORTCOTT, Gerald Francis - 26 February 1980

O

O'NEILL, Margarita (aka John Morris) - 9 June 1998

O'NEILL, Thomas (aka Lord Charles Leslie Falconer of Thoronton) - 9 June 1998

OAKES, Arthur - 15 February 2000

ORISHAGBEME, KD - 13 November 1987

OWUSU-NYANTEKYI, Kojo - 16 October 2001

P

PARKINSON, Peter Eric - 6 March 2000

PEPIN, John - 27 May 2004

PEROTTI, Angelo - 28 April 2006

PERSAUD, Norman Ernest (aka PERSAUD, Norman Siteram) - 22 February 1996

POMPHREY, Gloria Margaret Corinaldi - 2 February 1995

PRANKERD, Peter Henry - 18 November 1993

PRESCOTT, Joan - 8 March 1988

PRICE, Richard Thomas Clive - 19 March 1997

PURVIS, Paul Nigel - 3 December 2003

R

RATRA, Uday - 23 May 2003

RICHARDS, Miriam - 3 November 1998

RINEHART, Paul (aka Michael Stuart Rowe) - 15 July 1997

ROACH, Ion Curtis - 2 March 1998

ROBINSON, Arthur - 10 December 1992

ROBINSON, Frieda Alberta - 10 December 1992

ROBINSON, Max John - 12 May 1998

ROGERS, Gwendolen Rhoda - 8 March 1996

ROHRBERG, Monica - 24 March 1975

ROSATO, Anthony Leandro - 9 October 1995

RUSSELL, Frederick Boyd - 9 February 1965

S

SALAKOV, Andre John - 18 November 1999

SAMMY-JOE, Roggee Goodfellow (aka EKHAGUERE, Sammy Jasowa Osaigbovo) - 10 July 1989

SAMUELS, Graham - 22 July 2002

SAXENA, Ram Pratap - 21 November 2003

SAYER, George Frank - 7 July 1986

SCARR, Alexander Lowther - 7 December 1987

SCRIVEN, Geoffrey - 4 February 2000

SIMMONS, Kenneth William < - 26 June 2003

SIVASUBRAMANIAM, Markandu - 09 April 2008

SOARES, Delroy Anthony - 1 March 1999

SOUL, Robert Frederick - 28 October 1964

STAMOULAKATOS, Nicholas - 7 March 2000

STEVENS, Valerie Anne (formerly SCHWAB or SCHWAB-MORRIS) - 6 April 1984

SUJEEN, Basoodeo - 27 February 1996

T

TANNOCK, John Caldwell - 23 January 1962

TAYLOR, Boris Falcon - 7 October 1987

TEJENDRASINGH, Sardar - 10 April 1997

THOMPSON, Arthur George - 1 July 1958

THORNE, Dr Carl-Theo - 27 June 1973

TINGEY, William - 26 November 1986

TINSLEY, Robert - 14 December 1984

TOBIASINSKY, Barbara - 8 November 1988

V

VAN-DARI, Haroun El - 11 March 1988

VERNAZZA, Anthony - 9 April 1959

VIDLER, Barry Cornelius - 30 March 1998

W

WAKEFIELD, Violet Marion - 12 January 1984

WALKER, Denzil Keith - 21 October 1999

WARD, Alan Christopher Spencer (aka WARD, Alan Geoffrey, aka FORD, Alan) - 29 January 1997

WEBB, Albert James - 20 January 1984

WEBB, Eileen Stella Margaret - 20 January 1984

WILLIAMS, Betty Emma Meta - 8 July 1992

WILLIAMS, John - 22 April 1996

WILLIAMS, Richard Hugh - 20 December 1982

WILLIAMS, Richard Hugh - 16 May 1985

WILLIAMSON, Reverend Paul Stewart - 16 July 1997

WILLS, Geoffrey Donald Arthur - 22 July 1994

http://www.hmcourts-service.gov.uk/infoabout/vexatious_litigant/index.htm   10/19/2010

WOOD, Ellen Elizabeth - 25 June 1981

WOOD, Francis - 25 June 1981

WRAY, Bridget Deltora - 11 November 1996

Y

YEO, John Anthony (for a period of 10 years only) - 8 December 1999

APPENDIX TWO

List of Vexatious Litigants [2]

ALPHABETICAL LIST OF

VEXATIOUS LITIGANTS

[From the UK Court Service site]

NAME INDATE OF ORDER

ADAMS, Leslie James
May 20, 1966

ADOKO, Akena
May 20, 2004

ALEXANDER, Anthony
November 26, 2003

ALLAN, George Harvey
June 18, 1964

ALLAN, Theophilus Vincent
July 8, 1987

AMIN, Azad
July 12, 2000

ARNOLD, Dorothy Mignon (aka Gracie)
December 17, 1956

ARORA, Krishan Kumar (for a period of 12 years only)
July 23, 2001

AUBURN, Jack (aka MORTON, Herbert)
November 4, 1976

BADIBANGA, Kay Etienne
17 February 2003

BARNES, Peter Michael
December 4, 2002

BARRETT, Alan Gordon (for a period of 12 years only)
October 9, 2001

BARRETT, Stanley Arthur
October 20, 1955

BEBBINGTON, Ann Marjorie(aka EASTON, Ann Cholmondeley)
January 31, 1969

BECK, Annie Jane
July 22, 1936

BECK, William Winterburn
July 22, 1936

BECKER, Dorothy
March 13, 1969

BENTON, Paul
July 28, 2004

BISHOP, Malcolm Frederick
July 5, 2000

BLACKSTONE, James Luke
December 19, 1994

BLANK, Maurice
March 11, 1970

BLOY, Walter
June 17, 1993

BOALER, Bernard
May 15, 1914

BOOTHE-CHAMBERS,Michael (aka Mike Chambers)
June 14, 2001

BRANTSCHEN, Anne (aka Marsh-Read)
November 18, 1971

BRIDGEMAN, Albert
November 21, 1980

BROOKNER, Bernice Karen
November 18, 1997

BURGESS, Ralph
July 14, 2004

BURKE, Stanley
November 8, 1985

CADIGAN, Jeane Josephine
January 31, 1956

CAMERON, Sheila
July 29, 2004

CAMPBELL, John Dobson
July 29, 1997

CHITOLE, Dick Lucien
July 27, 2004

COLLINS, Alan David
December 9, 1996

COLLINS, Ann Margaret
December 9, 1996

COOPER, Barry
February 15, 1979

COOPER, Dan Colin
November 23, 1983

CORMACK, Jane
April 25, 1911

COUPE, Ellen
November 29, 1999

COVEY, Andy
October 6, 2000

CUTLER, Roy Edward
December 2, 1986

CUTTS, Oliver Alfred Sydney
March 4, 1992

DAISYSTAR LTD
December 1, 1997

DALTON, Emily
January 14, 1927

DAUNCY, Sandra
December 4, 1991

DAVIES, Maria Annie
June 5, 1888

DAY, Leonard
July 9, 1996

DENNIS, Cecilia
February 3, 1965

DE VRIES, Juda
November 7, 1986

DROZDOWSKI, Andrew Martin
April 6, 1998

EBERT, Geradjahu
July 7, 2000

EDGAR, David Alan
February 1, 2002

ELLIS, John Norman
October 25, 1949

EWING, Terence Patrick
February 12, 1990

FABIAN, Michael
June 18, 1997

FIELD, Royle (aka FIELD, Roy)
November 27, 1987

FIELD-ROYSTON, Mark A
November 3, 1997

FLETCHER, Simon William Peel Vickers
October 12, 1983

FOLEY, Harry Desmond
February 18, 1997

FOLEY, Lewis Frank (aka FOLEY, Frank Lewis)
February 18, 1997

FOY, Toneye
October 26, 1987

FRADKINA, Raisa
November 26, 2003

FRANKS, Fanny
July 22, 1936

GALLOWAY, John Murray (deceased)
March 27, 1990

GLACKEN, Betty Vera
July 9, 1947

GLEAVES, Roger Charles Augustine
June 25, 1982

GLEAVES, Roger Charles Augustine
March 7, 1985

GOBLE, Francis George
November 20, 1995

GOLDSTEIN, Dr Anthony Jonathan
December 12, 1995

GOLMICK, Greta Hedgwig Frieda Maria (aka GOLMICK-WAHL)
October 31, 1962

GOUGH, Bernard Alfred (also B A Gough Equipment Ltd)
March 20, 1995

GREEN, Alfred Edwin Ambrose
November 3, 1983

GREEN, Glenford
May 9, 2001

GREEN, Linbird
May 9, 2001

GUSH, Thelma
December 5, 1961

HALE, Ronald Gerald Derek
May 11, 1981

HALL, John Edward
April 30, 1945

HANNAM, Peter
October 20, 1988

HARALABIDIS, Nicholas
November 28, 1997

HAYWARD, Peter Rubery (aka LYELL, Sir Nicholas Walter, formerly HAYWARD, P R)
February 17, 1994

HELLYER, Michael Marshall
March 7, 2001

HENRY, Joseph Josiah
January 31, 1969

HODGSON, Francis
March 22, 1996

HOLLINGSWORTH, Bernard Hall
July 27, 1944

HUTCHINSON, Isabella
March 26, 1929

JAMIESON, John, Reginald
December 13, 2001

JOHNSON, Harry
February 26, 1996

JOHNSON, Kenneth
January 17, 1986

JONES, David Owen
December 16, 1983

JONES, Marcus David
March 20, 1989

JONES, David Robert
December 7, 2000

KHAIRA, Asa Singh
26 October 26, 2000

KALIBALA (male)
February 12, 1996

KING, Frank Charles
April 7, 1938

KING, Louisa Elizabeth
April 7, 1938

KNIGHTLEY, Betty
June 14, 1986

LANDAU, Audrey
March 3, 1994

LANDAU, Ivan Aubrey
May 11, 1992

LANGTON, Philip Sidney
February 10, 1966

LAWAL, Adekunle Adejare
March 11, 2004

LEWIS, Kess Thomas
November 17, 2004

LOFTUS, Robert
April 30, 1928

LONG, Helen May
July 10, 1969

LUCAS, Queenie Evelyn
December 1, 1986

LOWE, Nicholas John
January 14, 1998

MacCARTHY, Michael Reginald
December 19, 1962

MAHON, Kevin Dermot (for a period of 12 years only)
October 8, 2003

MARCUSON, Millie
October 29, 1894

MARLOW, George Edward
January 23, 1962

MARSHALL, Christopher
July 16, 1998

MATHEW, Thomas
February 15, 1991

MATTHEWS, Barry
November 14, 2000

MATTHEWS, Ida
October 30, 1959

MENSAH, Esther Modukpe Dzagbley
May 13, 2004

MENZIES, Rowan Gavin Paton
August 2, 1996

MILISSICH, Giovanni
May 20, 1892

MOORE, Barbara
May 18, 1962

MOORE, Edna May (aka SQUIRES, Dorothy)
March 5, 1987

MORRISS, Barbara, Ellen, Rhoda, Fielding
April 14, 1997

MOSS (aka MOFFAT), Gerald Deceased (!)

MOTTERSHEAD, Ruth Ann
March 29, 2000

MURPHY, John Edmund
October 25, 1984

MURPHY, Teresa
October 25, 1984

NEWMAN, Alfred Thomas
June 20, 1932

NEWMAN, Annie
June 20, 1932

NNADI, Alaoma Godwin
December 14, 1984

NORTCOTT, Gerald Francis
February 26, 1980

OAKES, Arthur
February 15, 2000

O'NEILL, Thomas (aka Lord Charles Leslie Falconer of Thornton)
June 9, 1998

O'NEILL, Margarita (aka John Morris)
June 9, 1998

ORISHAGBEME, K D
November 13, 1987

OWUSU-NYANTEKYIi, Kojo
October 16, 2001

PARKINSON, Peter Eric
March 6, 2000

PERSAUD, Norman Ernest (aka PERSAUD, Norman Siteram)
February 22, 1996

PITCHFORTH, Samuel Abraham
August 14, 1918

POMPHREY, Gloria Margaret Corinaldi
February 2, 1995

POTTER, Robert Henry
July 14, 1899

PRANKERD, Peter Henry
November 18, 1993

PRESCOTT, Joan
March 8, 1988

PRICE, Richard Thomas Clive
March 19, 1997

PURVIS, Paul Nigel
December 3, 2003

RATRA, Uday
May 23, 2003

RAWLINS, Caroline
February 5, 1889

RICHARDS, Miriam
November 3, 1998

RINEHART, Paul (aka Michael Stuart Rowe)
July 15, 1997

ROACH, Ion Curtis
March 2, 1998

ROBINSON, Arthur
December 10, 1992

ROBINSON, Frieda Alberta
December 10, 1992

ROBINSON, Louisa
May 15, 1914

ROBINSON, Max John
May 12, 1998

ROGERS, Gwendolen Rhoda
March 8, 1996

ROHRBERG, Monica
March 24, 1975

ROSATO, Anthony Leandro
October 9, 1995

RUSSELL, Frederick Boyd
February 9, 1965

SALAKOV, Andre John
November 18, 1999

SAMUELS, Graham
22 July 2002

SAMMY-JOE, Roggee Goodfellow
July 10, 1969

SAXENA, Ram Pratap
November 21, 2003

SAYER, George Frank
July 7, 1986

SCARR, Alexander Lowther
December 7, 1987

SCRIVEN, Geoffrey
February 4, 2000

SIMMONS, Kenneth William
June 26, 2003

SMURTHWAITE, Ellen Sarah
July 10, 1933

SOARES, Delroy Anthony
March 1, 1999

SOUL, Robert Frederick
October 28, 1964

STAMOULAKATOS, Nicholas
March 7, 2000

STEVENS, Valerie Anne (formerly SCHWAB or SCHWAB-MORRIS)
April 6, 1984

SUJEEN, Basoodeo
February 27, 1996

SUNNUCKS, Edith Vera Constance
April 8, 1949

TANNOCK, John Caldwell
January 23, 1962

TAYLOR, Boris Falcon
October 7, 1987

TEJENDRASINGH, Sardar
April 10, 1997

THOMPSON, Arthur George
July 1, 1958

THOMPSON, Robert
August 14, 1918

THORNE, Dr Carl-Theo
June 27, 1973

TINGEY, William
November 26, 1986

TINSLEY, Robert
December 14, 1984

TOBIASINSKY, Barbara
November 8, 1988

TORKINGTON, Elizabeth
May 22, 1889

TORKINGTON, John
May 22, 1889

VAN-DARI, Haroun El
March 11, 1988

VERNAZZA, Anthony
April 9, 1959

VIDLER, Barry Cornelius
March 30, 1998

WAKEFIELD, Violet Marion
January 12, 1984

WALKER, Denzil Keith
October 21, 1999

WARD, Alan Christopher Spencer(aka WARD, Alan Geoffrey aka FORD, Alan)
January 29, 1997

WASHINGTON, Marie
August 14, 1918

WEBB, Albert James
January 20, 1984

WEBB, Eileen Stella Margaret
January 20, 1984

WILLIAMS, Betty Emma Meta
July 8, 1992

WILLIAMS, John
April 22, 1996

WILLIAMS, Richard Hugh
December 20, 1982

WILLIAMS, Richard Hugh
May 16, 1985

WILLIAMSON, Reverend Paul Stewart
July 16, 1997

WILLS, Geoffrey Donald Arthur
July 22, 1994

WOOD, Ellen Elizabeth
June 25, 1981

WOOD, Francis
June 25, 1981

WOODS, Robinson
July 30, 1941

WRAY, Bridget Deltora
November 11, 1996

YEO, John Anthony (for a period of 10 years only)
December 8, 1999

[The above list was updated December 14, 2004 and is to the best of my knowledge complete,
although any omissions or inaccuracies in its transcription are entirely my own].

Back To Site Index

APPENDIX THREE

List of Vexatious Litigants [3]

Practice and Procedure Restriction of proceedings order	HER MAJESTY'S ATTORNEY-GENERAL	MS A P McCLUSKEY	THE HONOURABLE MR JUSTICE BURTON	09/06/2009
Practice and Procedure Restriction of proceedings order	HER MAJESTY'S ATTORNEY GENERAL	MR S DEMAN	THE HONOURABLE MR JUSTICE UNDERHILL	22/05/2006
Practice and Procedure Application/Claim	HER MAJESTY'S ATTORNEY GENERAL	MR V BRUCE	THE HONOURABLE MR JUSTICE LANGSTAFF	31/01/2006
Practice and Procedure Restriction of proceedings order	HER MAJESTY'S ATTORNEY GENERAL	MR S KUTTAPAN	THE HONOURABLE MR JUSTICE RIMER	24/11/2005
Practice and Procedure Restriction of proceedings order	HER MAJESTY'S ATTORNEY GENERAL	MR JAMES ROBERTS	THE HONOURABLE MR JUSTICE RIMER	25/05/2005
Practice and Procedure Restriction of proceedings order	HER MAJESTY'S ATTORNEY GENERAL	MR P PANDYA	THE HONOURABLE MR JUSTICE BURTON (PRESIDENT)	28/02/2005
Practice and Procedure Restriction of proceedings order	HER MAJESTY'S ATTORNEY GENERAL	MR D C D'SOUZA	THE HONOURABLE MR JUSTICE BEATSON	22/06/2004
Practice and Procedure Restriction of proceedings	HER MAJESTY'S ATTORNEY GENERAL	MR V BRUCE	THE HONOURABLE MR JUSTICE LANGSTAFF	01/01/2004

order

Practice and Procedure Restriction of proceedings order	Her Majesty's Attorney General	Mr O F Ayoivate	The Honourable Mr Justice Keith	30/10/2003	* New *
Practice and Procedure Restriction of proceedings order	HER MAJESTY'S ATTORNEY GENERAL	MR REGINALD TYRRELL	THE HONOURABLE MR JUSTICE BURTON (P)	04/06/2003	* New *
Practice and Procedure Restriction of proceedings order	Her Majesty's Attorney General	Mr S B Bennet	The Honourable Mr Justice Lindsay (President)	02/05/2001	* New *
Procedural Issues (obsolete topic) Employment Appeal Tribunal (obsolete sub-topic)	HER MAJESTY'S ATTORNEY GENERAL	MR C P ENGLAND	THE HONOURABLE MR JUSTICE LINDSAY (PRESIDENT)	19/02/2001	
Practice and Procedure Restriction of proceedings order	Her Majesty's Attorney General	Ms R King	His Honour Judge Peter Clark	04/05/2000	* New *
Procedural Issues (obsolete topic) Employment Appeal Tribunal (obsolete sub-topic)	HER MAJESTY'S ATTORNEY GENERAL	MR G WHEEN	THE HONOURABLE MR JUSTICE LINDSAY (PRESIDENT)	18/04/2000	

Geoffrey Wheen | 155

Practice and Procedure Restriction of proceedings order	Her Majesty's Attorney General	Mr O F Ayouvare	The Honourable Mr Justice Keith	30/10/2003	29/09/2010
Practice and Procedure Restriction of proceedings order	HER MAJESTY'S ATTORNEY GENERAL	MR REGINALD TYRRELL	THE HONOURABLE MR JUSTICE BURTON (P)	04/06/2003	29/09/2010
Practice and Procedure Restriction of proceedings order	Her Majesty's Attorney General	Mr S B Bennel	The Honourable Mr Justice Lindsay (President)	02/05/2001	29/09/2010
Practice and Procedure Restriction of proceedings order	Her Majesty's Attorney General	Ms R King	His Honour Judge Peter Clark	04/05/2000	29/09/2010

APPENDIX FOUR

EAT Lay Members [November 2004]

EAT Lay Members
November 2004

Ms S B Ayre
Ms C Baelz
Mr B Beynon
Mr K Bilgan
Mr D Bleiman
Dr A H Bridge
Mr D Chadwick
Ms R Chapman
Mr M Clancy
Ms S R Corby
Lord Davies of Coity CBE
Ms J L P Drake
Mr K Edmonson
Mr C Edwards
Mr I Ezekiel
Mr B V Fitzgerald
Mrs A Gallico
Mr P Gammon MBE, BA
Miss J A Gaskell
Mr B Gibbs
Mr T M Haywood
Ms A E Hibberd
Mr J W Hougham
Mr P Hunter
Mr P R A Jacques CBE
Mr D J Jenkins MBE
Mr J M Keenan
Mr D G Lewis
Mr A E R Manners
Miss A Martin
Mrs J M Matthias
Mrs M McArthur
Mr A G McQuaker
Ms G Mills
The Hon Dr William Morris OJ
Mr D A Norman
Ms D M Palmer
Mr P A L Parker CBE
Ms H Pitcher
Mrs M T Prosser
Mr A J Ramsden
Mr J R Rivers
Mr H Singh
Mr J C Shrigley
Mr M R Sibbald
Mr D G Smith

Mr M G Smith
Mr P M Smith
Dr W M Speirs
Mr S M Springer Esq. MBE
Mr R N Straker
Ms B Switzer
Ms P Tatlow
Mrs L S Tinsley
Mr R Thomson
Mrs R A Vickers
Mr B M Warman
Mrs D M Whittingham
Prof P D Wickens OBE
Ms S M Wilson
Mr G H Wright MBE
Mr S K Yaboah

APPENDIX FIVE

EAT Lay Members [December 2010]

EAT Lay Members
December 2010

Ms S B Ayre
Ms C Baelz
Mr B Beynon
Mr K Bilgan
Mr D Bleiman
Ms V E Branney
Ms R Chapman
Mr M Clancy
Ms J L P Drake
Mr K Edmonson
Mr C Edwards
Mr J D Evans CBE
Mr I Ezekiel
Dr B V Fitzgerald MBE LLD
Ms A Gallico
Mr P Gammon MBE BA
Miss J A Gaskell
Mr B Gibbs
Sir Alistair J Graham KBE
Mr A J Harris
Mr T M Haywood
Mrs A E Hibberd
Mr P Hunter
Mr D Jenkins OBE
Mr J M Keenan
Mr D G Lewis
Mr R A Lyons
Mr J D W Mallender
Mrs J M Matthias
Mrs M McArthur
Ms G Mills
Dr K C Mohanty JP
Mr F A M Motture
Mr D A Norman
Mr P L C Pagliari
Ms D M Palmer
Ms H Pitcher
Mr J R Rivers
Mr M R Sibbald
Mr H Singh
Mr D G Smith
Mrs G B Smith
Mr M G Smith
Mr P M Smith
Mr A J Stanworth
Ms N E F Sutcliffe

Ms B Switzer
Ms P Tatlow
Mr R Thomson
Mrs L Tinsley
Mr B M Warman
Mr D W Welch
Ms S M Wilson
Mr G M Worthington
Mr S K Yeboah

APPENDIX SIX

Advert regarding Judge, Employment Tribunals

00440: Salaried Employment Judge, Employment Tribunals (England and Wales)

ADVERTISEMENT

The Judicial Appointments Commission (JAC) is now inviting applications for the salaried post of Employment Judge of the Employment Tribunals.

Reference: 00440
Salary: £102,921
Number of vacancies: 14.5 with part-time working available
Closing date for applications: noon on 21 October 2010

There are 14.5 vacancies, to be filled on a full time or part-time basis, for immediate appointment to various regions across England.

Employment Judges preside over Employment Tribunals, whose jurisdiction involves the hearing of a wide range of employment-based disputes or issues. The largest number of cases concerns unfair dismissal. A substantial number of claims include allegation of discrimination, breach of contract, unlawful deductions from wages, transfer of undertakings and public interest disclosure. The hearings may serve to determine a case, or may be restricted to a preliminary issue or an interlocutory hearing for directions. Cases may involve one applicant or anything up to a complete workforce.

The vacancies are available in the following regions:

Newcastle - 3
Manchester - 1
Birmingham - 2
East Midlands - 2
London Central - 2
London North West - 1
London South - 1.5
London East - 2

The information pack includes the full eligibility criteria and the job description. It also describes the selection process, with relevant dates and advice on how to prepare your application.

The Judicial Appointments Commission selects candidates for judicial office. It does so on merit, through fair and open competition, from the widest range of eligible candidates.

Salaried Employment Judge of the Employment Tribunals

Job Description

Purpose of Office

1. The purpose of judicial office is to administer justice in accordance with the laws of England and Wales.

2. Employment Judges sit throughout England and Wales, currently in 12 Regional Offices, 9 ancillary offices and 12 or more hearing centres. They will be assigned by the President to sit in a particular Region. They may sit principally at one office in the region but must sit anywhere in the region when called upon to do so.

3. They may also be required, from time to time, to sit outside the assigned Region by the President when such a need arises. In the larger offices, 12 or more Tribunals will be sitting daily whilst in the smaller or rural offices, two or three Tribunals may be sitting daily. There are currently 12 Regional Employment Judges who are responsible to the President for the administration of justice in Tribunals in the area to which they are appointed.

4. Employment Judges may be appointed on a salaried (either full time or part-time) or fee-paid basis. These advertised posts are for salaried Employment Judges. All Salaried Employment Judges will be expected to undertake the full range of judicial duties.

General

5. The jurisdiction of an Employment Tribunal is summarised in the annex to this job description. Tribunal panels normally consist of the Employment Judge and two members, one from the employee panel and one from the employer panel. From time to time, Employment Judges sit without lay Members to decide matters of law and fact. The length of hearings varies considerably; the longest cases may take many days. Appeals from Employment Tribunals normally lie to the Employment Appeal Tribunal.

6. The provision of administrative support for Employment Tribunals is the responsibility of the Tribunals Service, which is part of the Ministry of Justice.

Main Activities

7. The main activities of the Salaried Employment Judge are as follows:

A. Case Management and preparation for Hearings

- Identifying the claims and issues in a case.
- Reading and assimilating papers in a case before the case management discussion or hearing commences.
- Undertaking interlocutory work, which may include:

- Initiating or considering requests for further and better particulars of claims and responses;
- Initiating or considering requests for discovery of documents;
- Drafting relevant questions for the parties to answer;
- Requests for Witness Orders;
- Giving directions for the future conduct of cases
- Preparing time estimates for hearings;
- Granting extensions of time where appropriate;
- Initiating or considering requests for amendments of claims or responses;
- Identifying the correct parties to proceedings and considering requests for joinder of parties;
- Identifying the claims and issues in the case
- Considering applications to strike-out;
- Deciding whether sample or test cases are appropriate and whether proceedings should be stayed;
- Deciding requests for postponements and adjournments;
- Offering advice to the administrative staff of the Tribunals on correspondence generally.
- Overseeing, in liaison with Tribunal staff, the progress of cases towards hearing and disposal so as to secure the most efficient dispatch of business compatible with the interests of justice.

B. Presiding over hearings

- Controlling (in accordance with the relevant law and practice) the manner in which cases are conducted.
- Ensuring that all parties are enabled to have their cases presented, and have them considered, as fully and fairly as possible. Parties may be represented by a wide variety of representatives, including solicitors and barristers (including Queen's Counsel), Citizen's Advice Bureau representatives, personnel officers, Trades Union officials and personnel consultants; or they may be unrepresented.
- Promoting in each case the most expeditious dispatch of business compatible with the interests of justice.
- Maintaining the authority and dignity of the Tribunal.
- Taking an accurate note of the evidence and the proceedings generally.
- Deciding issues of law and procedure which may arise during a case.
- Ensuring that there is a level playing field.
- Salaried Employment Judges should expect to conduct Hearings in the more complex cases.

C. Determination of applications with, if applicable, lay members

- Determining claims by finding facts from the evidence presented, applying the relevant law to the facts found and giving, where appropriate, a full oral Decision (which may subsequently be produced as the written Judgment and Reasons of the Tribunal).
- Assessing and making awards and deciding the amount and manner of payment.
- Giving any directions necessary to give effect to the Judgment
- Promulgating Judgments, and Reasons, timeously.

D. Other work

- Reviewing previous Judgments.
- Producing written Notes of Evidence if requested by the Employment Appeal Tribunal.
- Providing information and explanations in relation to the investigation of complaints.

Other Responsibilities

A. Keeping abreast of legal developments

- Employment Judges need to keep abreast of legal developments. This entails a substantial amount of reading not directly connected with the cases, which they are hearing.
- Employment Judges will be expected to become familiar with and to use the Employment Tribunals' computer system.
- All Employment Judges are required to attend training courses and undertake other training as appropriate.

B. Acting as a Mentor for newly appointed and other Fee Paid Judges

Other judicial and public duties

- Employment Judges are expected to assist from time to time when requested in training of other judicial colleagues and generally in meeting the judicial needs of the tribunal and assisting the Regional Employment Judge in improving the delivery of service to tribunal users in accordance with the Overriding Objective.
- Salaried employment Judges may be requested by the President to participate in development pilot projects, and some national aspects of judicial administration.

Note on the Jurisdiction of Employment Tribunals (England a Wales)

8.   Employment Judges preside over Employment Tribunals, whose jurisdiction involves the hearing of a wide range of employment-based disputes or issues. The largest number of cases concerns unfair dismissal. A substantial number of claims include allegation of discrimination, breach of contract, unlawful deductions from wages, transfer of undertakings and public interest disclosure. The hearings may serve to determine a case, or may be restricted to a preliminary issue or an interlocutory hearing for directions. Cases may involve one applicant or anything up to a complete workforce. This note is intended to give a flavour of the jurisdiction exercised by Employment Tribunals; it is not meant as a comprehensive list.

September 2010

Qualities and Abilities

Applicants for this selection exercise will be assessed against the following qualities and abilities:

1. Intellectual Capacity

- Expertise in your chosen area.
- Ability quickly to absorb and analyse information.
- Appropriate knowledge of the law and its underlying principles, or the ability to acquire this knowledge where necessary.

2. Personal Qualities

- Integrity and independence of mind.
- Sound judgment.
- Decisiveness.
- Objectivity.
- Ability and willingness to learn and develop professionally.

3. An Ability to Understand and Deal Fairly

- Ability to treat everyone with respect and sensitivity whatever their background.
- Willingness to listen with patience and courtesy.
- Ability to enable parties to present their case.

4. Authority and Communication Skills

- Ability to explain the procedure and any decisions reached clearly and succinctly to all those involved.
- Ability to inspire respect and confidence.
- Ability to maintain authority when challenged.

5. Efficiency

- Ability to work constructively with others (including leadership and managerial skills where appropriate)
- Ability to organise time effectively and produce clear reasoned judgments expeditiously (if required).

Fair Treatment

Equality and fair treatment is at the centre of all the JAC does.

Under the Constitutional Reform Act 2005 we must appoint on merit and that combined with a wide pool of high quality applicants will ensure that the most meritorious candidates will succeed and that the best judges will be appointed. Merit and equality therefore go hand in hand. That is why the JAC makes huge efforts to ensure our processes are fair and all applicants receive equal treatment.

Our guiding principle is 'diversity in the field, merit in the selection'

APPENDIX SEVEN

Correspondence with Essex University

We do not believe that it is anything at all to do with our applicant portal, myessex, in which the applicant's information is used by the University only for the purposes of admissions processing and is not accessible on the internet (including by search engines).

I do hope that this clarifies the situation and provides you with some reassurance but please do let me know if you have any further queries and I will do my best to answer them.

Yours sincerely

From: Geoffrey Wheen [mailto:gwheen2@yahoo.co.nz]
Sent: 15 September 2010 08:50
To: Vice-Chancellor at Essex
Subject: internet entry

Professor Colin Riordan
Vice-Chancellor
University of Essex

Dear Vice-Chancellor

On 30 August 2010 I applied to enrol for a PhD in Criminology with Essex University, and was subsequently told my application was being processed by the Admissions office. Today, out of curiosity, I searched on the internet for "myEssex geoffrey wheen" and was taken aback to find [as the first and most prominent entry on the page] "Attorney General v Wheen" etc,, involving the Employment Appeal Tribunal and Court of Appeal a mere 10 years ago, about which I have disclosed the relevant documents and my riposte and criticisms in my recently published book "Moral Beaks and Claws". So anybody can now judge for themselves whether anything is and was untoward, as can you and your colleagues, since it and my other books formed part of my application.
I tried various other permutations on the internet and failed to get the same result. Without inside knowledge the chances of linking me with your University and then publishing the connection on the internet under your banner are, in my view, nil. So how could anyone link me with Essex University? At my end apart from myself only my partner is aware of any such link, and we told nobody.
The motive behind this latest smear/entry is obvious, coming as it does with the publication of various revelations about the case and appeal in question. At this stage I can only surmise who is responsible [although past history is a strong guide] but apart from computer-hacking the link must, in all probability, have come from Essex U or its contacts. If it did not only have my privacy rights been breached I can see no earthly reason why a 10 year-old carcass could have any bearing on or relevance to my PhD application. Given that processing of the latter entails checking qualifications apart from Reading University I can see no logical reason why any other body or person would or should be aware of my connection and contact with Essex University. If, therefore, other parties were made so aware please advise me who they are and why they were given the information. Otherwise I will proceed on the basis that no other parties are involved.
Thank you.

Geoffrey Wheen

From: "Illsley, Monica" <illsmp@essex.ac.uk>
To: "Murphy, Richard S D" <rmurphy@essex.ac.uk>
Cc: "Brooke, Keith N" <kbrooke@essex.ac.uk>
Sent: Wednesday, September 15, 2010 7:51 PM
Subject: RE: internet entry

Thank you so much Richard. I will respond using this info an= see what happens.

Monica

From: Murphy, Richard S D
Sent: 15 September 2010 13:48
To: Illsley, Monica
Cc: Brooke, Keith N
Subject: RE: internet entry

Monica,

I think you are right – it is the "geoffrey whee=" component of the search term that is delivering the reference to t=e tribunal case at the top of the results list and that the "myessex" component is largely irrelevant. I=think further proof of this can be obtained by searching for "+m=essex geoffrey wheen" which makes Google return entries that must in=lude the word myessex – the tribunal case is not returned as a result.

It is worth noting that searching for "myessex geoffre= wheen" in other search engines doesn't return the tribunal ca=e.

Returning to Google, their returns to a query are based on s=veral technical areas: information harvesting and indexing, page ranking, =nd query matching. All of these are complex, semi-secret black boxes (and an important part o= their continuing commercial success) so I'm afraid that it is a mys=ery as to exactly why Google returns the tribunal case as the first ranked=item when entering the query "myEssex geoffrey wheen".

What is clear is that Google's indexing includes fairl= strong links between the words "geoffrey" "wheen"=and his employment tribunal cases.

Although we can't say for certain, it is likely that t=e association with the word "myessex" and "geoffrey whee=" comes from a source other than the University. Myessex is used elsewhere (blog site: bloggers.myessex.co.uk, a news=archive site: zonicholas.net/myessex) and these may have caused index entr=es at some point. In addition there are large numbers of spam websites who=e purpose is to return links from queries, including typing errors, to a variety of sites for dating, medication, por=ography, etc. These tend to mix up huge numbers of words (and mis-spelling= -- mysex?) that already well-indexed to capture search query traffic=

What I think we can say to Mr Wheen that we've looked =nto his comment and we believe that Google returning links to his tribunal=cases when "myessex" is used in the query with "geoffrey wheen" is as a result of othe= myessex uses -- not the University's myessex - including spam =ites. We do not believe it is anything at all to do with his use of our ap=licant portal, myessex, in which the applicant's information is used by the University only for the purposes of admissions processing a=d is not accessible on the internet (including by search engines).

I referred this to Keith Brooke who has clarified and confir=ed the above. Keith has some detail should you need it at any point. <=o:p>

11/17/2010

From: "Murphy, Richard S D" <rmurphy@essex.ac.uk>
To: "Ilsley, Monica" <ilsmp@essex.ac.uk>
Sent: Tuesday, September 21, 2010 11:48 PM
Subject: RE: internet entry

Monica,

I think that it is worth using some of Sara's observations to reinforce the point about myEssex applicant portal information not being accessible except by the applicant (only their own details) and a limited number of University staff (solely for the purpose of processing applications).

This means that because we recognise the importance of managing personal information, a) we apply technical security measures to myEssex to prevent unauthorised access to people and automated systems such as search engines ("searchbots") and b)we invest considerably in ensuring that staff are aware of, and act in accordance with, proper data protection practice. I'm somewhat hesitant to mention the internal audit report as it may be requested.

I can't immediately obtain details of system security and firewalls – it may be better not going into detail anyway. We will have look at some log information to confirm our security but given the huge (really huge) size of our logs, I don't propose that we attempt to identify Mr Wheen's accesses at this stage.

Richard

Richard Murphy
Director of Information Systems

From: Ilsley, Monica
Sent: 21 September 2010 13:10
To: Murphy, Richard S D
Subject: FW: internet entry

Some useful content here I think that I will use in my reply to Mr Wheen. Is there something in the suggestion to check with Bret that our systems have not been tampered with?

Monica

From: Stock, Sara
Sent: 21 September 2010 13:00
To: Ilsley, Monica
Subject: RE: internet entry

Hello Monica

I'm not totally sure what he means, either!

I think we need to reassure him about two things. First - the system used. I think either Bret Giddings or Keith Brooke would be able to supply information on My Essex and the network – how secure it is, the firewalls and systems etc we have in place. They should also be able to confirm that we have ways of seeing if someone has hacked into our systems and that, to the best of our knowledge, they have not

11/17/2010

Geoffrey Wheen | 169

From: Geoffrey Wheen [mailto:gwheen2@yahoo.co.nz]
Sent: 21 September 2010 06:39
To: Illsley, Monica
Subject: Re: internet entry

Monica Illsley

Not only do I fail to understand the relevance of the penultimate para of your e-mail to what has occurred having done more research and conducted a series of random and objective tests, none of which remotely bear out your contentions I can no longer accept your explanation, effectively shifting the blame onto Google's shoulders, especially as your failure to advise me who Essex U has contacted does nothing to alleviate or allay my concerns.
Thank you.

Geoffrey Wheen

From: Geoffrey Wheen <gwheen2@yahoo.co.nz>
To: "Illsley, Monica" <illsmp@essex.ac.uk>
Sent: Mon, 20 September, 2010 7:19:23 PM
Subject: Re: internet entry

Monica Illsley

As I said in my e-mail I tried various permutations before I wrote, and none of them produced the same result. Five minutes ago [as I have done regularly over the past few days] I repeated the process for "geoffrey wheen" and got the same result as I have for the last few weeks - references to my books.. So either you are using a different search engine [mine is Google] or something inexplicable is going on about which Essex U apparently knows nothing. That being so I am pursuing the matter elsewhere. Thanks for the info.

Geoffrey Wheen

From: "Illsley, Monica" <illsmp@essex.ac.uk>
To: "gwheen2@yahoo.co.nz" <gwheen2@yahoo.co.nz>
Cc: Vice-Chancellor at Essex <vc@essex.ac.uk>
Sent: Mon, 20 September, 2010 5:50:14 PM
Subject: FW: internet entry

Dear Mr Wheen

I am writing on behalf of the Vice-Chancellor in response to your e-mail communication of 15 September.

I have consulted with our IT services team, and we've found that the word "myessex" appears to be completely redundant in the search you were using in Google. As an illustration of this you may care to try searching on just "geoffrey wheen" or even "mysurrey geoffrey wheen" or any such permutation which all bring back exactly the same result. This I think shows that there is no particular connection with the University of Essex. It does appear to be a peculiarity of the Google search engine; as other search engines do not behave in the same way.

11/17/2010

From: Stock, Sara (sstock@essex.ac.uk)
To: gwheen2@yahoo.co.nz
Date: Fri, 7 January, 2011 11:45:54 PM
Cc:
Subject: Your FOI request on criminology PhDs

Dear Mr Wheen

I am writing to respond to your FOI enquiry of 6 December 2010. I note your email received this morning regarding when this is due. The 20 working days allowed does not include the 3 public holidays that the UK has had since then and now. I also explained at the time of seeing clarification from you that the stop clocks when we seek clarification. A single day has been added to account for that. I am therefore responding within the time frame.

The University of Essex does not actually offer a PhD in criminology. Students are attached to a department and within the scope of supervision in that department at the time can select an area of study of their choice. This means that we cannot search our database for students researching a PhD in criminology.

What I have done with colleagues is to look at the published titles of theses from the Sociology department (which you can see on the library catalogue http://serlib0.essex.ac.uk/search/d?SEARCH=Sociology+thesis) Where we have identified a thesis title as being in the area of criminology we have then pulled out what information we have on the student who produced that thesis. We have also asked supervisors of current students to identify those working on some area of criminology.

I have focussed on the Department of Sociology as I have assumed that you interest lay with this department, and because criminology as a research area is generally only listed under the Sociology department in our postgraduate prospectus http://www.essex.ac.uk/prospectus/pg.pdf. It is possible that students in the School of Law, and departments of history and psychology might also have written PhDs with covering some aspects of criminology. You can look at the lists of theses for each department on the library catalogue. http://libww.essex.ac.uk/Information_Skills/theses.htm The other reason for excluding PhDs from these departments is the time taken. I have had to go through paper files of students by hand to find some of this information. To do so for three more departments I consider would mean that your request would exceed the limit of what is considered in the Act (section 12) to be a reasonable timeframe to spend on a request.

The data we have drawn together does not answer all of your questions. During the application process we do not generally ask for details of professional qualifications, research experience or publications; the focus is normally on academic qualifications. Some more recent application forms have asked for work experience, but not all the forms on file asked this question. Many PhD applicants will, of course, be BA or MA students and will not yet have got round to having papers published, or work experience. Where we still hold complete files for students I have gone through the files by hand to look at the application form. Some students did give information on work experience, but in many cases this information was not collected and is not held.

Student files are kept for six years after they end their relationship with the University (through graduation or withdrawal) and thereafter only the bare minimum is kept. Records older than this do not include entry qualifications. This is led by data protection legislation and is clearly set out in our retention schedules. http://www2.essex.ac.uk/rm/records/schedules.shtm

The Data Protection Act means that we are limited in the information that we can give out that might identify living individuals. I am afraid this is more complex than just stripping out a name from data, as it "is" often possible to identify a person from a set of information other than their name. In any case, by searching the library catalogue for the tiles of theses you will immediately find the name of the person. I have therefore split the information. I have given the list of titles as one set. You can look these up on our library catalogue (see link given above) and will see the name of the person writing each thesis, and the date of publication. You should note that there are fewer titles than there are students – this is because some students did not complete their PhDs, and we do not hold titles in such cases. The second set of information is the age, nationality, gender and (where we hold it) the academic qualifications of each candidate.

The final set of information shows the work experience and professional qualifications noted by students. Only two noted professional qualifications on their applications, and eleven mentioned their work experience or employment history. All three sets of information are contained in the attached spreadsheet – each set is on a different tab. Please let me know if you have any difficulty opening the spreadsheet.

I am sorry not to be able to give you exactly the information that you wanted. I hope you can understand the reasons for this and that the information I have been able to obtain is useful to you.

To return to your email received this morning, you mention your other request about your references. That application, because it was about you, was not treated under the Freedom of Information Act, but under the Data Protection Act, which allows us 40 days (working and holidays) to respond. You seem to feel that the University of Essex had refused a response. I have sent our response to you in my email of 23rd December in which I explained that I simply wanted to double check with Admissions. I have just been across to Admissions and they confirm that, as I explained to you on 10th and 23rd December that the only references we hold for you are your own letter and the Reading reference.

As ever, if you have any questions about this information or this email do please contact me.

Regards

Sara

Mrs Sara Stock
University Records Manager
University of Essex
Wivenhoe Park
Colchester
CO4 3SQ

Tel. (01206) 874853
E-mail: sstock
For general Freedom of Information queries please e-mail: foi
(non-Essex users should add @essex.ac.uk to create full e-mail addresses)

APPENDIX EIGHT

List of PhD [Criminology] applicants

PhD in Criminology at Essex

No	age	nationality	sex	academic qualifications	offered place
1	31 Taiwan		F	BA	2008
				MA	
2	43 United Kingdom		M	BA	2002
				BA	
				LLM	
				MA	
3	32 Taiwan		F	BA	2006
				MA	
4	47 United Kingdom		F	BA	2004
				MA	
5	30 Thailand		F	BA	2009
				MA	
6	30 Greece		M	BA	2001
				BA	
7	35 United Kingdom		M	BA	2004
				MA	
8	31 Vietnam		M	BA	2008
				MA	
				European Master Public Health	
9	32 Kyrgyzstan		F	MA	2008
10	36 United Kingdom		F	MSC	2007
11	45 United Kingdom		M	MA	2006
12	38 United Kingdom		M	BSC	2006
13	55 United Kingdom		M	BA	2003
14	42 China		F	MA	2002
15	28 United Kingdom		M	BSC	2001
16	24 United States		F	MA	2001
17	23 United Kingdom		F	BA	2004
18	25 United Kingdom		F	MA	2004
19	24 United Kingdom		F	MA	2005
20	36 Saudi Arabia		M	MA	2005
21	32 Nigeria		M		1988
22	35 United Kingdom		F		1988
23	25 United Kingdom		M		1989
24	44 United Kingdom		M		1992
25	33 United Kingdom		M		1993
26	36 Iran (Islamic Rep)		M		1993
27	52 United Kingdom		M		1994
28	47 United Kingdom		F		1994
29	31 United Kingdom		M		1995
30	34 United States		F		1995
31	37 United Kingdom		F		1997
32	34 Saudi Arabia		M	MA Sociology	1996
33	27 United Kingdom		F		1997
34	26 Taiwan		M		1998
34	No data No data		F		1986
35	No data No data		F		1985
36	No data No data		F		1982
37	No data No data		M		1977

CHAPTER THREE

Muck Spreaders

According to bumff downloaded from the internet the U.K. Office for Judicial Complaints [OJC] "investigates complaints about misconduct of judicial office holders." Being a bit simple, naively it crossed my mind that sticking derogatory material on the internet for worldwide public consumption for over a decade at public expense for no good, logical or, so far as I could see, legal reasons might conceivably amount to "misconduct". How dumb can you get? Of course it isn't. Whatever the dictionary says to the contrary it can't be, considering that not even fitting up innocent bystanders, branding them murdering terrorists, concocting evidence against them, threatening them with firearms inside police stations and above all banging them up and keeping them there for as long as possible thanks to Lord Denning and his disciples collectively merely amount to a glorified "mistake" [aka "miscarriage of justice"] which, after all, anybody can make. Some mistake. Some bullshit. Some system of Justice, ha-bloody-ha. Below, for the record, is my complaint dated 18 October 2010 to the OJC.

COMPLAINT

1 - I am a UK citizen. Living abroad, I see no good reason to supply my current address or phone number unless required to do so by law and because doing so is unnecessary, as my e-mail address should suffice and is invariably used by both sides for correspondence purposes.

2 - I complain about continual, persistent, unjustified and unnecessary breaches of my human and civil rights over more than 10 years caused by the actions of various judges inside the Employment Appeal Tribunal and Court of Appeal. Such actions breach my privacy rights under Section 6 and Articles 8 and 17 of the Human Rights Act 1998.

3 - The acts in question comprise the insertion of publications on the internet about me for over a decade, starting in year 2000, about which I was completely unaware until I was tipped off earlier this year. Not only is the continual insertion of these publications a total and pointless waste of public money it is motivated by malice and is

unlawful.   In the latter respect according to information on the internet the onus is on the public authority to prove not only that it has exercised proportionality [by interfering with my rights only so far as is strictly necessary to achieve a specific purpose set out in the European Convention on Human Rights] but also that it is not using a sledgehammer to crack a nut. It has made no attempt to prove either, because it can't. If the abuse of my rights is in line with my rights under the HRA and Convention I am entitled to know how and why.

4 - Following my request to the Ministry of Justice for information under the Official Information Act I have been advised by the Tribunals Service [a] that the first insertions on the EAT website would have been arranged by the EAT President at the time [meaning the esteemed Judge Lindsay} and [b] the current cost of hosting the EAT website is 700 pounds a month, regardless of the number of judgments added to the database each month. That being so, for the privilege of Lindsay trying to make me look stupid throughout the world for over 10 years the taxpayers – not him, akin to sponging M.P.'s – have already forked out about 80,000 pounds, give or take. Money well spent, by his standards, especially in a recession. People who

have to work for a living might think it's slightly over the top, or in his terminology "disproportionate".

5 - Yesterday I downloaded 5 different entries about this issue. Knowing who I'm dealing with, there may well be others. I am enclosing four of them; one would not print for some reason. Whereas the Tribunals Service refer to the EAT website [see above] only two were found there. Under "eat vexatious litigants" I found - in suitably bold lettering, ensuring the prominence and significance to those of similar mentality - Enclosure 1, relating not just to the EAT judgment, but the Appeal decision, again over 10 years old. On page 3 of the same webpage was an item "HMAG v King", also featuring yours truly. Then another gem under "geoffrey wheen" [Enclosure 2], one more under the name of Lindsay himself [Enclosure 3] and just for good measure, "myEssex geoffrey wheen" [Enclosure 4] on Essex University's website of all places, presumably because I'd had the temerity to apply for enrolment there. Needless to say the University deny any involvement, while failing to explain how an outsider could have known about the link between us. Are all these on the EAT website, or is some malicious moron spending yet more public

money on other sites trying to gag critics and dissenters?

6 - Yes, these ermined upholders of human rights and their perks and pensions have certainly gone to town in the last decade, not just by fixing the outcome and membership pf Appeal Courts but by squandering public money proving what many people already know about them and their methods. They have even managed to stop their victims suing them for malice, while they continue dispensing their brand of junk/"New Labour" justice. Whereas the EAT and CA smears have been dishing the dirt on the world-wide internet with an audience of billions for a decade convicted criminals are entitled to protection when their convictions become spent under the Rehabilitation of Offenders Act. What's more, publishers of spent convictions can be sued for libel. I don't happen to be a criminal, and individuals like Lindsay aren't going to get away with treating me worse than one.

7 - It's pretty clear that Lindsay started the ball rolling, that this abuse of my rights is on-going and he's now retired or dead. No matter. Since apparently he could and did authorize insertion[s] on the internet he and his successors could have

stopped them any time over the last 10 years. The same goes for the Court of Appeal, whose members at my appeal included Mummery [a past President of the EAT] and Keene [if not ditto, a member of the EAT, leftie and mate of the Blair entourage], who being one of "them" were ideally qualified to rubber-stamp the treatment wearing their "independent' uniforms. Strange too that the individual under whose auspices all this has been going on – the Attorney General – knew and did nothing either. Perhaps they didn't because their attitude is they can do what they like, and to hell with anyone else and their human rights. Shades of Iraq and ruin.

8 - So what have Lindsay and his ilk proved and achieved, and what is the point? Do they seriously imagine that I, a man of 70, would have any direct dealings with that lot ever again, that I'd grovel before them for the right to bring proceedings against tin-pot political bodies which have been penalizing men throughout the entire term of the last discredited Government? Or maybe they think I won't write another book about them and their notable achievements.

9 - Finally, if you refuse to deal with my complaints please supply reasons and advise me who will address them.

It didn't take long for the bureaucratic bullshitters to swing into action. Despite my complaint having been made [on a separate form supplied by the OJC] against "Judge Lindsay and his successors" and my also supplying the names and addresses of the bodies involved – the Employment Appeal Tribunal and Court of Appeal respectively – the next day much to my surprise I was advised by an individual named Michael Scarff that my complaint was merely "about Judge Lindsay". By return e-mail I told him "I'm afraid I don't understand" and explained why. True to form Scarff ignored my e-mail. After all, he works for the U.K. Government – rendering him superior to the rest of us – and it's not his job to explain to idiots like me why he's always right. Nevertheless, silence conveys a message. My interpretation of it – not unusual when I'm dealing with The Establishment – was that they're trying to prevent this from spreading, by producing the customary, predictable in-house whitewash.

So two days later I wrote to Ken Clarke, the U.K.'s Justice Secretary, who was obviously impressed with my arguments. So much so that they were "answered" [if I may debase the word] by e-mail nearly 3 weeks later by one of his minions in what looked suspiciously like a stereotyped "push-off" format: in bureaucratic jargon, standard letter number 1234 7B referring me to a lawyer, any lawyer, as if I'd just arrived from Mars. Thanks Ken. I'll remember your help at the next election – if you've not been kicked upstairs by then.

Although the draft letter below was not sent to Ken Clarke [instead I sent him an abridged version by e-mail], it encapsulates not only what I felt at the time – and still do, even more so – but the salient issues, about which he and others responsible did nothing, which is absolutely typical of the head-in-the-sand attitudes prevailing in U.K. Governments, regardless of their political hue and hubris.

Rt. Hon. Kenneth Clarke QC MP,

Secretary of State for Justice

I am addressing you about apparent ongoing breaches of the law by the UK Government, about which I enclose a copy of my complaint to the Judicial Complaints Office [which evidently only concerns itself with alleged "misconduct"], which outlines the gist of the relevant facts and issues. Whether or not perceived misconduct has taken place is beside the point for present purposes, namely whether the actions of the

UK Government have, in my case, been contravening the European Convention on Human Rights and the Human Rights Act 1998 for over a decade, and continuing.

When asked to justify the legality of its actions the Tribunals Service has answered me by citing Rules and Procedures "laid down by Parliament, which set out how it must operate". Really, on both counts? So, in effect, if the assertion is true the legislators, both Houses of Parliament, enacted administrative procedures demanding that details of vexatious litigants be inserted on the internet and left there indefinitely? I don't believe it. The Tribunals Service also refers me to the Employment Tribunals Act 1996 and the Employment Appeal Tribunal Rules 1993. Then I'm told the EAT has discretion to determine what operational practices to adopt, and that under Paragraph 18.8 of the Practice Directions judgments "may" be posted on the EAT website if so directed by the Registrar or a judge. In other words, the criterion is which side one or other of them got out of bed that morning. Or more likely, on which side of the political fence they belong. Nor, in my case, has this smear-publishing been restricted to the EAT website. For instance, when I last checked it was on the website not only of Essex University but that of another University to whom I had the temerity to apply for a job some 12 years ago. But to some being a white, English male is enough for the abuse to start and continue.

And just in case the Tribunals Service don't know it, exercising discretion is not tantamount to being ordered to do or not do something by Parliament. It's the opposite. So "must" doesn't arise.

Nor, apparently, does having to act as it has by virtue of "primary legislation", per the HRA. It's pretty clear in the latter what public authorities are required to do and not do and why, and that only "primary legislation" [which Rules and other administrative niceties are invariably not] counts if the public authority is attempting to justify conflicting interest creating unavoidable breaches of the HRA and European Convention. And even discretion is not a licence to trample on other people. It has to be exercised in a fair and reasonable manner, of which there is no evidence in my case. So-called "judicial independence" does not extend to being given carte-blanche to do whatever one likes. Judge Lindsay and others of like mind and disposition must have known about the global destructive power of the internet, so adopted and perpetuated its use as their weapon of choice. The Convention and HRA were born and exist in part to curb judicial abuses of power, which grow by the minute.

To the best of my knowledge the only mandatory obligation on the EAT regarding publication lies in Section 33[5] of the Employment Tribunals Act 1996, which requires the insertion of a copy of an "order" [not details of the case] in two specific publications, the London Gazette and the Edinburgh Gazette, largely for the benefit of legal practitioners. One insertion in 2 newspapers. Once. That's enough to satisfy the statutory, mandatory provision.

The purpose of this letter is not to persuade the UK Government it's in the wrong, because we know from past experience that its policy is to deny the undeniable come hell or high water. I am trying to get this matter resolved amicably and civilly without recourse to litigation. At the moment I can see no legal, moral or ethical justification for the way the UK Government and its agencies have behaved, which in my view is completely over the top – the nut to be smashed by the juggernaut was presumably me - and probably unlawful right from the start. Indeed, it demonstrates a complete disregard and contempt for me and my rights enshrined in the European Convention and the HRA.

On the face of it I have strong grounds to sue the UK Government [for which I do not need to seek the permission of anybody] for what it has done to me and my family for over a decade. But I'm not a lawyer, so I may be up a gum tree. If so it would save us both a lot of time and trouble [and public money] if I were told in what way. I wouldn't bother asking the last Government, because I knew what to expect from the lot who have caused this and many other problems for UK citizens. If you can tell me why I'm wrong and I agree I'll trouble you no more. Otherwise, I'll pursue the matter elsewhere wherever and however I can.

Thank you.

....

Below is a copy of my letter sent to Alan Rusbridger, the Editor of "The Guardian" newspaper, which he was good enough to ignore.

26 October 2010

Enclosed is my complaint dated 18 October 2010 to the Office for Judicial Complaints, for potential publication in whatever form you deem appropriate. Whereas I thought I was complaining about illegalities, egregious breaches of my privacy and human rights and abject waste of public money the OJC has chosen to treat my complaints as one of "misconduct" to be investigated [whitewashed?] by one of its own, Mr. Justice Nicholas Underhill [the latest EAT President, as was Judge Lindsay], over a leisurely, time-wasting 3 months or so. All very independent, objective and convincing, I don't think. Equally predictable are the deafening silences resulting from my e-mails to Ken Clarke himself and the Cabinet Office, and my fax to Google HQ. And to complete the roll-call, let's not forget the majority of the panel sitting at my belated appeal, Mummery LJ and Keene LJ, without whose entirely independent, fair, objective and conflict-free interests this situation would, and could, never have arisen.

....

Meanwhile on 3 November 2010 the OJC delivered its considered verdict, by exonerating itself not just from any blame but having a go at me for having the audacity to complain. The nub of it runs as follows:-

'I am bound to say that the complaint seems to me wholly misconceived since it involves no question of judicial conduct; nor in any event can I see how there can be a legitimate objection to a judgment delivered publicly being publicly available on the website". Having exonerated all-and-sundry [including himself, since he participated in what took place and obviously sees nothing untoward] he then says he has no jurisdiction to investigate the complaint since it involves him and his predecessors. Prefaced by his expression "Even if I were wrong about that" [see Appendix 1].

The fact that this bullshit was penned by "The Honourable Mr. Justice Underhill" – who just happened to be the current President of the Employment Appeal Tribunal with a vested interest in the outcome and probably a crony of Lindsay - was naturally irrelevant at least in the eyes of those to whom the art and practice of sleight-of-hand-and-mouth are commendable attributes.

So, to summarise, although Underhill and the OJC knew from the outset any investigation into a complaint involving people with a vested interest must be carried out by those with no such interest not only did they take no notice but were happy to issue a whitewash concocted by one of them. Moreover, even though he makes out that what counts is his opinion – and that's all it is, and happens to be dead wrong – whether or not Underhill is right or wrong is beside the point. Either way he's passing judgment about the conduct of himself and his predecessors in response to a complaint which started out on one basis and has now evolved into another about the way my complaint was dealt with. In other words, what Underhill and the OJC assert ain't worth a bean.

In effect Underhill was not only trying it pull the wool over my eyes on several counts he was issuing his legal opinion that any objection to a judgment delivered publicly being publicly available on the internet - he expediently chose to overlook or ignore the inconvenient fact that most people might see a distinction between one and approaching four thousand internet smears – is illegitimate. Before I continue, one must remember that this is England's finest speaking, a land of bilk and funny, where acting as defendant, prosecutor, judge and jury is "legitimate", thereby rendering those who complain about it and its practitioners bastards.

Although blinkered Luddites like Underhill obviously don't realize it - what else can you expect from a judge? - the rest of humanity knows full well there's a world of difference between sticking a smear in the local rag and spreading it exponentially via the internet. Hence the phenomenal success of Google, whose vast income is derived from doing little else but advertising others' products on the internet. In his enlightening [at least to me] judgment of a case featuring Google UK Limited and Google Inc [1] the redoubtable libel judge and animus of "Private Eye" magazine [2] The Honourable Mr. Justice Eady said that as at 31 March 2009 some 1.59 billion users were accessing the internet, and between January 2005 and 2009 the number of publicly indexable web pages – pages that a search engine like Google could access – had rocketed from 11.5 to 39 billion and climbing. Which also explains why Lindsay et al select this option, and why when one of their victims challenge what's been done in the name of "justice" Establishment props like Underhill play silly-buggers by pretending black is white, a mountain is a molehill and the "public" means not a tiny clique of deadbeat lawyers in the backwater of England but everybody treading The Earth, even though almost none of them understand or care one way or the other because the all-important "public knowledge" means the right to know shit – even though knowing ain't worth knowing except to twisted sadists and members of the Flat Earth Society, aka English judges. Unlike the rest of us special exceptions do, of course, apply to exceptional individuals and their families, such as the Tory M.P. who on "coming-out" about his homosexual preferences appealed for the privacy of his family to be respected [3]. Since when did this hypocritical twit and junior minister in the U.K. Government give a damn about families and privacy until the issue involved him and his own?

Although he is not exactly popular in some quarters – why should popularity count where judges are concerned? – in his judgment [1] Judge Eady expanded my knowledge of internet law and practice. Before that I am not ashamed to say I was pretty clueless about both. Although it may be a heinous crime to computer-buffs starting at age five to be ignorant about the worldwide bible of mice and men – exemplified by a comment in the documents I obtained from Essex University "Doesn't Mr. Wheen understand how the internet works?", which at least was relatively polite, by using my name instead of say the more accurate "this idiot" and suppressing an overwhelming desire to add a final exclamation mark after the question mark - it's all a matter of priorities, as it has always been. So despite the open-mouthed disbelief of the short-trousered I feel neither shame nor discomfort at being computer-illiterate. Indeed there's much to be said for being the last of a dying breed - the pre-P.C. generation who didn't want to learn a new and wholly indecipherable computer language, hardly ever watched the inexorably boring "in-programme" "Click" on B.B.C. t.v. and had a thick Windows XP manual [designed for the non-thick] which had scarcely been opened, never mind pored over. Why should I have to explain my disinterest in computers any more than in the working of my car? Both seemed to be the province of insufferably boring twits endlessly prattling on in pubs far and wide, presumably to convince their audience Einstein had nothing on them. Is this the latest way to get laid? And what else did these know-alls know, if not nothing?

Necessity may be the mother of invention, but in my case ignorance was the precursor of action.

Whereas lack of know-how is not only acceptable but inevitable at some point being taken advantage of becomes intolerable. Sooner or later the age-old excuse "we've done nothing wrong" – which usually means "prove we have" - starts wearing thin. The latest examples came from a bevy of sources, including Essex University and the U.K. Information Commissioner The latter – shades of Lindsay and Underhill, coincidentally or not, since all work for the same employer – stuck to the same, erroneous line. That the only thing that mattered was U.K. law – a transparently false, if not fraudulent, spiel. If nothing else by insisting that the U.K. Data Protection Act had [amended later to "probably"] not been breached it proved not only that his horizons began and ended at the cliffs of Dover – a nonsensical attitude where use and abuse of the global internet was concerned, as he and other con-merchants must have known all along – but his claims of "independence" were looking decidedly flaky and shaky. All the more reason, then, to agitate the tree of knowledge and see what fruits landed.

I started by consulting a local IT specialist, who confirmed my preconceptions that no system was foolproof or secure from hackers, and – for a fee – without expending much time or effort to the task he could show me how to hack into my own P.C. files, e-mails and correspondence, and insert derogatory entries about me on the internet, camouflaged to look realistic. How did this square with Essex U's version, IT specialists included? And how did it relate to the fact that I was dealing with the U.K. Government, which throughout my lifetime had acquired a reputation of conducting dirty and unlawful operations, including computer hacking and mail interception by the likes of MI5? [For copies of the relevant correspondence see Appendix 2].

Below is a summary of the main events.

- On 27 September 2010 I made what I thought was a routine, if not token, subject access request to MI5 under the U.K. Data Protection Act, requesting "All information and copies of documents held about me by you". Fully expecting nothing, I added "In anticipation of your habitual refusal to comply kindly send your reply to my e-mail address"
- The next day I told the MI5 Data Controller the following:-

"I can only speculate who might have info [sic] about me, and can only say someone apparently with malicious intent has been posting derogatory smears about me on the internet [10 years after the event] connecting me with the Attorney General and a third party who denies any involvement. To do that, at this stage it is entirely conceivable that some Government body or agency has been intercepting my communications and/or e-mails with or without legal authority. Consequently I want to know if MI5 is involved or implicated in any way and/or has any info [sic] or documents about me. If you have none or refuse to release any please advise me by e-mail. Otherwise kindly send them [if feasible] by e-mail attachment".

- To date, despite the fact that MI5 told me in writing that a letter had been posted to me on 6 December 2010, no answer has been received from M.I.5., its boss or the Home Office, the I.C.O., Dennis Skinner M.P., or the U.K. Cabinet Office, to which I also belatedly complained more in hope than expectation. Likewise my requests for a copy to be e-mailed to me have been ignored.
- As a last resort, I intended to file a complaint with the Investigatory Powers

Tribunal – until I spotted who its President was. Who else but my old acquaintance Lord Justice Mummery, who had done so much for me in the past, in his previous capacity as an "independent" member of the Court of Appeal? No need to waste my time on that wild goose chase.

.Almost inevitably the omnipresent Google was a player in my case. And equally inevitably it denied any wrong-doing, although only after it had pretended not to have received my complaints to it and I had had to enlist the help of the Better Business Bureau. A copy of my letter is reproduced below.

15 September 2010

Managing Director , Google , USA

Dear Sir

By searching one of your websites [myEssex geoffrey wheen] today and previously I found an entry at the top of the page to "Attorney General v Wheen", ie me. This case [and the subsequent appeal to the UK Court of Appeal, details of which have been, and are, on the internet] was concluded 10 years ago, yet their continued insertion on the internet is not only clearly malicious I am now linked to Essex University, which could only have happened through breaches of UK privacy laws and/or unlawful computer hacking into e-mail correspondence. As the current aforesaid entries are by no means the first or only ones implicating the previous UK Labour Government and its cronies kindly advise me:-

1 - who or what body arranged for one or both entries to be inserted on the internet and kept there over the last decade under Google's banner?

2 – from what date[s] onwards did it begin?

3 – as it is UK taxpayers money being spent, at what daily, weekly or yearly cost?

4 – what law permits this outrageous conduct to occur?

5 – how can these internet entries be deleted permanently?

Thank you.

....

For once, and for good reason I prefer to heed the word of someone who, superficially at least, has acquired the knowledge [albeit thanks to the testimony of experts] and no vested interest in the outcome, to wit, Judge Eady. To me, Eady's pronouncements [1] carried even more significance. A fundamental doubt in my mind about jurisdiction [i.e. where any legal proceedings could and should be brought] seemed to have been answered. Below I quote relevant extracts from paragraphs 31 and 32 of his judgment:-

"The legal submissions in this case were made against the background of well established principles in relation to the court's jurisdiction in respect of tortuous publications, including on the internet. It has long been established that publication takes place, for the purposes of a defamation claim, where the relevant words are heard or read…. As to publication on the internet, it has been held that "If a publisher publishes in a multiplicity of jurisdictions it should understand, and must accept, that it runs the risk of liability in those jurisdictions in which the publication is not lawful and inflicts damage". Then [in paragraph 32] "there is a principle that the jurisdiction in which the tort was committed is to be regarded as *prima facie* the natural forum for the dispute".

And although it was exonerated in that particular case and trotted out the usual "not me, guv" excuse to me Google was still in the loop. The evidence showed not only that I had complained to Google and been ignored it had only answered after the Better Business Bureau intervened and squeezed out a response. But so far as I could tell it had done nothing to remove the offending material from the internet. If I had interpreted Eady correctly this could be construed as authorization or acquiescence. In his words, "Having the power to remove it, it had chosen not to do so".

That Thailand seemed to be the right and proper venue to bring legal proceedings against the U.K. Government [and any other defendants] was re-confirmed in the Thai legal Codes and in an article posted on the internet by a firm of lawyers based in Bangkok [4]. Slowly but surely I was making progress.

Knowing that other victims of this brazen and crude system of naming–and–shaming on the internet – the latter-day equivalent of being pilloried in the stocks – existed it occurred to me that a class action suit might be brought against the U.K. Government. So I broached the subject with a dozen or so lawyers spread far and wide, but apart from a couple of well-meaning and courteous exceptions precious little ensued. This neither surprised nor deterred me, because in my experience most lawyers are gutless wonders when push comes to shove and their wallets are involved. A specimen of the letter I sent is at Appendix 3.

What their reaction would have been had I raised the issue of how internet damages might be assessed was probably even more predictable. Allowing for the fact that the laws in Thailand were very different to those in The West [11] it struck me that the principle enunciated in *Rylands v Fletcher1868* [5], which created the tort of strict liability, might at least be arguable. In those bygone days flooding of adjacent land arising from the unforeseen escape of water was the cause of action, but in subsequent developments it was held that an interest in land was not necessary in order to bring a claim. In which case, why shouldn't the principle apply when malicious and/or irresponsible individuals introduce intrinsically harmful and dangerous elements onto the territory of the internet? And why shouldn't they incur liability for their actions as and when those elements escape? If strict liability were the criterion, as it should be, they would pay the penalty, as the rest of us are expected to do.

Meanwhile, while the wool-makers were spinning their yarns I'd been doing some research and consulting some local lawyers about the law in

Thailand, which thankfully bears little resemblance to the English version. Having previously sent him an e-mail dated 15 September 2010 [see Appendix 4], which he ignored, the upshot was I faxed a Notice dated 11 November 2010 [on behalf of myself and my Thai partner] to the U.K. Attorney-General. Its contents are reproduced below.

LEGAL NOTICE

NOTICE OF REQUIREMENTS FOR REMEDIAL ACTION AND POTENTIAL LEGAL PROCEEDINGS

Attention : Attorney-General, Government of the United Kingdom, England

Subject : Wilful, persistent and unlawful breaches of the Constitution and other laws of Thailand

Particulars :

At or about April 2000 the Government of the United Kingdom [hereinafter called "the offender"] arranged for the posting of one or more entries on the global internet, wherein Geoffrey Arnold Wheen [hereinafter called "Wheen"] was denounced and derided as a vexatious litigant. Those entries have continued unabated ever since.

The appeal process upholding that condemnation, which has also been running on the internet for over a decade, was flawed and biased. The offender ensured that any appeal rights under its own judicial process ended at that point by demanding a deposit of 20,000 pounds should Wheen attempt to further appeal to the House of Lords [which only considered appeals involving the public interest] and if necessary the European Court.

Despite Wheen's protests and complaints about these internet entries, which breach U.K. and European Human Rights laws, not only has the offender done nothing to remedy the damage caused to him and his family one of the individuals responsible has claimed Wheen has no reason to complain.

Wheen has every right to sue wherever harm and damage has been caused to him and his reputation throughout the last 10 plus years, including in Thailand, which he has frequented since 2000 and where he is now retired. So too has his family [about whom there is no defence, since they played no part in any of the preceding events] about all of whom the offender has displayed the same callous indifference and disrespect as that shown to Wheen.

Knowing the scope, readership and impact of entries on the worldwide internet by its actions the offender has willfully, persistently and maliciously breached the laws of numerous countries, including the Constitution and other laws of the Kingdom of Thailand, about which, its citizens and residents, it has shown a contemptuous disregard and disrespect for their legal and civil rights. Wheen, his partner Amporn Suwannara and their family have all suffered loss, humiliation and damage at the hands of the offender, which, among other breaches of the law, has infringed the following laws of Thailand:-

S. 35 of the Thai Constitution, which bestows rights of privacy, dignity and reputation for Wheen and his family

Article 17 of the International Covenant on Civil and Political Rights [to which both Thailand and the UK are signatories] outlawing "unlawful interference", and "unlawful attacks on one's honour and reputation".

S. 423 of the Thai Civil and Commercial Code, whereby the offender must prove firstly that the defamatory statements were true [which will be refuted, since the proceedings giving rise to their existence and publication were unfair and unsound, and were not conducted under Thai law and proceedings] and secondly were and are "substantially justified", which is virtually impossible to prove anywhere, especially in Thailand, over a period exceeding 10 years.

TAKE NOTICE therefore that with this notification we require you, within the next 21 days, to take the following measures to remedy the harm caused and recompense us for your repeated breaches of our legal rights, failing which we will institute legal proceedings, including bringing a class action suit if appropriate, without further prior notification.

Remedial Measures and Compensation Required

1 – the removal from the internet and any other publications of all the relevant entries

2 – the insertion of a formal apology [in wording, in a place and of a size to be agreed by the undersigned] on the internet and in "The Bangkok Post", "Thai Rath" and "The Guardian" for a continuous period of 3 months

3 – payment of compensation of 20 million Thai baht made payable to the Thai bank account of Geoffrey Arnold Wheen, who occupies the same Thai residence as his undersigned partner, Amporn Suwannara

Should litigation arise we also intend to sue for criminal defamation and cruel and unusual punishment and claim punitive and exemplary damages arising from the offender's malice, misconduct, bias and intentional disregard for our protected rights and for the severe, intentional and repetitive torts.

This Notice has been produced and sent after consultation with a lawyer practicing in Thailand.

Signed and Dated

....

Here again I was dealing with an individual whose predecessor [in name but not title] had brought the U.K. proceedings against me, whose title was on the internet entries and who therefore had a vested interest in trying it on. Which duly happened, under the name of my previous contact, one James Ross. For all I know he may just have been following orders. The problem was in my book where he was concerned his credibility had gone, so whatever he said had to be treated with a mountain of salt. Again he didn't disappoint. Having ignored my request to acknowledge receipt of my Notice the response dated 15 November 2010 was blunt, acrid and designed to put me in my place:- "The Attorney-General is not responsible for material published on the internet by others. Therefore, I am afraid to say that this office is unable to assist you in this matter". Nice try, but wide of the mark again.

So, in a nutshell, in U.K. terms the position so far was:-

Minister of Justice – seek legal advice from bodies located entirely in England

Attorney-General – get lost, whoever you are

OJC – what's and where's the beef?

ICO – the Data Protection Act clears the offender of any wrong-doing

MI5 – we say we've sent you a letter, so whether you've received it or not, our file is closed

Essex University – nothing to do with us, matey

The shock from these earth-quaking, gob-smacking reactions and revelations merited publishing on the internet, preferably by WikiLeaks, but Julian Assange seemed to have more important things on his mind and was incommunicado. Even relatively small fry like Max Clifford didn't seem to understand that mine was a riveting story tailor-made for the tabloids – at the right price, need I add. I've got my pride to fall back on. If nothing else, I'm no Cheap Charlie, whatever the bar-girls say behind my back and to my face.

Time for The Grinders-Down to have another go. Having been advised by me on 30 November 2010 that I'd served a Notice on the Attorney-General, was not interested in whatever else the OJC had to say on the subject and would treat any further attempt to contact me as a breach of my privacy rights what else would it do but take not a blind bit of notice of my Notice, proceed regardless and issue another whitewash? To what end? To confirm what I'd known about them and their methods for an eternity? Best treat it with the contempt it deserves and another breach of my privacy rights.

Reverting to earlier events, it was natural and logical to approach the U.K. Attorney-General, since he instigated the vexatious proceedings against me, and might be expected to know why they were apparently so important as to justify their continued presence on the internet over the last decade, the tab for doing so and who made the relevant decisions. So I produced and sent a list of items, which elicited an immediate response from the ubiquitous James Ross. I make no apologies for dwelling at some length about our exchange, since it exemplifies the dismissive and bombastic attitude adopted by far too many bureaucrats I experienced towards freedom of information legislation and those who attempted to utilize it. [A particularly egregious example of recent lineage was the U.K.'s Serious Fraud Office, which just happens to fall under the aegis of the Attorney General [see my book *III A Fraud*].

By e-mail dated 19 September 2010 - sent simultaneously to the Minister of Justice – and by virtue of the Freedom of Information Act I requested from the Attorney-General all documents, records and information in [their] possession regarding the undermentioned matters:-

1 – a list of UK Attorney-Generals from 1995 to now

2 – the exact dates Jack Straw and Ken Clarke became the UK Ministers of Justice and accountable for the actions of the Attorney-Generals

3 – the respective amounts of public money expended from the date[s] of original insertion[s] until now on publishing on the internet "Attorney General v Wheen EAT on 18 April [2000] Employment Appeal Tribunal" and the Court of Appeal decision re the same case

4 – the exact dates such internet advertising began

5 – on the authority of which UK Government Minister[s] and/or individual did this advertising begin?

6 – the law which permits anyone to publish this information 10 years after the event

7 – if you deny responsibility, who is responsible and what evidence do you have?

8 – against how many other individuals has the EAT issued similar orders to that referred to in 3 above?

9 – if those cases are on the internet, where and under what heading?

10 – the amount of money expended by the UK Government on intercepting, recording and hacking into communications to and from myself and the legal authority for doing so.

The Tribunals Service's answers to points 1 to 10 [dated 10 November and 23 December 2010 are at Appendices 5 and 6. Although they are much more informative than can be said of the feeble efforts of the A.G. inevitably gaps in my knowledge still remain. Plus yet another mystery. The still unexplained references by the Ministry of Justice to the Admin Court, its non-transcribed judgment and my application which failed at the permission stage. About which only two possibilities existed. Either I was suffering from acute amnesia – including not only about making an application to the Admin Court but being the subject of a hearing and judgment by that Court, about all of which my mind was a complete blank – or I wasn't. In which case what was going on, and why no explanation? The refusal of Roger Davies and his bosses to answer my questions – apparently because they considered it was the job of the "independent" Information Commissioner to come up with an answer – was hardly likely to inspire confidence or trust in any of them. But who cares one way or the other where they dispense their services and smears? [See the correspondence at Appendix 7]. But at least dealing with that body was not like pulling teeth, and, to its credit, a damn sight better than when we last crossed swords over my earlier FOI Act requests.

As for the A.G., and items 2, 3, 4, 5, 8 and 9 James Ross answered "we do not hold this information". When I pointed out it was his job to help me locate the relevant information he referred me to his initial answer, which in part said "matters regarding employment tribunals fall within the jurisdiction of the Ministry of Justice", to which he knew I had made an identical request on 19 September 2010.

He did, however, state that neither Jack Straw nor Ken Clarke [the respective Ministers of Justice] were/are accountable for the actions of the Attorney-General's Office. [Notice how he tacked on the suffix "Office" to the information I actually requested].

At the second time of asking he answered item 1. Which left items 6, 7 and 10. Taking them in turn, the answers were:-

6 – "This is not a request as stated by the FOI act [sic], but is *in fact* a request for *advice* [my italics]. He suggested I seek independent legal advice. When I challenged him about his contentions he iterated that I was seeking advice, presumably as "fact" rather than his opinion. But what's the difference where lawyers are concerned, or even minions who work for lawyers?

7 – here his answer was "This not a request as stated by the FOI act"[sic]. He stuck to this answer after I pointed out he had not answered my request.

He also contended items 6 and 7 were "questions", [6 clearly isn't] as if they are not permissible.   But they are, as confirmed in information published on the internet by the Information Commissioner [6].

10 – according to Mr. Ross "You [meaning me] are making a very serious allegation of criminal activity being perpetrated against your being" [My being? What's that, legal jargon or just nonsense?].   He then continues "If you have evidence of such activity taking place, then you will need to inform your local police authority for investigation".

Quite rightly, he avoids doing the very thing I'm proscribed from asking for.   No, instead of suggesting or even advising me to visit the local cops he tells me what I "need" to do, as if he's my boss at work, and I don't know any better, including about the commodity he seems to take for granted. Trust in the police, local or otherwise. Under challenge and my request for an internal review [which he refused off his own bat] Ross' answer changed to "Your question 10 is also one that does not fall under the Act" [it wasn't a question, it was a request for factual information, which he evaded twice]. He continued "like I said in my previous e-mail, you are making very serious allegations. [Suddenly and inexplicably the single "allegation" becomes "allegations", which in AG Speak and PC Plodland are invariably "very serious", trivial or not. If these "allegations" – which are nothing of the sort – are indeed "very serious" how would Ross describe say rape, incest, torture and murder, I wonder? I shudder to think. As for "miscarriages of justice", about which the U.K. judiciary, along with its victims, have acquired some expertise and experience how can they best be described? Why do "consistent" and "inconsequential" spring to mind? Still, forget about reality, pretend and go to the cops as instructed, regardless}.

After putting up with similar obstruction from other U.K. Government bodies I let loose by telling Peter Fish [the lawyer who was supposed to deal with internal reviews in the A.G.'s office] what I thought about the answers I'd been given and Lord Goldsmith's "advice" about the Iraq War. The big Fish left it to the tiddler to reject my request for an internal review – invariably a complete waste of time and money, but nevertheless a prerequisite to complaining to the Information Commissioner, who unlike people working together inside the same organization on occasion bears some superficial, passing resemblance to independence and objectivity. In keeping with their renowned refusal to countenance criticism about them and their own I was treated to another lecture coupled with a veiled threat.

Changing tack yet again Ross this time said "You [meaning me] are claiming that a criminal offence has taken place against your person, as you will know this would be a matter for the police to investigate". Although Ross makes these "serious allegations" against me I said no such thing. Incredible though it seems for somebody working in a Department which spends the whole time dishing out advice and lectures about the law apparently he was totally unaware of the fact that in certain circumstances intercepting communications is not illegal under U.K. law, let alone a "criminal act" [7].

Nor would the police – local or otherwise – be the slightest bit interested, if past contact with them about anything is any guide. But Mr. Ross was determined to put me in my place. Warming to his task he concludes that I am making "other allegations that this office is implicit [does he mean implicated?] in the killings of innocent civilians in a foreign country, this is wholly inappropriate and slanderous" [I think he means libelous, but who cares about legal niceties?]" blah blah blah. Really? Well, if he says so I must be guilty as charged, even though again my e-mail said nothing of the sort. Could this be another attempt to consign me to the "spent force" dustbin? Or maybe an effort to re-write history and tragedy, air-brushing the roles played by the leading players? Come to think of it, why not blame me and a few billion others for the Iraq debacle? Over to you, U.K. Government.

I complained to the Information Commissioner, whose Decision Notice – which he was clearly reluctant to issue – is at Appendix 8 [See also the correspondence at Appendix 9]. To peruse that document – produced by a supposedly independent individual who clearly isn't – an undiscerning reader would get a completely false impression of what happened, which doubtless played a part in the decision to stick it on the internet. For instance, he says the A.G. answered all my questions. If by asserting he didn't have the answer to most of them amounts to an answer, which according to the disingenuous I.C.O. it does, a negative thereby becomes a positive.

As the correspondence proves, James Ross refused to answer point 10, and told me to get lost – a reaction tried by another individual employed in the Ministry of Justice – because he clearly did not understand U.K. law. If Ross knew what he was talking about, which he obviously didn't and [with the connivance of the ICO] tried to extricate himself later his answer would and should have been entirely different. As I told the ICO on 23 September 2010 in certain circumstances it is not a criminal offence to intercept communications, so Ross' belligerent mouthings about my making serious accusations about criminal activity was and is drivel, as is the ICO's interpretation of the correspondence, including between us. When the penny finally dropped, or more likely he was put in the picture by somebody else, Ross' dogmatic certainty evaporated, he then trots out the very Act about which I was always aware and he was seemingly clueless, then cites it to me as if our previous stances never existed. Somehow the reality and the attempted con get lost in the version concocted by the ICO. Could a lawyer have played a part in this fantastic, unbelievable production?

It gets better. Having refused to correspond further and to conduct a review of his own answer – which no other body I've dealt with has done, and renders the concept of a "review" farcical – on a completely false and defamatory premise Ross then stood on his head, presumably because somebody had told him he was talking cobblers. So what does he do? Having refused to engage in further correspondence and to conduct a review of his own conduct and decisions the Attorney-General, in the shape of James Ross, then decides, out of the blue, that the Freedom of Information Act does, after all, apply to point 10 and supplies another answer predictably saying nothing worth knowing. Meanwhile the ICO said the Attorney-General [under whose name the proceedings against me were taken and the internet smear appears] was wrong about the law, because it was the Data Protection Act, not the Freedom of

Information Act, which applied. The ICO then tried to shovel all this under the carpet. After I made it clear that his version was flatly contradicted by what the Attorney-General had actually said the ICO decided to issue a Decision Notice for insertion on his web-page. The Attorney-General then repeats his earlier refusal to provide any information, this time under the Data Protection Act.

In the latter, dated 10 January 2011 the A.G. says "A communication may only be intercepted if this is done pursuant to a warrant issued under the Regulation of Investigatory Powers Act 2000". Again, that statement is plainly wrong in law and practice. Not only does the Act say no such thing, interceptions occur without any warrant, legally and illegally, and with increasing regularity, impunity and complete disregard for the rights of the victims, often for the most fatuous, petty and petty-minded reasons [See, for instance, 8]. And since the law is being used as it was never intended and Section 19[1] of the Regulation of Investigatory Powers Act is the catch-all justification for total silence and official secrecy it says the following:-

"Where an interception warrant has been issued or renewed, it shall be the duty of every person falling within subsection [2] to keep secret all the matters mentioned in subsection [3]". But what says the law when no such warrant has been issued? No warrant, no relevance. From that and the Attorney-General's answer we know: that if and when a warrant is issued no law-breaking occurs, as I knew all along. And James Ross obviously didn't. Otherwise his ridiculous rant about "very serious allegations" of "criminal activity" and going to the local police would make no sense, as they didn't to me. But what if no warrant had been issued? Then Section 19{1} was inapplicable, secrecy and all. Then another alternative. The interception had been going on without any warrant, which according to the A.G. was not only unlawful it didn't happen. Then another scenario. A warrant had been issued belatedly because I'd contacted the Thai Attorney-General about law-breaking by the U.K. Government, the U.K. Government knew this because it had been intercepting my communications and it knew it would be asked about this in any litigation. Added to which, before our Petitions were sent I had served a formal Notice on the U.K. Attorney-General regarding the intention to sue. Par for the course in a country where the law and individual rights ceased to have any meaning long ago. So threats, retaliation, snooping, spying, lying, propaganda, conspiracy and the U.K. Government's panoply of dirty tricks were only to be expected, since that's all it and the lawyers it employs seem to know about [9]. All of which help to explain several events, including the failure of MI5's "letter" to arrive at all. Could it be it never existed, or was never posted, or was stopped from being delivered? All of which would scarcely matter if, as I repeatedly requested, a copy had been e-mailed to me. About which MI5, the Home Office, the ICO and others involved maintain a stubborn silence, since revealing it might be too incriminating.

So on what legal grounds has the U.K. Government got the right to issue a warrant against anybody, myself included? Apparently it's enough for you to be a "person of interest", although that sounds a bit too wishy-washy to me. Having the audacity to exercise your rights in another country might well be enough in their eyes, although some people might regard setting the spooks on you, poking collective noses into somebody's private life and papers and issuing derogatory and erroneous decisions for posting on the internet smacked, if not stank, of intimidation and retaliation. Other than that, what sort of case for a warrant could possibly have been concocted against me?

National security, preventing or detecting crime, preventing disorder, public safety, protecting public health, or in the interests of the economic well being of the United Kingdom seem to be the qualifiers [10], although I didn't realize the U.K. had an economy which was "well". How about being designated a "spent force" who refuses to stay mum? That's a much more promising approach, coupled with more defamation, courtesy of the U.K. Attorney-General's Office and ICO.

APPENDIX ONE

Letter dated 3 November 2010 from President of EAT

The Hon Mr Justice Underhill
President of the Employment Appeal Tribunal

Employment Appeal Tribunal
Audit House
58 Victoria Embankment
London EC4Y 0DS

Telephone 020 7273 1022

3 November 2010

Dear Mr Wheen,

The Office for Judicial Complaints forwarded me your Complaint dated 18 October 2010 complaining (as I understand it) that a judgment of Mr. Justice Lindsay making a restriction of proceedings order against you appears on the Employment Appeal Tribunal website. I am bound to say that the complaint seems to me wholly misconceived since it involves no question of judicial conduct; nor in any event can I see how there can be a legitimate objection to a judgment delivered publicly being publicly available on the website. But even if I were wrong about that, I have myself no jurisdiction to investigate the complaint since it relates to myself and my predecessors as President. I have notified the Office accordingly.

Yours sincerely,

Nicholas Underhill

The Honourable Mr. Justice Underhill

APPENDIX TWO

Information and Correspondence regarding MI5

Fascism, state terror and power abuse

This web-page is dedicated to all those working in Britain's Diplomatic and Intelligence services who, like David Shayler, Annie Machon, Craig Murray and Katherine Gun, put democracy and their country before private gain, the occult or foreign control.

The Secret State: Britain's Intelligence Agencies: MI5 (Counterintelligence/Home Office/MOD) and MI6 (Intelligence/Foreign Office/MOD)

Why does us Brits' MI5 logo include an occult symbol, 'the all seeing eye', as part of her 1950's to 1970's official insignia? And pentagram illusions (try looking at the MI5 *Rectum Defendae* 'roses' close up then as a distance) in their current insignia? If you know why, please

The SS - 'Security Service' (official title), MI5, is Britain's domestic military intelligence division. The SIS or 'Secret Intelligence Service', MI6, is Britain's foreign military intelligence division. Though described as 'services' they are a cross between government departments and plain clothes military units operationally controlled foreign powers.

Known as *The Secret State* (nicknamed *The Permanent Government* in Ramsey and Derril's book *Smear!*) they operate as a 'state within a state' having only token democratic accountability. They go to great lengths, including lying to elected ministers and use of the archaic 'Official Secrets Act' to stave off embarrassing revelations about what a waste of our public money many of their operations are... and to deflect all scrutiny of their work. The IOPS (Information Operations Planning System) department of MI6 plants stories beneficial to the *secret state* to gullible/bribed journalists in newspapers and on newswires. Champions of the arbitrary telephone intercept they appear to be safe haven for occultists as well as 21st Century gestapo elements.

The Guardian's Big Brother surveillance special **http://www.guardian.co.uk/bigbrother/privacy/**

To request access to personal data MI5 hold on you under Part II, section 7 of the data protection act 1998 write to: The Data Controller, The Security Service, PO Box 3255, LONDON, SW1P 1AE. The search will cost £10.00 and you will be refused any information. But you can appeal, as have Norman Baker MP, Mohammed Al Fayed, and me.

MI5 and the Christmas Tree bites - secret political vetting at the BBC - seperate page

Background reading matter:
'Defending the Realm: MI5 and the Shayler Affair', Mark Hollingsworth and Nick Fielding, Andre Deutsch, 1999.
'The Big Breach, From Top Secret to Maximum Security' Richard Tomlinson, 2001
'Spycatcher, the Candid Autobiography of a Senior Intelligence Officer, Peter Wright, Heinemann, 1987.

UK intelligence agencies' news

04Sep06 - Belfast Telegraph - Tomlinson: the spy who was left out in the cold

02Jul06 - Telegraph - Revealed: how the BBC used MI5 to vet thousands of staff

06Jul06 - Belfast Telegraph - Secret millions row over new MI5 HQ

22Dec05 - Yorkshire Today - Shadowy alliance haunts Stormontgate

19Dec05 - Bilderberg.org - Shayler 'Blair was an MI5 agent'

13Sep05 - Bristol Evening Post - N.11 THE WORK OF SECURITY CHIEFS

18Aug05 - Times - Top secret intelligence unit will quit Belfast for new role in Iraq

Mar05[added] - Observer - There is no case for torture, ever

11Feb05 - Evening Standard - Key Kelly pair helped appoint MI6 chief

From: Geoffrey Wheen (gwheen2@yahoo.co.nz)
To: Enquiries@mi5.gov.uk;
Date: Tue, 7 December, 2010 8:50:20 AM
Cc:
Subject: Re: Obtaining Information

Security Service

Given the inevitable delay through your sending me a letter why can't your response be transmitted to me now by e-mail attachment, especially if you have no information to give me?
Thanks.

Geoffrey Wheen

From: Contact Us <Enquiries@mi5.gov.uk>
To: Geoffrey Wheen <gwheen2@yahoo.co.nz>
Sent: Mon, 6 December, 2010 9:23:44 PM
Subject: RE: Obtaining Information

Dear Mr Wheen

Thank you for your email. A letter has been sent to you today in relation to your OPA enquiry.

Kind Regards

The Enquiries Team
The Security Service

From: Geoffrey Wheen [mailto:gwheen2@yahoo.co.nz]
Sent: 03 December 2010 00:35
To: Contact Us
Subject: Re: Obtaining Information

MI5

I reckon the 40 days allotted to supply your response about me expired some days ago, so where is it and why the unexplained delay?
Thanks.

Geoffrey Wheen

From: Geoffrey Wheen <gwheen2@yahoo.co.nz>
To: Contact Us <Enquiries@mi5.gov.uk>
Sent: Mon, 18 October, 2010 8:22:40 PM
Subject: Re: Obtaining Information

Security Service

Thank you.

http://nz.mg4.mail.yahoo.com/dc/launch?.gx=1&.rand=99cfqa55jt6tb   12/7/2010

From: casework@ico.gsi.gov.uk (casework@ico.gsi.gov.uk)
To: gwheen2@yahoo.co.nz;
Date: Thu, 9 December, 2010 4:46:08 PM
Cc:
Subject: Information Commissioner's Office - response[Ref. RFA0349888]

9 December 2010

Case Reference Number RFA0349888

Dear Mr Wheen

Thank you for your email, your comments have been noted.

You raised a question about why an answer to another DPA request you made should be sent to you by letter rather than via e-mail or e-mail attachment.

A data controller may choose to send information in response to a request in the post when enclosures need to be sent as they may believe it is a more secure way of sending information. If you have a preference to how you wish to receive the information I would suggest informing the data controller at the time of making your request. However it is important to note that although the DPA states that information should be provided to an individual in permanent form, it does not allow an individual to demand what format it is sent in. Therefore, if a data controller decides for example, that there is too much information to send in an email attachment they may decide to send it in the post.

I hope you find the above information helpful.

Yours sincerely

Charlotte Haywood
Case Officer
First Contact Group

---

http://nz.mg4.mail.yahoo.com/dc/launch?.gx=1&.rand=dc5blcl0n1jsu   12/9/2010

From: Geoffrey Wheen (gwheen2@yahoo.co.nz)
To: casework@ico.gsi.gov.uk;
Date: Sat, 18 December, 2010 6:19:07 AM
Cc:
Subject: complaints

ICO
UK

I complain about the following :-

1 - Ministry of Justice - by its own word its FOIA review was due yesterday - predictably it hasn't arrived

2 - Among other things, I am also still awaiting your verdict re the actions of Roger Davies of that Dept - your ref RFA0305281. The letter I received yesterday from a Richard Goodman of the Ministry of Justice is still beyond my ken, since no attempt is made to address the points about which I specifically complained and am most concerned, namely Davies' references to an "Admin Court", its "judgment" and an "application" which "failed at the permission stage", about all of which I had no prior knowledge and are utterly meaningless to me, yet Richard Goodman has left you to explain. Or try to explain away at your pace and in your good time. How peculiar that Davies' bosses - who have access to the relevant material - prefer to pass the buck and expect me to accept what you tell me on their behalf sometime down the line. Based on past and current events there's not much chance of that happening now or later

3 - MI5 - its answer to my DPA request was late to begin with, a letter was apparently sent to me by post on 6 December [a mere 12 days ago and counting] and predictably [and deliberately?] has still not arrived. It has ignored my e-mail to send its response to me by e-mail, which when I raised the issue with you instead of your pursuing the matter with the spooks you shrugged it off - your ref RFA0349888

4 - AG - another instance of obstruction and tardiness. My ignored e-mails to you of 13 and 14 December refer - your ref RFA0364561.
Thanks.

Geoffrey Wheen

From: Geoffrey Wheen (gwheen2@yahoo.co.nz)
To: public.enquiries@homeoffice.gsi.gov.uk;
Date: Tue, 28 December, 2010 1:56:32 PM
Cc: gwheen2@yahoo.co.nz;
Subject: complaint re MI5

Home Office
UK

I understand you are responsible for MI5, about which the corres below refers, and has been ignored. I have still received no response to my DPA request due on 27 November, also inexplicably and supposedly posted on 6 December - over 3 weeks ago - nor any answer from MI5 or the ICO why it can't be e-mailed to me. About that, according to Section 7[1][c] Data Protection Act I'm entitled to have the relevant information communicated to me "in an intelligioble form" - which includes via e-mail, as has happened with every other body I've dealt with. So the decision is mine, not MI5's or any other data controller's. So where is the information, why hasn't it been sent to me by e-mail, and why have my complaints and queries been ignored?
Thanks.

Geoffrey Wheen

From: Geoffrey Wheen <gwheen2@yahoo.co.nz>
To: casework@ico.gsi.gov.uk
Cc: gwheen2@yahoo.co.nz
Sent: Thu, 23 December, 2010 3:43:36 PM
Subject:

ICO
UK

Further to my unanswered e-mail of 18 December [your ref RFA0349888], the reply from MI5 has still not arrived, despite its telling me it was posted on 6 December - 16 days ago. Moreover both it and you have ignored my request for it to be e-mailed to me, which considering it is a "letter" which will doubtless say nothing worth knowing by me or anybody else, is not only the most logical but practical method to use.

All of which started 3 months ago, because this body couldn't be bothered publishing basic info on its website re DPA procedures and fees, compelling me to apply twice. Receipt of my last and current appln was ackd by it by e-mail on 18 October, so its reply should have been sent to me by 27 November at the latest - long before the customary annual airport farce and laughable alibis in the UK began.

Consequently you can regard this as a complaint of tardiness and refusal by MI5 to supply the information I requested and have paid for. Ditto the failures/refusals by the AG and Ministry of Justice to supply FOI and DPA info respectively.

Thank you.

Geoffrey Wheen

http://nz.mg4.mail.yahoo.com/dc/launch?.gx=1&.rand=cq3cq8i1o9ijc   12/28/2010

Home Office

Direct Communications Unit

Switchboard 020 7035 4848   Fax: 020 7035 4745 Textphone: 020 7035 4742
E-mail: [illegible]   Website: www.homeoffice.gov.uk

gwheen2@yahoo.co.nz
Mr Geoffrey Wheen

Reference: T23000/10

30 December 2010

Dear Mr Wheen,

Thank you for your e-mail of 28 December to the Home Office concerning a complaint about MI5. I have been asked to reply.

The issue you have raised is a matter for the Information Commissioner's Office (ICO). I note from your e-mail that you have already been in touch with ICO. In doing so, you have taken the right course of action.

If you wish to pursue this matter further, I suggest you forward your enquiry to the ICO for their continued action.

Yours sincerely,

Mrs M Lockmun
Direct Communications Unit

From: Geoffrey Wheen (gwheen2@yahoo.co.nz)
To: skinnerd@parliament.uk;
Date: Sat, 1 January, 2011 10:54:20 AM
Cc:
Subject: Re: complaint re MI5

Dennis Skinner M.P.
House of Commons
UK

I am seeking your help re the corres below because I am being messed around, don't believe what I've been told and living in Thailand [as the UK Govt and MI5 know full well, through their having obtained my address etc on the pretext of confirming my identity under the Data Protection Act] have no M.P. to whom I can turn or complain re this increasingly apparent cover-up and other malpractices. If, therefore, you can assist me it would be much appreciated, because based on my past experience the supposedly independent ICO doesn't and won't take any notice.
Thank you.

Geoffrey Wheen

From: Geoffrey Wheen <gwheen2@yahoo.co.nz>
To: casework@ico.gsi.gov.uk
Sent: Thu, 30 December, 2010 9:33:47 PM
Subject: Re: complaint re MI5

ICO
UK

Re below, the Home Office has referred me to you. Needless to say MI5's answer has still not arrived - 24 days after its supposed posting, and over a month after the deadline to send its reply to me, about which neither you nor that body have lifted a finger to sort things out. Meanwhile how strange that the last letter posted to me from London was dated 22 December 2010 and took only 6 days to arrive over the Christmas holiday.
Thank you.

Geoffrey Wheen

From: Geoffrey Wheen <gwheen2@yahoo.co.nz>
To: public.enquiries@homeoffice.gsi.gov.uk
Cc: gwheen2@yahoo.co.nz
Sent: Tue, 28 December, 2010 1:56:32 PM
Subject: complaint re MI5

Home Office
UK

I understand you are responsible for MI5, about which the corres below refers, and has been ignored. I have still received no response to my DPA request due on 27 November, also inexplicably and

http://nz.mg4.mail.yahoo.com/dc/launch?.gx=1&.rand=foc6t73oo3i02   1/1/2011

From: Geoffrey Wheen (gwheen2@yahoo.co.nz)
To: public.enquiries@homeoffice.gsi.gov.uk;
Date: Tue, 4 January, 2011 5:06:05 AM
Cc: mayt@parliament.uk;
Subject: Re: complaint re MI5

Mrs. M Lockmun
Home Office
UK
Re yours of 30 December 2010,
1 - the Home Secretary [to whom this is copied], not the Information Commissioner [who as usual has done nothing to sort out this issue] is accountable to Parliament for MI5
2 - the UK Government has taken 10 pounds from me for information from MI5 which I have never received. It also demanded details of my address, bank account and other personal and sensitive information on the pretext of identifying me to no useful purpose, thereby breaching my privacy rights
3 - its telling me MI5 posted a "letter" to me [late, naturally] on 6 December - which now seems extremely implausible - does not discharge the contractual obligation owed to me, since I paid for information, not unproven, unfulfilled and empty assertions about posting that information. What's more and worse, that information / letter could and should have been sent to me by e-mail, as I specifically requested in my original letter and e-mailed request made to MI5 on 27 and 28 September 2010, which it ignored, along with my subsequent requests and complaints
4 - I am entitled to, and want, a copy of that letter either from MI5 or the Home Office. What the ICO does sometime never is beside the point
5 - MI5 has either been complying with UK law or it hasn't. That was one of the reasons for my subject access request to it, amplified in my e-mail of 28 September 2010 to Laurence Brett, MI5 Data Controller. If it has been intercepting my communications I'm entitled to know:-
[a] whether or not its actions are and have always been lawful
[b] whether or not, and if so when, the Home Office has ever issued a warrant authorising such interceptions
[c] how much public money has been expended on such interceptions

You, not the Information Commissioner or anybody else, can and should answer those questions here and now. Please do so to my e-mail address.

Finally [for now] it must be said that not only is this whole ridiculous and time-wasting episode deplorable somebody might wonder why, if its hands are clean, MI5 would choose to act as if they aren't for no logical or positive reason. Am I supposed to believe what I'm told after all this juvenile nonsense?
Thank you.

Geoffrey Wheen

From: "public.enquiries@homeoffice.gsi.gov.uk" <public.enquiries@homeoffice.gsi.gov.uk>
To: gwheen2@yahoo.co.nz
Sent: Thu, 30 December, 2010 8:41:57 PM
Subject: complaint re MI5

Reference : T23000/10

Thank you for your e-mail enquiry of 28/12/2010 6:56:32 AM

A reply is attached.

http://nz.mg4.mail.yahoo.com/dc/launch?.gx=1&.rand=cem0p0vdp961o   1/4/2011

From: Geoffrey Wheen (gwheen2@yahoo.co.nz)
To: pscorrespondence@cabinet-office.x.gsi.gov.uk;
Date: Thu, 3 February, 2011 11:19:58 AM
Cc: gwheen2@yahoo.co.nz;
Subject: payment

Cabinet Office
UK Govt

I am addressing your office because requesting information from MI5, the Home Secretary, Home Office and Information Commissioner is like talking to a brick wall.
On 6 October 2010 I posted a [second] subject access request to MI5 under the Data Protection Act, enclosing personal details about me and a cheque for ten pounds. Receipt of that communication was acknowledged by e-mail, and [after the time allowed to reply] I was told a letter had been posted to me on 6 December 2010. That letter - if it exists, which I very much doubt - has never arrived. What's more, my several requests to the aforementioned Depts for a copy to be e-mailed to me have all been ignored.

I have just received my latest bank statement from England, showing that the above-mentioned cheque was only debited to my account on 19 January, ie 105 days after it was sent and 44 days after MI5 claims it posted its non-existent reply to me. Consequently please advise me the following:-
1 - why can't I get a copy of the MI5 letter to me sent to me by e-mail, since I've paid for it?
2 - since when has the UK Government sent replies to DPA requests before the application fee has been paid, never mind 6 weeks beforehand?
3 - where has my cheque been all that time?
4 - why has the UK Govt banked it weeks late and still given me nothing in return?

Thank you.

Geoffrey Wheen

Geoffrey Wheen | 229

APPENDIX THREE

Specimen Letter
to Lawyers

From: Geoffrey Wheen (gwheen2@yahoo.co.nz)
To: gmason@masonlawdc.com;
Date: Sun, 24 October, 2010 9:45:55 AM
Cc:
Subject: Re: privacy class action

Gary Mason
Mason Law LLP
Dear Sir

I am a retired Brit living in Thailand, who wants to sue the UK Govt for inserting derogatory and damaging entries about me on the internet for over 10 years, [which I only found out about earlier this year, thanks to a tip-off from a foreign friend] breaching my privacy rights under the UK Human Rights Act and European Convention on Human Rights. So far as I can see under UK jurisdiction any breach of the HRA and Convention can only be legally justified if the UK Govt had no alternative than to act as it has done by virtue of "primary legislation". It fails on both counts, plus its actions are wholly disproportionate, given that I committed no criminal offence. Even those who have done once their convictions are "spent" under the Rehabilitation of Offenders Act they are entitled to, and given, protection from privacy invasion under that Act and libel laws. Consequently I regard the actions of the UK Govt as wholly indefensible under its own laws. However, because the Convention applies to numerous countries whose populations have access to the internet [thereby multiplying the exposure and damage incalculably] I see no legal reason why proceedings for invasion of my privacy rights should not be brought against the UK Govt in any one or all of them, especially where very restrictive privacy laws apply and are enforced and class action suits are accepted practice, eg France and Holland. About that, because hundreds of other victims of this internet abuse created and perpetuated by the UK Govt exist [I have downloaded lists of them] opt-out class action and claims for substantial if not punitive damages on a contingency fee basis seem appropriate..
Could you please advise me whether you can assist, bacause I badly need expert help and support, especially fighting a juggernaut.
If you can't help me, do you know who can?
Thank you.

Geoffrey Wheen

APPENDIX FOUR

E-Mail dated 15 September 2010 to U.K. Attorney General

From: Geoffrey Wheen (gwheen2@yahoo.co.nz)
To: complaints@attorneygeneral.gsi.gov.uk;
Date: Wed, 15 September, 2010 10:33:55 AM
Cc:
Subject: complaint

Dominic Grieve Esq
Attorney General
UK Government

Dear Sir

On the internet are references to Attorney General v Wheen, meaning me. Since this juvenile drivel is 10 years old and I thought the Labour Government, its sexist policies, cronies and pals had departed;-
1 - when did you first know about the above-mentioned internet entries?
2 - what justification do you have for their continued presence?
3 - apart from the obvious attempt to smear and ridicule me, what point are you and they trying to make?
4 - who authorised these entries and when?
5 - who first arranged for these entries to be put on the internet and on what date?
6 - who approved and kept them on the internet for the last decade?
7 - so far, what has been the total cost to the taxpayer of doing so?
In answer to queries 4-6 inclusive, I would appreciate the names of those concerned.

I would be grateful if you would reply in person or confirm that whoever does so is speaking on your behalf and with your full authority.

Thank you.

Geoffrey Wheen

APPENDIX FIVE

Information from
Tribunals Service

Tribunals Service
Employment

Employment Policy Team
3rd Floor
Alexandra House
14-22 The Parsonage
Manchester
M3 2JA

DX 743570 Manchester 66

T 0161 833 6316
E: paula.sidgreaves@tribunals.gsi.gov.uk

Minicom 0845 7673722
(Helpline for the deaf and hard of hearing)

Mr G Wheen
gwheen2@yahoo.co.nz

Our ref: FOI/67604/10/PS

10 November 2010

Dear Mr Wheen

Subject: Freedom of Information Request

Thank you for your email of 19 October 2010 addressed to the Data Access and Compliance Unit in the Ministry of Justice. In your email you made a request under the Freedom of Information Act 2000 (FOIA) for:

> 1 - regarding the members of the EAT from 1999 until now, please advise me in each case their:-
> [a] identity and position held
> [b] legal and/or professional qualifications, if any
> [c] dates of appointment and entry into, and departure from, office
> [e] remuneration
> [f] who appointed them, and by what process
> [g] any previous public positions held
> 2 - in addition to the above, I request all and any other information which can lawfully be supplied to me regarding the following EAT members:-
> [a] Mr Justice Lindsay [ex-President]
> [b] Mr D Chadwick
> [c] Mr P R A Jacques CBE

Your correspondence has been forwarded to me because I am responsible for dealing with requests for information the Employment Tribunals (ET), Employment Appeal Tribunals (EAT) and Tribunals Service (TS).

I can confirm that the Department does hold the names of the judiciary at the EAT from 1999 and are provided below.

President of the EAT:
Sir Thomas Morison 1996 – 1999
Sir John Lindsay 1999 – 2002
Sir Michael Burton 2002 – 2006
Sir Patrick Elias 2006 – 2008
Sir Nicholas Underhill 2009 – to date

Resident Judges of the EAT:
England & Wales
His Honour Judge Peter Clark prior to 1999 to date
His Honour Judge McMullen QC prior to 1999 to date
Scotland
Lady Smith 2005 to date
Lord Johnston 1996 – 2005.

It may be helpful if I explain that judiciary at the EAT are High Court, Circuit or Scottish Court of Session judges. Other judges visit the EAT for a month or two at a time.

All judges who sit at EAT are appointed in England and Wales, with the exception of the Honourable Lady Smith who is appointed in Scotland.

As the information you are seeking is already available in the public domain, it is exempt from disclosure under Section 21 (Information accessible to the applicant by other means) of the FOIA.

Further information about the role of and appointment of judges can be found on the Judiciary of England and Wales website. The website includes a list of the individual judges and the date of their appointment, the role of the different judges (i.e. High Court, Circuit etc) and how they are appointed. The information can be found in the section 'About the judiciary' at the following internet address:

http://www.judiciary.gov.uk/about-the-judiciary

Further information about individual judges and the Presidents can be found by entering the name of the individual judge in the search facility on the website.

A biography of the Hon Lady Smith can be found on the Scottish Court website at the following internet address: http://www.scotcourts.gov.uk/biographies/smith.asp?dir=session

Details of judicial fees and salaries are published on the Ministry of Justice website at the following internet address:

http://www.justice.gov.uk/publications/judicial-salaries-fees-2010.htm

Information in relation to the legal and/or professional qualifications and any previous public positions held by the judges you are seeking would be considered the personal data of another person, and disclosure would be unfair to that other person who is the subject of the data.

It might be helpful if I explain that the information you are seeking in relation to Mr D Chadwick and Mr PRA Jacques CBE is the personal information of those individuals and therefore would be exempt under section 40(2)(b) of the FOIA because the personal data would be disclosed to a third party. This would contravene the principles of the Data Protection Act 1998 in respect of the fair processing of personal data because the Lay Members would have a reasonable expectation that the Department will keep their personal details (such as their qualifications, background etc) confidential.

The Lay Members of the EAT have practical experience in employment relations, either on the employers side (for example as personnel directors) or on the employees' side (for example as trade union leaders). When two lay members sit on a tribunal there will be one from each side. Lay Members are appointed by the Lord Chancellor following an open recruitment exercise.

If you are unhappy with the result of your request for information, you may request an internal review within two calendar months of the date of this letter by writing to:

Data Access and Compliance Unit
Information Directorate
Ministry of Justice
6th Floor - Zone B
102 Petty France
London
SW1H 9AJ   e-mail: data.access@justice.gsi.gov.uk

If you remain dissatisfied after an internal review decision, you have the right to apply to the Information Commissioner's Office under Section 50 of the FOIA. You can contact the Information Commissioner's Office at the following address:

Information Commissioner's Office
Wycliffe House
Water Lane
Wilmslow
Cheshire SK9 5AF   Internet: https://www.ico.gov.uk/Global/contact_us.aspx

Yours sincerely

Paula Sidgreaves
Employment Policy Team

APPENDIX SIX

Information from Tribunals Service

 Tribunals Service

Craig Robb
Head of Employment Policy
Tribunals Service
5th floor
Victory House
30-34 Kingsway
London
WC2B 6EX

Mr GA Wheen

Gwheen2@yahoo.co.uz

T – 0207 273 8666
E – Craig.Robb@tribunals.gsi.gov.uk

Our ref: FOI/68089/10/CR

23 December 2010

Dear Mr Wheen

Freedom of Information Act 2000 (FOIA) – Outcome of Internal Review

Thank you for your email dated 21 November 2010 requesting an Internal Review in relation to your request under the Freedom of Information Act 2000 (FOIA). Please accept my sincere apologies for the delay in responding to your request.

I have reviewed the Department's original decision and have concluded that the response was incorrect insofar that the names of the Lay Members of the EAT should have been provided. However, I also find that the original decision in relation to the qualification and background of the Judiciary and Lay Members are the personal information of those individuals and therefore exempt from disclosure. My findings are as follows.

Background

On 19 October 2010 you asked the Department, under the FOIA, for information under the following headings:

1. regarding the members of the EAT from 1999 until now, please advise me in each case their:-
    - [a] identity and position held
    - [b] legal and/or professional qualifications, if any
    - [c] dates of appointment and entry into, and departure from, office
    - [e] remuneration
    - [f] who appointed them, and by what process
    - [g] any previous public positions held
2. in addition to the above, I request all and any other information which can lawfully be supplied to me regarding the following EAT members:-
    - [a] Mr Justice Lindsay [ex-President]
    - [b] Mr D Chadwick
    - [c] Mr P R A Jacques CBE

The Department responded to your request by email on 10 November 2010 informing you that the information the Department did hold the names of the Judiciary at the Employment Appeal Tribunal (EAT) from 1999 to date and included the names and dates of the Judges.

The response then explained that the role and appointment of Judges was already in the public domain and could be found on the Judiciary or England and Wales website. Therefore, this information was exempt under Section 21 (information accessible to the applicant by other means) of the FOIA.

In addition the response advised that the details of judicial fees and salaries were published on the Ministry of Justice website and the link to the relevant pages of the website were provided to assist you with your enquiries.

In relation to your request about the legal, professional qualification and any previous public positions held by the Judges, Mr D Chadwick and Mr PRA Jacques CBE, the response advised that this information was considered to be the personal information of those individuals and therefore exempt under Section 40(2)(b) of the FOIA.

You requested a review of the Department's decision by email dated 21 November 2010. In your email, you said that the information you were seeking was not solely in relation to the Judges at the EAT but also the Lay Members. In addition you asked for information as to the identity of those members with a Trade Union background.

Having conducted an Internal Review of the Department's decision, I have found that the

- The Department should have sought clarification as to whether you were seeking information about Judges or Lay Members and considered your request accordingly;
- The fees payable to EAT Lay Members are published on the Ministry of Justice website, therefore this information is exempt under Section 21 (reasonably accessible) of the FOIA; and
- The legal and/or professional qualifications and details of any previous public positions held by the Lay Members, and the dates of their appointments is the personal information of those individuals and therefore exempt under section 40(2)(b) (personal information) of the FOIA;

The basis of my decision is set out below.

Reasons

Your original request was misinterpreted as seeking the information in relation to members of the Judiciary at the EAT and the Department should have asked you to clarify the scope of your request. I apologise for this oversight.

The names of the Lay Members at the EAT are held by the Department and are provided on the attached documents. The first attachment contains the names of the current Lay Members as of December 2010; the other attachment contains the names of the Lay Members of the EAT in November 2004. Despite extensive searches of electronic and manual records the Department has been unable to locate the details or a list of the Lay Members from 1999.

The details of all judicial fees and salaries (including Lay Members) are published on the Ministry of Justice website, and include the fees payable to Lay Members of the EAT. Lay Members receive a daily fee for sitting at the EAT and the fee in detailed at the bottom of page 2 of the list available at the following internet address:

The personal information of the Lay Members such as their qualifications and backgrounds is their private information and is exempt from disclosure under section 40(2)(b) (personal information) of the FOIA. The personal information of an individual cannot be disclosed to a third party because this would contravene the principles of the Data Protection Act 1998 in relation to the fair processing of the personal data. The information provided by Lay Members as part of the recruitment process is provided in confidence and it is entirely reasonable that they would expect this information to remain confidential.

Lay Members (and other Judicial office holders) are appointed through a fair and open selection to the standards for such exercises set by the Judicial Appointments Commission (JAC). There is a selection and interview process before the selection panels make recommendations for appointments to the Lord Chancellor.

However there have not been any recruitment campaigns for Lay Members at the EAT since 2003 prior to the establishment of the JAC in 2006. The campaign would have been the responsibility of the former Department for Trade & Industry (DTI); this is because the EAT was part of the Employment Tribunals Service a former executive agency of the DTI. Although DTI would have been responsible for the recruitment campaign the actual appointment would have been made by the then Lord Chancellor.

Further information on the role of the Judicial Appointments Commission and details of the selection policy can be found on the website at the following internet address:

Conclusion

In summary, therefore, I am satisfied that the original decision by the Department was incorrect on the basis that:

- the Department should have sought to clarify the scope of your request to include Lay Members; and
- the names and dates of appointment of the Lay Members at the EAT should have been provided.

However I am also satisfied that the original decision by the Department was correct on the basis that:

- information sought in relation to the fees payable to Members (both judicial and lay) is already available through the Ministry of Justice website and therefore is accessible otherwise than under the FOIA and so is exempt information under section 21(1); and
- information sought in relation to qualification, background and personal details of the Members (both judicial and lay) is personal information and disclosure of this type of information would breach the fair processing principle of the DPA and so is exempt information under section 40(2)(b).

I hope that the Department's decision is now clear. However, if you are dissatisfied with the findings of this Internal Review, you can complain to the Information Commissioner, at the following address:

APPENDIX SEVEN

Information from
Ministry of Justice

 **Ministry of JUSTICE**

Mr G Wheen

Our Ref: 67752

Data Access and Compliance Unit
Postal Point 6.25
Floor 6
102 Petty France
London
SW1H 9AJ

T 020 3334 5493
F 020 3334 2245
E Data.Access@justice.gsi.gov.uk

www.justice.gov.uk

24 November 2010

Dear Mr Wheen,

RE: Request for an Internal Review

Thank you for your email dated 25 October 2010 in which you expressed dissatisfaction with the Department's response to your Freedom of Information Act (FOIA) request and asked for an Internal Review of that decision. Your request has been passed to me for investigation as I carry out Internal Reviews for the Ministry of Justice (MoJ) related matters.

The purpose of an Internal Review is to assess how your Freedom of Information request was handled in the first place.

In your email of 19 September, you requested information regarding

1 - a list of UK Attorney Generals from 1995 to now
2 - the exact dates Jack Straw and Ken Clarke became the UK Ministers of Justice and accountable for the actions of the Attorney Generals
3 - the respective amounts of public money expended from the date[s] of original insertion[s] until now on publishing on the internet "Attorney General v Wheen EAT on 18th April [2000] Employment Appeal Tribunal" and the Court of Appeal decision re the same case
4 - the exact dates such internet advertising began
5 - on the authority of which UK Government Minister[s] and/or individual did this advertising begin?
6 - the law which permits anyone to publish this information 10 years after the event
7 - if you deny responsibility, who is responsible and what evidence do you have?
8 - against how many other individuals has the EAT issued similar orders to that referred to in 3 above?
9 - if those cases are on the internet, where and under what headings?
10 - the amount of money expended by the UK Government on intercepting, recording and hacking into communications to and from myself and the legal authority for doing so.

On 13 October MoJ responded to you confirming that the department does hold some of the information that you had requested and released that information to you.

You have queried MoJ's response to your request by stating:

'Re your answers dated 13 October to my two recent FOI requests, as the entries about me are not restricted to the EAT website I request an internal review because the answers to items 3 and 4 are incomplete and if like items 3 and 4 you do not have the answer to item 10 I should have been told, and am entitled to know, who does'.

I have reviewed the way in which your case was handled and have looked at the basis of the original decision.

I am sorry that the response you received did not cover all aspects of your request.

In your particular case, the Admin Court Judgment was never transcribed and the judgment was not paced on Bailii, (who the Court of Appeal uses as their service provider for the purpose of publishing judgments online). The reason for this is that your application failed at the permission stage. The Admin Court only transcribes and places judgments of substantive hearings on Bailii. If a case fails at permission stage then it would not progress to the Court of Appeal. I have run a search of 2000-2001 cases and I can confirm that there is no judgment posted on Bailii.

have provided the web link to Bailii for your convenience.

I can confirm that we do not hold information regarding the intercepting, recording and hacking into communications but you can find more information about the general issue of interception on the Interception of Communications Commissioner website. I have provided the web link to that site for your convenience.

If you are dissatisfied with the findings of this internal review, you can complain to the Information Commissioner, at the following address:

Information Commissioner's Office
Wycliffe House
Water Lane
Wilmslow
Cheshire
SK9 5AF

Yours sincerely

Roger Davies
Data Access & Compliance Unit

Roger Davies

From: Geoffrey Wheen [mailto:gwheen2@yahoo.co.nz]
Sent: 24 November 2010 13:18
To: Davies, Roger
Cc: casework@ico.gsi.gov.uk
Subject: Re: Internal Review.

Roger Davies
Min of Justice
UK

I have no idea what you are talking about, because I have no record of any "Admin Court" being involved at any stage. About this issue, I attended the Appeal Court in The Strand twice. On the first occasion I was given consent to proceed with my appeal against the EAT decision to a full appeal hearing. The latter took place in December 2000 before 3 Lord Justices of Appeal, namely Nourse, Mummery and Keene. Your telling me at this point in time that my "application failed at the permission stage" thanks to a decision made by the "Admin Court" in a "Judgment" it supposedly issued without my knowledge are all utterly beyond my comprehension in the light of all the documentary evidence, including postings on the internet, and what actually took place then and since. Consequently I request immediate clarification on all 3 counts, because on the face of it your current version confounds reality. Thank you.

Geoffrey Wheen

From: "Davies, Roger" <Roger.Davies@justice.gsi.gov.uk>
To: gwheen2@yahoo.co.nz
Sent: Wed, 24 November, 2010 5:34:31 PM
Subject: Internal Review.

http://nz.mg4.mail.yahoo.com/dc/launch?.gx=1&.rand=3l6kcg3btmppg   12/3/2010

From: Geoffrey Wheen (gwheen2@yahoo.co.nz)
To: pscorrespondence@cabinet-office.x.gsi.gov.uk;
Date: Fri, 3 December, 2010 11:43:38 AM
Cc: gwheen2@yahoo.co.nz;
Subject: Re: complaint re civil servant

Sir Gus O'Donnell
Head of UK Civil Service
Cabinet Office
UK

Dear Sir

Having had my previous e-mail dated 25 November to the Cabinet Office ignored, I am now writing to you again.
The answer given to me in the e-mail below concerns a FOI review I requested, about which I have already complained to the Information Commissioner, who judging by past experience after an interminable delay at best will do next to nothing about it. However, whatever he does is beside the point, and probably outside his terms of reference anyway.

The issue is no longer about the FOI. It is whether Roger Davies, or any other Govt employee, has any right to issue purported facts about me which in my eyes are nonsensical balderdash and then dismiss my queries about them by referring me to somebody else, while he hides behind the FOI Act, itself denuded by bureaucrats notably inside the Ministry of Justice. What he's done isn't a matter for the ICO, it's one for you, as Davies' boss. Either the statements he has made are true or they aren't. I gave him the chance to explain himself. In response he tells me to get lost. That's a disciplinary matter, because on the face of it either he knows what he's talking about and I don't [and want to know what's been going on behind my back] or he's up a gumtree.

So either I get a rational explanation and/or apology [if justified] from you or I don't. The ball is now in your court, because I've no intention of dropping the matter, waiting for or accepting some half-baked excuses from the ICO as and when the cows come home.
Thank you.

Geoffrey Wheen.

From: "Davies, Roger" <Roger.Davies@justice.gsi.gov.uk>
To: Geoffrey Wheen <gwheen2@yahoo.co.nz>
Sent: Wed, 24 November, 2010 9:39:01 PM
Subject: RE: Internal Review.

APPENDIX EIGHT

Decision Notice dated 11 January 2011 from ICO

From: OperationsSupport (opssupport@ico.gsi.gov.uk)
To: gwheen2@yahoo.co.nz;
Date: Wed, 12 January, 2011 8:57:57 PM
Cc: casework@ico.gsi.gov.uk; Richard.Sisson@ico.gsi.gov.uk;
Subject: [Ref. FS50350791]

Dear Mr Wheen

Please find attached an electronic version of the Decision Notice FS50350791
dated 11 January 2011. I have copied below the covering letter:

Mr Geoffrey Wheen
gwheen2@yahoo.co.nz

11 January 2011

Dear Mr Wheen

Freedom of Information Act 2000: Section 50(1)
Attorney General's Office

Please find enclosed a Decision Notice issued under section 50(1) of the Freedom
of Information Act 2000. This Decision Notice relates to your complaint about a
request for information that you submitted to the Attorney General's Office on 19
September 2010.

Your complaint has been carefully considered and in this case the Commissioner
has found substantively in favour of the Attorney General's Office, although it has
been found in breach of a procedural matter.

The enclosed Decision Notice sets out the reasons for this decision.

If you disagree with any aspect of the attached Decision Notice, you have the right
to appeal to the First-Tier Tribunal (Information Rights). Contact details for the
First-Tier Tribunal (Information Rights) are included in the Decision Notice.

The Decision Notice includes details about you and the public authority. This is to
ensure that there is no doubt as to the request for information to which the Notice
relates. The Commissioner will publish the decision on the ICO website, but will
remove all names and addresses of complainants.

Although public authorities may choose to reproduce this Decision Notice, the
Commissioner would expect that they would take similar steps. The Commissioner
considers that these may be necessary in order to comply with the requirements
of the Data Protection Act.

You should write to us if the public authority fails to comply with any steps specified by the Commissioner in the Decision Notice.

It is important to note that the Commissioner's power to commence legal
proceedings in this situation is discretionary and although we
will investigate the matter, formal action will not be appropriate in all cases.

I hope the above information is of assistance.

Yours sincerely

Richard Sisson
Case Officer
Complaints Resolution Group 1

Yours sincerely

Beryl O'Donnell

Beryl O'Donnell   Operations Support Officer

Information Commissioner's Office, Wycliffe House, Water Lane , Wilmslow, Cheshire SK9 5AF.
T. 01625 545691 F. 01625 524510 www.ico.gov.uk

ico.

Freedom of Information Act 2000 (Section 50)

Decision Notice

Date: 11 January 2011

Public Authority:	Attorney General's Office
Address:	20 Victoria Street
	London
	SW1H ONF
Complainant:	Mr Geoffrey Wheen
Address:	gwheen2@yahoo.co.nz

Summary

The complainant made a request for information to the public authority consisting of 10 separate elements. The complainant's complaint to the Commissioner has focused only on part 10 of the request. The Commissioner finds that the public authority breached section 17(1) of the Act by failing to handle part 10 as a request under FOI and not citing a relevant exemption in a timely manner. The Commissioner finds that section 40(5) of the Act should have been applied to part 10. The information requested, if held, would be the personal data of the complainant and as such the public authority is under no obligation to confirm or deny under the FOI Act whether it holds the relevant information.

The Commissioner's Role

1. The Commissioner's duty is to decide whether a request for information made to a public authority has been dealt with in accordance with the requirements of Part 1 of the Freedom of Information Act 2000 (the "Act"). This Notice sets out his decision.

ico.

The Request

2. The complainant made the following request on 19 September 2010:

'By virtue of the Freedom of Information Act I now request all documents, records and information in your possession regarding the undermentioned matters:-

1 - a list of UK Attorney Generals from 1995 to now

2 - the exact dates Jack Straw and Ken Clarke became the UK Ministers of Justice and accountable for the actions of the Attorney Generals

3 - the respective amounts of public money expended from the date[s] of original insertion[s] until now on publishing on the internet "Attorney General v Wheen EAT on 18th April [2000] Employment Appeal Tribunal" and the Court of Appeal decision re the same case

4 - the exact dates such internet advertising began

5 - on the authority of which UK Government Minister[s] and/or individual did this advertising begin?

6 - the law which permits anyone to publish this information 10 years after the event

7 - if you deny responsibility, who is responsible and what evidence do you have?

8 - against how many other individuals has the EAT issued similar orders to that referred to in 3 above?

9 - if those cases are on the internet, where and under what headings?

10 - the amount of money expended by the UK Government on intercepting, recording and hacking into communications to and from myself and the legal authority for doing so.'

3. The public authority responded to the complainant's request on 20 September 2010. The public authority provided a response to all 10 parts of the complainant's request. In order to meet its obligation to provide advice and assistance under section 16 of the Act, the public authority also confirmed that

ico.

information regarding employment tribunals would be held by the Ministry of Justice.

4. The complainant responded to the public authority on 20 September 2010, by questioning the responses of the public authority and by requesting further advice and assistance. The complainant asked to be advised who would hold the requested information if the public authority did not. The complainant stated that he believed part 10 not to be an accusation of criminal activity (asserting this action to be going on) but a request for the figure of expenditure, he believes to exist.

5. The public authority provided further advice and assistance to the complainant on 21 September 2010. In this it reiterated that information regarding employment tribunals would be held by the Ministry of Justice. It maintained its stance that part 10 was an accusation of criminal activity. Finally, the public authority provided a further copy of the list of Attorney Generals, following the complainant being unable to locate the previous list provided to him.

6. On 22 September 2010, the complainant requested an internal review, focussing solely on part 10. He maintained his position that the information could be considered a request under the Act, as it related to a specific figure (this assumed that the accused activity had occurred).

7. The result of the internal review was provided to the complainant on 22 September 2010. The public authority restated its position that part 10 was an accusation of criminal activity and was therefore unable to treat it as an FOI request.

The Investigation

Scope of the case

8. On 23 September 2010 the complainant contacted the Commissioner to complain about the way his request for information had been handled. The complainant specifically asked the Commissioner to consider the public authority's handling of part 10 of his request.

ico.

9. The complainant also raised other issues that are not addressed in this Notice because they are not requirements of Part 1 of the Act.

10. The Commissioner (for the reasons set out below) has determined that part 10 of the request is a valid request for information. On that basis, the Decision Notice and its analysis is directed solely towards that part.

Chronology

11. On 04 November 2010 the Commissioner wrote to the complainant to provide a preliminary view on the case. He explained to the complainant that the public authority should have applied the exemption under section 40(1) of the Act, as the requested information, if held, would likely be considered the complainant's personal data as defined by section 1(1)(d) of the Data Protection Act 1998 (the DPA). However in circumstances where the information sought by the complainant is likely to be that person's personal data, the Commissioner would treat this as being a valid subject access request under section 7 of the DPA.

12. The public authority wrote to the complainant on 26 November 2010 to explain that it had conducted a review of its initial decision. It explained that it had been incorrect in stating that part 10 of the request fell outside of the Act and had now considered it.

13. The public authority informed the complainant that it neither confirmed nor denied that it held information relevant to part 10 of the request. In making this response, the public authority explained that it was relying on section 44(1)(a) and 44(2) of the Act (Prohibitions on disclosure). It further explained that, in order to intercept personal communications (as the public authority was alleged to have done by the complainant) a warrant would be necessary under the Regulation of Investigatory Powers Act 2000. Section 19 of this Act prohibits the disclosure of the existence of such a warrant. The public authority therefore asserted that this provided a statutory bar to the confirmation or denial of the existence of the information and of its release, if held.

14. The complainant made a further complaint to the Commissioner on 30 November 2010 about the public authority's refusal to confirm or deny holding the information he seeks. The Commissioner responded, explaining that the

requested information, if held, would still be the personal data of the complainant under section 40(1). The Commissioner explained that section 40(1) of the Act is an absolute exemption and therefore encouraged the complainant to make a subject access request under the Data Protection Act.

15. The complainant raised further arguments regarding the case on 30 November 2010. On the basis that the complainant was not content with the explanation provided to him in relation to part 10 of his request, the Commissioner decided to make a formal decision on this part and issue a Decision Notice.

Analysis

Substantive Procedural Matters

16. Section 17(1) states that:

'A public authority which, in relation to any request for information, is to any extent relying on a claim that any provision of Part II relating to the duty to confirm or deny is relevant to the request or on a claim that information is exempt information must, within the time for complying with section 1(1), give the applicant a notice which-

    (a)   states that fact,

    (b)   specifies the exemption in question, and

    (c)   states (if that would not otherwise be apparent) why the exemption applies.

17. Section 10(1) of the Act states that a request for information made under section 1 of the Act must be complied with not later than the twentieth working day following the date of its receipt.

18. The Commissioner is satisfied that the wording of part 10 of the complainant's request constitutes a request for information. He gains support for this view in the decision of the Information Tribunal in Barber v IC (EA/2005/0004) which confirmed that a request which makes an accusation or is based on an assumption which the authority disputes is still a valid request.

19. Therefore in failing to issue a valid refusal notice within 20 working days of the request in respect of part 10 of the

complainant's request the public authority failed to comply with section 17(1) of the Act.

Exemptions

20. The Commissioner considers that the public authority should have cited section 40(5)(a) in its response to part 10 of the complainant's request, on the basis that the information he seeks would constitute his own personal data.

21. Section 40(1) states that:

'Any information to which a request relates is exempt information if it constitutes personal data of which the applicant is the data subject.'

Subsection (5)(a) states that:

'The duty to confirm or deny:

    (a)   does not arise in relation to information which is (or if it were held by the public authority would be) exempt information by virtue of subsection (1)'.

22. For this exemption to apply, the data referred to must, if held, constitute personal data under the DPA. The DPA defines personal data as:

'...data which relate to a living individual who can be identified
    (a) from those data, or
    (b) from those data and other information which is in the possession of, or is likely to come into the possession of, the data controller,

and includes any expression of opinion about the individual and any indication of the intention of the data controller or any other person in respect to the individual'.

23. The Commissioner has considered the terms of the complainant's request for information against the context provided by this request and is satisfied that the information the complainant seeks, would, if held, amount to his 'personal data'. The information sought in respect of part 10 of the request would relate to the complainant: It is information referenced to himself, relating to his interaction with third parties in a context which is personal to the complainant.

ico.

24. Furthermore the Commissioner has decided that the public authority is not obligated under the Act to confirm or deny whether or not any information is held by it (following section 40(5)) or to supply any information if so held (section 40(1)). The Commissioner has determined that part 10 of the complainant's request should be considered under the provisions of the DPA. He will now go on to do this separately.

25. Because of the above, the Commissioner feels it is unnecessary to consider the later application, by the public authority, of section 44(1)(a) and (2) of the Act.

The Decision

26. The Commissioner's decision is that the public authority did not deal with the request for information in accordance with the Act: the public authority did not initially recognise part 10 of the request as a valid request for information and did not issue a refusal notice citing an exemption for this part of the request within 20 working days.

Steps Required

27. The Commissioner requires no steps to be taken.

Other matters

28. Although they do not form part of this Decision Notice the Commissioner wishes to highlight the following:

29. The Commissioner wishes to emphasise that the disclosure of information under the FOI Act constitutes the disclosure of information into the public domain, without restriction. Furthermore, apart from whether determining whether a request is vexatious or repeated, a public authority cannot take into account the identity of a requestor when dealing with a request made under the Act.

30. Therefore the Commissioner expects public authorities, when responding to requests for information which would, if held, constitute the personal data of the requestor, to handle the

7

ico.

request in the first instance as a Subject Access Request under section 7 of the Data Protection Act 1998.

ico.

Right of Appeal

31. Either party has the right to appeal against this Decision Notice to the First-tier Tribunal (Information Rights). Information about the appeals process may be obtained from:

> First-tier Tribunal (Information Rights)
> GRC & GRP Tribunals,
> PO Box 9300,
> Arnhem House,
> 31, Waterloo Way,
> LEICESTER,
> LE1 8DJ

> Tel: 0845 600 0877
> Fax: 0116 249 4253
> Email: informationtribunal@tribunals.gsi.gov.uk.
> Website: www.informationtribunal.gov.uk

32. If you wish to appeal against a decision notice, you can obtain information on how to appeal along with the relevant forms from the Information Tribunal website.

33. Any Notice of Appeal should be served on the Tribunal within 28 (calendar) days of the date on which this Decision Notice is sent.

Dated the 11th day of January 2011

Signed ....

Alexander Ganotis
Group Manager – Complaints Resolution

Information Commissioner's Office
Wycliffe House
Water Lane
Wilmslow
Cheshire
SK9 5AF

ico.

Legal Annex

Freedom of Information Act 2000

General Right of Access

Section 1(1) provides that -

"Any person making a request for information to a public authority is entitled –

(a)   to be informed in writing by the public authority whether it holds information of the description specified in the request, and

(b)   if that is the case, to have that information communicated to him."

Time for Compliance

Section 10(1) provides that –

"Subject to subsections (2) and (3), a public authority must comply with section 1(1) promptly and in any event not later than the twentieth working day following the date of receipt."

Duty to provide Advice and Assistance

Section 16(1) provides that -

"It shall be the duty of a public authority to provide advice and assistance, so far as it would be reasonable to expect the authority to do so, to persons who propose to make, or have made, requests for information to it".

Refusal of Request

Section 17(1) provides that -

"A public authority which, in relation to any request for information, is to any extent relying on a claim that any provision of Part II relating to the duty to confirm or deny is relevant to the request or on a claim that information is exempt information must, within the time for complying with section 1(1), give the applicant a notice which -

10

ico.

(a)   states that fact,

(b)   specifies the exemption in question, and

(c)   states (if that would not otherwise be apparent) why the exemption applies."

Personal information

Section 40(1) provides that –

"Any information to which a request for information relates is exempt information if it constitutes personal data of which the applicant is the data subject."

Section 40(5) provides that –

"The duty to confirm or deny-

(a)   does not arise in relation to information which is (or if it were held by the public authority would be) exempt information by virtue of subsection (1), and

(b)   does not arise in relation to other information if or to the extent that either-

(i)   he giving to a member of the public of the confirmation or denial that would have to be given to comply with section 1(1)(a) would (apart from this Act) contravene any of the data protection principles or section 10 of the Data Protection Act 1998 or would do so if the exemptions in section 33A(1) of that Act were disregarded, or

(ii)   by virtue of any provision of Part IV of the Data Protection Act 1998 the information is exempt from section 7(1)(a) of that Act (data subject's right to be informed whether personal data being processed)."

Prohibitions on disclosure

Section 44(1) provides that –

"Information is exempt information if its disclosure (otherwise than under this Act) by the public authority holding it-

(a)   is prohibited by or under any enactment,

11

ico.

(b)   is incompatible with any Community obligation, or

(c)   would constitute or be punishable as a contempt of court."

Section 44(2) provides that –

"The duty to confirm or deny does not arise if the confirmation or denial that would have to be given to comply with section 1(1)(a) would (apart from this Act) fall within any of paragraphs (a) to (c) of subsection (1)."

Data Protection Act 1998

Basic interpretative provisions

Section 1(1) provides that -

In this Act, unless the context otherwise requires—

"data" means information which—

(a) is being processed by means of equipment operating automatically in response to instructions given for that purpose,
(b) is recorded with the intention that it should be processed by means of such equipment,
(c) is recorded as part of a relevant filing system or with the intention that it should form part of a relevant filing system,
(d) does not fall within paragraph (a), (b) or (c) but forms part of an accessible record as defined by section 68; or
(e) is recorded information held by a public authority and does not fall within any of paragraphs (a) to (d);

"data controller" means, subject to subsection (4), a person who (either alone or jointly or in common with other persons) determines the purposes for which and the manner in which any personal data are, or are to be, processed;

12

"data processor", in relation to personal data, means any person (other than an employee of the data controller) who processes the data on behalf of the data controller;

"data subject" means an individual who is the subject of personal data;

"personal data" means data which relate to a living individual who can be identified—

(a) from those data, or
(b) from those data and other information which is in the possession of, or is likely to come into the possession of, the data controller,

and includes any expression of opinion about the individual and any indication of the intentions of the data controller or any other person in respect of the individual;

Right of access to personal data

Section 7 provides that –

(1) Subject to the following provisions of this section and to sections 8, 9 and 9A, an individual is entitled—

(a) to be informed by any data controller whether personal data of which that individual is the data subject are being processed by or on behalf of that data controller,

(b) if that is the case, to be given by the data controller a description of—

(i) the personal data of which that individual is the data subject,

(ii) the purposes for which they are being or are to be processed, and

(iii) the recipients or classes of recipients to whom they are or may be disclosed,

13

ico.

(c) to have communicated to him in an intelligible form—

> (i) the information constituting any personal data of which that individual is the data subject, and

> (ii) any information available to the data controller as to the source of those data, and

Regulation of Investigatory Powers Act 2000
Offence for unauthorised disclosures

Section 19 provides that -

(1) Where an interception warrant has been issued or renewed, it shall be the duty of every person falling within subsection (2) to keep secret all the matters mentioned in subsection (3).

(2) The persons falling within this subsection are—

> (a) the persons specified in section 6(2);

> (b) every person holding office under the Crown;

> (c) every member of the staff of the Serious Organised Crime Agency;

> (ca) every member of the Scottish Crime and Drug Enforcement Agency;

> (e) every person employed by or for the purposes of a police force;

> (f) persons providing postal services or employed for the purposes of any business of providing such a service;

> (g) persons providing public telecommunications services or employed for the purposes of any business of providing such a service;

14

Geoffrey Wheen | 257

ico.

(h) persons having control of the whole or any part of a telecommunication system located wholly or partly in the United Kingdom.

(3) Those matters are—

(a) the existence and contents of the warrant and of any section 8(4) certificate in relation to the warrant;

(b) the details of the issue of the warrant and of any renewal or modification of the warrant or of any such certificate;

(c) the existence and contents of any requirement to provide assistance with giving effect to the warrant;

(d) the steps taken in pursuance of the warrant or of any such requirement; and

(e) everything in the intercepted material, together with any related communications data.

(4) A person who makes a disclosure to another of anything that he is required to keep secret under this section shall be guilty of an offence and liable—

(a) on conviction on indictment, to imprisonment for a term not exceeding five years or to a fine, or to both;

(b) on summary conviction, to imprisonment for a term not exceeding six months or to a fine not exceeding the statutory maximum, or to both.

(5) In proceedings against any person for an offence under this section in respect of any disclosure, it shall be a defence for that person to show that he could not reasonably have been expected, after first becoming aware of the matter disclosed, to take steps to prevent the disclosure.

(6) In proceedings against any person for an offence under this section in respect of any disclosure, it shall be a defence for that person to show that—

(a) the disclosure was made by or to a professional legal adviser in connection with the giving, by the

15

ico.

adviser to any client of his, of advice about the effect of provisions of this Chapter; and

(b) the person to whom or, as the case may be, by whom it was made was the client or a representative of the client.

(7) In proceedings against any person for an offence under this section in respect of any disclosure, it shall be a defence for that person to show that the disclosure was made by a legal adviser—

(a) in contemplation of, or in connection with, any legal proceedings; and

(b) for the purposes of those proceedings.

(8) Neither subsection (6) nor subsection (7) applies in the case of a disclosure made with a view to furthering any criminal purpose.

(9) In proceedings against any person for an offence under this section in respect of any disclosure, it shall be a defence for that person to show that the disclosure was confined to a disclosure made to the Interception of Communications Commissioner or authorised—

(a) by that Commissioner;

(b) by the warrant or the person to whom the warrant is or was addressed;

(c) by the terms of the requirement to provide assistance; or

(d) by section 11(9).

APPENDIX NINE

Correspondence regarding Decision Notice etc.

From: James Ross (James.Ross@attorneygeneral.gsi.gov.uk)
To: gwheen2@yahoo.co.nz;
Date: Mon, 10 January, 2011 10:33:21 PM
Cc:
Subject: Data Protection Act request

Dear Mr Wheen
10 - the amount of money expended by the UK Government on intercepting, recording and hacking into communications to and from myself and the legal authority for doing so."
The Information Commissioner's Office has suggested that we should treat this request as a request for access to your personal data under section 7 of the Data Protection Act. We have now reconsidered your request on that basis.
In order to make a request under section 7, you would normally be required to provide proof of identity and pay a fee of £10.00. However, we will not require this from you on this occasion, as we consider that the matters your request relates to are exempt from section 7 by virtue of section 29(1)(a) of the Data Protection Act (data processed for the prevention or detection of crime). Therefore, we will not be providing the information you have requested, and indeed we can neither confirm nor deny that this office holds such information.
A communication may only be intercepted if this is done pursuant to a warrant issued under the Regulation of Investigatory Powers Act 2000. Section 19 of that Act prohibits the disclosure of the existence of such a warrant; the content of the warrant, the details of the issue of the warrant, the existence and contents of any requirement to provide assistance with giving effect to the warrant, the steps taken in pursuance of the warrant, and everything in the intercepted material together with any related communications data. This provision is a statutory recognition of the prejudice to the prevention and detection of crime that would be caused by the disclosure of such details.
If this office held information related to intercepted communications, it would be contrary to section 19 to disclose it, and it would prejudice the prevention and detection of crime. Equally, if this office were to confirm those cases where it did not hold such information, this would lead to the inference in other cases that the absence of such a confirmation indicated that this office did hold information related to intercepted communications. That would also be contrary to section 19, and would prejudice the prevention and detection of crime. Therefore, I can neither confirm nor deny that this office contains such information. This is in accordance with the principles recognised by the Information Tribunal in Baker v Information Commissioner (EA/2005/0002).
Yours sincerely
James Ross
Freedom of Information Officer

****

The Attorney General's Office is located at 20 Victoria Street, London SW1H 0NF

Please visit our new website www.attorneygeneral.gov.uk.

All communications sent to or from the Attorney General's Office may be subject to recording and/or monitoring in accordance with relevant legislation.

The information included in this email is of a confidential nature and is intended only for the addressee. If you are not the intended addressee, any disclosure, copying or

From: casework@ico.gsi.gov.uk (casework@ico.gsi.gov.uk)
To: gwheen2@yahoo.co.nz;
Date: Mon. 17 January, 2011 10:06:17 PM
Cc:
Subject: data protection case (Attorney General's Office)[Ref. RFA0364561]

17 January 2011

Case Reference Number RFA0364561

Dear Mr Wheen

When I last wrote to you, I explained that when we receive data protection complaints, our obligation is to make an assessment. An assessment is the Information Commissioner's view about whether an organisation has followed the rules of good practice for handling information in the Data Protection Act 1998 (the DPA).

I also explained that our aim is to ensure that organisations deal with personal information properly in the future. Our assessment decisions can help us to decide whether we should take action against a particular organisation.

Our decision

I wrote to the Attorney General's Office (AGO) about this matter and have now received its response. On the basis of all of the information provided by you and the AGO, we have decided that it is unlikely that the AGO has complied with the requirements of the DPA in this case.

This is because they did not recognise that point 10 of your freedom of information request was a request for your personal data. I understand that the AGO has now treated this point as a subject access request and written to you. As you are aware, the subject access right is not an absolute one and organisations can use exemptions in certain circumstances. Should an organisation use any exemptions, it is under no obligation to provide any information or explanation to the requester about anything it has withheld.

We are satisfied that the AGO now responded to your request appropriately under the DPA.

The Information Commissioner has decided that further regulatory action is not required at this time.

When deciding whether regulatory action is appropriate, we take into account the organisation's general record of compliance with the DPA (including any previous assessments we have made) and any other information that is in our possession (including information given during the course of those assessments).

Having considered all the information that we hold about the AGO, we are satisfied that it takes its obligations under the DPA seriously and that we need take no further regulatory action at this point.

Next steps

However, most organisations want to put things right when they have gone wrong and learn from complaints that are raised with them. We have therefore asked the AGO to consider the information we have provided during the course of this assessment and take steps to prevent the situation from happening again.

We will keep a record of your complaint and take this assessment into account if we receive further complaints about the AGO. The information we gather from complaints may form the basis for action in the future.

Thank you for bringing this matter to our attention.

Yours sincerely

Joy Corne
Lead Case Officer - Complaints Resolution Group 1
Direct dial number 01625 545844

---

http://nz.mg4.mail.yahoo.com/dc/launch?.gx=1&.rand=fmrpo0dhueifg   1/18/2011

From: Geoffrey Wheen (gwheen2@yahoo.co.nz)
To: casework@ico.gsi.gov.uk;
Date: Wed. 19 January, 2011 12:29:07 PM
Cc: gwheen2@yahoo.co.nz;
Subject: my complaints

ICO
UK

In the light of your Decision Notice FS50350791 dated 11 January 2011 - which, apart from other privacy issues I regard as defamatory as it is substantially inconsistent with what actually occurred and the erroneous and intimidatory statements and accusations made at the time by the employee of the Attorney-General - and your having had sufficient, if not plenty of, time to deal with my outstanding complaints I am now terminating our correspondence regarding these and any other matters, which will now be dealt with elsewhere, including in my impending legal action against the U.K. Government, of which you and he are employees. If you choose to pursue your stated intention to publish your Notice in its original or an amended form on your website or elsewhere - about which I was not consulted and object - you will do so against my wishes, and in the knowledge that I will pursue the issue on legal and other grounds.

Henceforth kindly refrain from contacting me again, as I am entitled to be left alone by virtue of my privacy and other rights, about which the U.K. Government seems to be singularly indifferent.
Thank you.

Geoffrey Wheen

CHAPTER FOUR

Private Hedge

Among my favourite definitions of privacy [1] – for an overview of which see [2] - I number the following:-

- The "right to be left alone" – U.S. Justice Louis Brandeis
- "The desire of people to choose freely under what circumstances and to what extent they will expose themselves, their attitude and their behavior to other people" – Alan Westin, author of "Privacy and Freedom"
- "The right of the individual to be protected against intrusion into his personal life or affairs, or those of his family, by direct physical means or by publication of information" – Calcutt Committee, U.K. [1].

In my case the latter has the most resonance, with its reference to intrusion by publication. Anybody perusing relevant information displayed on the internet might wonder whether the community of spooks waste our money doing other than opening files on and snooping into the lives of those of a different disposition on some contrived pretext or other just to justify their somewhat sordid choice of occupation. [For other specimens of State hacking, see 3 and 4]. Perhaps it's less the squalor, more the humbug and hypocrisy that goes with it. Decades ago they were supposedly uncovering Reds beneath beds, now it's terrorists with unpronounceable monikers who, like their predecessors were sleeping amongst us since childhood, suddenly emerging like some latter-day Rip Van Winkle. And does the contrived and phony message – and the expected gratitude - ever change? After all, they, so they and their political masters assert with false modesty, are merely doing their "duty", ensuring we can walk the streets, sleep safe and sound in our or whatever other bed is close at hand, protecting and preserving the British way of life. One from which millions, myself included, had had a bellyful and couldn't wait to flee. As if they will let you. To them the right to privacy – the right to be left alone, wherever you are, whatever you're doing and with whom – is non-existent, laws or no laws. Better still, why not invent a system allowing them to snoop and pry at will, legal or not? One based on the English model, so open to widespread abuse and corruption. One that can be used to intimidate and threaten anybody who stands in their way, who disagrees with their despotic tyranny, who opposes authoritarian thuggery. In a word, "them".

According to some inadvertently humorous blurb I spotted recently on the internet the ghost of Peter Wright – or Banquo, depending on how one visualizes MI5 – had finally been put to rest, never to return. No longer would we be dismayed, even appalled, by the antics of a bunch of looney, loose cannons burglarizing their way round London, petering the unsafe safes of nonentities like the Prime Minister, to wit one Harold Wilson, who later became the victim of a vicious whispering campaign whose orchestration had nothing whatever to do with law-abiding organizations like MI5 and the CIA. Still, it did the trick. Wilson quit, the smears and books persist to this day and the half-witted evil-doers gloat. Not much change there, nor in the end-justifies-the-means law-breaking.

As a rule, globally and domestically one's rights are supposedly protected by laws. Unfortunately, laws conveying "rights" – any rights, even to exist - are useless if they are ignored, abused and/or unenforced. In some countries the "right" to privacy is non-existent. In others breaches of privacy rights are strictly enforced. In yet more, least said the better.

Of course, occasionally [or should I suggest all-too-often?] things do go pear-shaped, but are soon forgotten – or, being a British balls-up, have a habit of being shoveled under the rug for later disposal. Some people – quick, open a file on them – might think or even say that killing an unarmed, innocent and defenceless Brazilian on the tube was a bit extreme. Until they heard the explanations, resulting in the *promotion* of the individual in overall charge of the operation, who just happened to be a woman. Murder, bungling incompetence and downright lies about what happened we can tolerate, even encourage – but accusations of sexist discrimination, never. As for the trigger-happy Special Branch – or should I say the Dirty Buggers? - weren't they also involved in the assassination of four unarmed Irish, who they branded terrorists but actually weren't, just like the Brazilian electrician singled out for target practice? Or was it Thatcher's heroes, the SAS? Perhaps both. Who cares when you're dead at their hands? "Death on the Rock" they called it. Yet for some reason I can't help thinking that "Death" doesn't do justice to the victims and their families. Compared to them I shouldn't complain, even if the buggers and shakers are watching my every move, reading this text as it crystallizes on the screen. Such is the lot of any person "of interest" to them. Judging by the bald statistics, who isn't, in The Holy Hole? Let's see. Extrapolate the number of secret files on individuals – a mere 272,000 in 2006[4] - until now, and what do you get? Owzabout a dump not worth living in, as I've known since I was a kid? May our Saviour in all His glorious manifestations protect and preserve Thai culture against societies whose best products resemble such as George double-Ya Bush and his pet Cheshire cat Blair [5].

Being signatories to the Universal Declaration of Human Rights and to the International Covenant on Civil and Political Rights the Governments of Thailand and the U.K. thereby agreed to abide by all the terms and conditions therein, although you'd hardly believe it, judging by the actions and reactions of one of them. Some of the most relevant Articles are quoted below.

Universal Declaration of Human Rights [6]

Article 1 – All human beings are born free and equal in dignity and rights. They are endowed with reason and conscience and should act towards one another in a spirit of brotherhood.

Article 10 – Everyone is entitled in full equality to a fair and public hearing by an independent and impartial tribunal, in the determination of his rights and obligations and of any criminal charge against him.

Article 12 – No one shall be subjected to arbitrary interference with his privacy, family, home or correspondence, nor to attacks upon his honour and reputation. Everyone has the right to the protection of the law against such interference or attacks.

Article 18 – Everyone has the right to freedom of thought…………

Article 19 – Everyone has the right to freedom of opinion and expression; this right includes freedom to hold opinions without interference and to seek, receive and impart information and ideas through any media and regardless of frontiers.

Article 26 – 1. Everyone has the right to education……………higher education shall be equally accessible to all on the basis of merit.

Article 29 - 2. In the exercise of his rights and freedoms, everyone shall be subject only to such limitations as are determined by law solely for the purpose of securing due recognition and respect for the rights and freedoms of others and of meeting the just requirements of morality, public order and the general welfare in a democratic society.

Article 30 – Nothing in this Declaration may be interpreted as implying for any State, group or person any right to engage in any activity or to perform any act aimed at the destruction of any of the rights and freedoms set forth herein.

The core provisions of the <u>International Covenant on Civil and Political Rights</u> are contained within Articles 6 to 27. Of those, Article 7 prohibits "degrading punishment" – which I reckon includes the maintenance of a 10 year smear on the internet, Article 14 recognises and protects a right to justice and a fair trial and Article 17 mandates the right to privacy [7]. As the latter varies slightly from its counterparts I quote it in full, below:-

Article 17

1. No one shall be subjected to arbitrary or unlawful interference with his privacy, family, home or correspondence, nor to unlawful attacks on his honour and reputation.
2. Everyone has the right to the protection of the law against such interference or attacks.

Regionally, Article 8 of the <u>European Convention on Human Rights</u> provides a right to respect for one's private and family life, his home and his correspondence, subject to certain restrictions "in accordance with the law" and "necessary in a democratic society". What these expressions mean is anybody's guess, but needless to say those empowered with enforcing the law have not been slow to breach it as they saw fit. Consequently on the one hand telephone tapping, for instance, is lawful and on the other it isn't. And in case of doubt snooping is legit provided it's "necessary" – what isn't, in the eyes of authoritarians who conduct torture under the premise that the end justifies the means? – and "proportionate" As usual, all's very clear and convincing – I don't think [8].

Under U.K domestic law two Statutes in particular embody one's rights to privacy.

Article 8 of the Human Rights Act 1998 corresponds in number and content with that of the European Convention on Human Rights. Although the definition of "correspondence" [which can include communications by letter, phone, fax and e-mail] is broad a "public authority" can still interfere with one's privacy rights provided the legal basis justifying interference is clear and its aim was either national security, public safety, protection of the economy, prevention of crime, the protection of health or morals or the protection of the rights and freedoms of others [9]. [This seems to resonate with Big Brother's Buggers' Charter, of which more later]. Not quite carte-blanche for State-snooping, but well on the way.

The Data Protection Act 1998 contains a number of key principles, and affords rights to the individual that data about them:-

[a] will not be used in any way that may potentially cause damage or distress

[b] should only be processed fairly and lawfully

Under Section 55 of the Act it is unlawful for outside parties such as hackers and impersonators to obtain unauthorized access to personal data [10].

Not last or least, a word about Big Brother's Buggers' Charter. No, not entry to the priesthood. Although certain individuals inside the Attorney General's office may not be aware of the fact, interception of communications [e.g. eavesdropping on phone calls, opening and reading letters and e-mails] is a regular and usually lawful feature of daily life. Hardly surprising – except to law-punchers and crunchers - considering the threats posed by actual, potential or even suspected terrorists and organized criminal gangs. Not only the Security Services but the police and HM Customs and Excise supposedly do no wrong [and plenty of right] with interception warrants endorsed by the Secretary of State [usually the Home Secretary], the Security Service or Chief Constables under the Regulation of Investigatory Powers Act 2000. Needless to say, despite the inevitable cock-ups on all sides [11] and stitch-ups [12] the show must go on, with another trio of B's - burglary, bugging and bribing – topping the taxpayers' bill [13], some of them contemptible, if press reports are to be believed. Among the dross, spying on and bugging of the families of the four Deepcut depot army victims, who were found shot dead in mysterious and highly suspicious circumstances. This secret intelligence operation, conducted jointly by MI5 and the Army's Special Investigation Branch, was launched, so we are told, to enable them to find out what the families "were up to" [watching "Coronation Street" on the box, perhaps?] and whether they were planning concerted action. So what's wrong with that, and what business is it of MI5? Haven't the spooks got more important things to do with our money, like monitoring every word I write and say? [14].

Finally, a word about morality, equality and justice – meaningless and worthless concepts within some political and judicial systems. Under the U.K.'s Rehabilitation of Offenders Act 1974 some criminal convictions must be ignored after a time, starting from the date of conviction. Thereafter the conviction is "spent", but unlike me [as the QC Jay would want it] the offenders, or forces, aren't. On the contrary, they are afforded legal and judicial protection, courtesy of the aforesaid Act. Once their time is spent provided they don't re-offend cons need not disclose their past transgression to potential employers, insurers and in civil court proceedings. All very laudable and humanitarian.

What's more, publication of a spent conviction can be defamatory [and result in payment of libel damages] if motivated by malice. So what are the rehabilitation periods after which convictions become spent? For adults, 5 years for most custodial sentences, 7 years for prison sentences up to 6 months, and 10 years for prison sentences between 6 months and 2.5 years. [15].

Remember, we are talking about convicted criminals, which I am not, as our Lords and Masters will know all too well, although judging by historical and recent events they seem to be bending over backwards – which is unusual for The Buggers – to produce/plant/concoct "evidence" to prove otherwise. Why bother? After all, my offence is far more serious than any committed by felons. It might be termed "exposure" – of what these hypocritical agents of "morality" are and do. To them that is intolerable. They can't stand, and will not countenance, hearing the truth about themselves. A bunch of conspirators who fit up innocent patsies courtesy of corrupt trials and rigged Appeal Court panels. Individuals who, morally, spiritually and ethically, are infinitely worse than those they judge from on high. So it is only fitting – or is it fitting-up? – that my civil offence should remain on the internet for public display, delectation and general piss-taking for over 10 years. In other words, compatible with my having been convicted of a crime for which I'd been sentenced to over two-and-a-half years in the slammer. What type of offence might that be, for a first-time offender? Robbery? – not serious enough. Armed robbery? – depends on the victim and the weapon. How about armed robbery of a bank with a shotgun? Yeah, but was it real and loaded? And was it all a mistake, brought on by your drug-taking girlfriend being pregnant for the eighth time in seven years, thanks to six different partners? No, it's got to be something really indefensible for a first offence 2.5 stretch not to be overturned in The Strand. Talking of which, let us not forget that the judicially motivated and activated smears about me not only take different guises [for instance, by infiltrating entries about my books - see Appendix 1, which was downloaded as recently as 22 January 2011] they show no signs of abating. What's more, even though the aforesaid piece of judicial junk ostensibly concerns an individual named Mr. Barker just in case anyone should be in any doubt what its real purpose was why not finger me in the headline – in BLOCK CAPITALS, for the benefit of all the myopic blockheads out there, and why not insert [in slightly smaller type-face] my full name, lest some Mongolian English student should lose sleep over who the evil transgressor really is. Why not indeed, when the watchword is "watch it, nobody"?

You might even construe my punishment as a death sentence, imposed by a system which never fails to amaze and appal in equal measure. Here's the latest example of hypocrisy par-excellence. All five justices of the U.K. Supreme Court decided that convicted paedophiles and rapists should have the right to appeal against their being on the sex offenders register for life, without any chance of a review. Under this barbaric system of "justice" anyone sentenced to 30 months or more imprisonment for a sexual offence is put on the register for life, supply the police with their personal details and any change of address [which by a strange coincidence occasionally find their way to unauthorized vigilantes like tabloid newspapers] and when the "pervs" travel abroad. No doubt trips to exotic places like Thailand [where I reside] make the nether regions of the spooks and other State snoopers quiver and judder with excitement. Not surprisingly the aforesaid ermined quins and the threesome before them decided that such treatment amounted to "indefinite" registration and therefore breached the offenders' human rights, including that to privacy [26].

In response, after a prolonged bout of Thatcher watching, finger-wagging and a good wigging, Dave-the-Rant-and-Rave and darling of The Rabid Right and Invariably Wrong could scarcely contain his pent-up fury at not getting his own way. Erupting like a non-spent but nonsensical Mount Vesuvius Dave discarded his life-long beliefs and love affair with Lora Norda and, displaying his freshly-brushed sabre gritted teeth and white knuckled launched into a spontaneous attack – which he'd practicing in front of the very full-length mirror used by his heroine, or in her case, pseudo-heroine, the Leaderene, prior to another notable performance before a packed house of pissed nonentities at P.M.'s question time. Stridently mimicking the maestro giving expert testimony after several rehearsals D.C. Cameron knew his lines by heart. "No, no no", then for good measure "more no". Pausing for effect and to remove his bike-clips he amplified his point. "We the people – who are all in it together – can't have those johnnies over there" – swiveling and pointing with a jabbing, stabbing forefinger in the general direction of the nearest edifice, which happened to be the local fish market – "telling us, the people, who are in the shit together, what to do. Noooooo, and more no, what we the people need above all else is a Bill of Rights. One more bill won't make much difference to what we the people haven't got, which is nothing". Looking skywards for inspiration he spotted none other than Mrs. T-bone punching the air like a demented striker who's just head-butted both goalposts and linesmen. Or is it assistant referees? Or linespersons? Taking this gesture as a sign of encouragement he then launched into yet another boring lecture about his vision of Britain , which he'd filched from a speech by Presidente O"bamarama. Whereupon his audience of two decided enough is plenty, and headed for the nearest tavern, where Mrs. T was holding forth and signing copies of her best-selling autobiography entitled "I am the greatest, and you're not".

And so the insanity continues ad nauseam. The message seems to be that judges can't interpret and enforce the law? For some reason I thought the Human Rights Act and European Convention were exactly that. Not to mention international Covenants and Conventions. We know where Dave and his pal George Osborne were at least some of the time. Nowhere, because they didn't exist. And later? How about helping Norman Lamont to devalue the pound – again – after a bruising, losing slugging match against George Soros, from which he's prospered and the country's gone further down the plughole? Bollocks such as Cameron yaps, as I witnessed and winced at recently while watching CNN may be O.K. for those who know next to nothing about English history and its institutions, but at the end of the day what would a Bill of Rights – or any other fancy, foul confection - accomplish, let alone change? Justice? In that place? Don't make me laugh. Last word on the subject. Wrong to stick details of sex-offenders in a "register" [no mention of the worldwide internet] for life. Fine to do the opposite in my case. So who are the criminals, and who isn't? Watch this space, as the snoopers are supposedly doing. Privacy? Say that again. Owzabout devising another law upholding our right to shit on people who have the temerity to dispute what we are and do. No trial or frilly briefs necessary. Case proved. Back to dirty business as usual.

The powers exercised by the Employment Appeal Tribunal and its President in particular are contained in Section 33 of the Employment Tribunals Act 1996, whereby a restriction of proceedings order was issued against me. Under subsection [5] of Section 33 "A copy of a restriction of proceedings order shall be published in the London Gazette and the Edinburgh Gazette". [By contrast, by virtue of Section 42 [5] of the Supreme Court Act 1981 a copy of any order made under that Act only needed to be published in the London Gazette]. Before either step was taken the decision-makers were duty bound to consider and implement any relevant provisions of the U.K.'s Human Rights Act 1998 [hereinafter called the HRA].

Mirroring the European Convention on Human Rights, Article 8 of the HRA says:-

1. Everyone has the right to respect for his private and family life, his home and his correspondence.
2. There shall be no interference by a public authority with the exercise of this right except such as is in accordance with the law and is necessary in a democratic society in the interests of national security, public safety or the economic well-being of the country, for the prevention of disorder or crime, for the protection of health or morals, or for the protection of the rights and freedoms of others [16].

So any interference with that right – which must be by a "public authority" - can only be justified if [a] the interference is lawful and [b] it is necessary in order to produce outcomes specified in Article 8 e.g. national security. Since "everyone" is accorded this right all I should need to prove is I exist – whereupon I automatically receive the aforesaid rights –and that I was the victim of some "interference" with my rights. The internet entries produced in evidence prove all three. At that point the onus swings onto the public authority responsible for interfering with my right to privacy to prove both [a] and [b] enumerated above, i.e. that its interference was in accordance with the law and was "necessary" for one or more of the specific reasons. Unless the public authority can prove both its interference is unlawful.

Needless to say, for the edification of all the ignoramuses out there, the legal fraternity have been hard at work dissecting some of the bumff, and sticking it on the internet [17]. "Family life" means your relationship with your "close" family, including an unmarried male and female living in a stable relationship. Your home means where you currently live. [But does that run to a cardboard box near Waterloo Station, a ramshackle jalopy, public toilets or even the top of a wall, which, I seem to recall, the delectable Marianne Faithfull once occupied, doubtless to the consternation of the local postman or woman?]. Unsurprisingly, your correspondence includes letters, phone calls and e-mails, attracting Article 8 challenges to police and secret service snooping and hacking. With that in mind Articles supposedly bestowing a right to an effective remedy and prohibiting abuse of rights [e.g. 13 and 17] begin to look a bit sick, like the U.K. itself. So too the following reassurance – headed "What does the Human Rights Act mean for our Courts and Judges"? - plucked from the internet. According to its anonymous source, who judging by its contents has recently escaped from 20 years solitary confinement,

"The Human Rights Act helps them to protect individuals' Convention rights. And they are able to check that the rights of the wider community are properly balanced, if individuals' rights have to be affected, the public authority will need to show that it is not using a sledgehammer to crack a nut. This is often referred to as 'proportionality': interfering with rights only so far as it is necessary in order to achieve a specific purpose set out in the Convention". All very convincing, except that in my case an internet smear lasting 10 to 11 years does seem a tad over the top – as over-proportioned as a Jayne Mansfield look-alike, you might say – and try as I may I just can't find any reference in the Convention to any "purpose" even vaguely resembling that enunciated by Jay Q.C., the sledgehammer whose stated objective was to crack that crazy nut, by creating a "spent force" zombie, incapable of thought, deed or criticism of him and his ilk, previously known as Geoffrey Wheen.

To avoid liability under Section 6[2] HRA the onus is on the public authority to prove it had no alternative i.e. was compelled, under <u>primary legislation</u> [i.e. Acts of Parliament] than to act as it did. So what did it do to me? Firstly, it started and finished legal proceedings against me. Not that it had to, as can be shown in umpteen other cases recorded on the internet about which the same public authority has done absolutely nothing. There never was any liability on it to act as it did against me. I was picked on for entirely extraneous and improper reasons. Had it not pursued its vindictive course of action none of the succeeding events would have occurred. Its next step was to publish what it had done. Here what it should have done, as determined by Parliamentary legislation [the primary legislation] was clear enough. Under the enabling Act the public authority had to publish a copy of its <u>order</u> in the London Gazette and

Edinburgh Gazette. Once. But while the legislators decided otherwise the readership of these select publications was obviously not wide enough to satisfy the appetite of the rapacious Employment Appeal Tribunal. To hell with publishing our order just once in two publications read only by the legal fraternity. This guy Wheen, who just happens to be our first pick for "the treatment" because he's had the temerity to challenge and criticize what we do and say has got to be taught a lesson he won't forget, permanently put in his place, or as our worthy advocate at the Court of Appeal put it , Wheen's destiny was to become a "spent force" – an Orwellian zombie with no rights to think, speak or act, naturally. So what did the public authority do? The opposite of what Parliament intended. Stick not just the order but the details on the internet, available for consumption, delectation and schadenfreude of the masses – billions of them. And while we're at it, do the same with the Court of Appeal decision. And keep up the treatment not for a day, two days, a week, a month, a quarter, or even a year. How about a decade or more, or forever – at somebody else's expense, naturally. So in terms of compulsion, the public authority's responsibilities ended immediately after it published a copy of its order once in two specific newspapers in or around the year 2000. The rest was not only unnecessary and uncalled for it emanated from pure malice and utter disregard for me, my family and whatever legal protection we were entitled to.

The individual who apparently took or authorized these actions knew perfectly well what he was doing, why, whose political aims he was pandering to and the ensuing, inevitable effects of his actions. He, after all, was the President of the Employment Appeal Tribunal, who, like others of gross rank, pay, pensions and perks, might be expected to know the relevant law backwards. Which to him obviously excluded irrelevant, irritating inconveniences like the Human Rights Act, about which the obligations on him and his compatriots were crystal clear. Instead of abiding by it, if his actions are anything to go by, it might just as well not have existed. Trying to argue that he acted as he did because he had no alternative by virtue of other principal legislation is fanciful. S.33[5] of the Employment Tribunals Act of 1996 says no such thing, and so far as I can see neither do the EAT Rules and Practice Directions [mere administrative tools] - which in any case are not "primary legislation". Nowhere in the relevant legislation under which he was empowered to act is the slightest suggestion that he had to do what he did or indeed that his actions were fair or reasonable in the context of the relevant primary legislation. So by doing it anyway he was acting ultra vires, presumably because English judges think and act as if they can do what they want. Isn't that one of the main reasons human and civil rights were created, and became enshrined in international and domestic laws? To curb and control rogue-elephant judges who should never have been appointed in the first place, regard their so-called "independence" as a ticket to make up the law as they go along, throw their weight around and intimidate and threaten victims of their junk justice?

Nor is the individual in question the only one to blame. Other people knew what was going on, stood by, enjoyed the show, spread the dirt and did nothing to stop it. For over 10 years. Who might they be? For a start, how about other EAT members and employees, not to mention a few hundred lawyers inside various Ministries, including those appointing members of the EAT? Weren't they all obliged to consider the relevance of the HRA from the outset and every moment since? Yet none of them, along with politicians, lifted a finger or raised a protest, for over a decade.

Their failure to act , which obviously includes failure to remove the offensive internet passages, is equally unlawful under Section 6[5] of the HRA. Compare that to vote-winning, politically-motivated initiatives by the sad and lonely Alan Johnson.

Then there was and is the small matter of a bunch of laymen making quasi-judicial decisions and dishing out insults dressed up as legal judgments which – along with lists of miscreants - were subsequently posted on the internet. Who do these prats think they are, just because they've acquired this power thanks to the likes of Mr. Gormless, Alan Johnson, himself an academic duffer who achieved his rightful level of accomplishment by delivering junk mail? As for the worthies who rejected my appeal, since when were Mummery and Keene independent and impartial? Given whence they came their mate Underhill might also have just been going through the motions. [For a more detailed account of this charade see my book *Moral Beaks and Claws*]. After dealing with that crowd and others of similar disposition somehow I suspected that, given the chance, the Thai judiciary would have interpreted the Thai Constitution, and especially its Sections 40[2] and 81, vis-a-vis the events which occurred at the hands of the U.K. Employment Tribunals, Employment Appeal Tribunal and Court of Appeal in a somewhat different fashion. But just try suing that lot and the trial judge [25] who couldn't see fraud if it were a Californian Redwood standing lone and forlorn in the Ghobi desert. Hence yet more lies and libels on the internet, of which the following are a few choice samples.

- From the LexisWeb webpage, under the heading "Wheen v Smithmann European Homes and another [2000] All ER [D] 836, on 15 July 2010 I downloaded an extract which, in part, stated : "Principal discovering agent's deception prior to paying commission". Another internet entry regarding the same case asserted it was a "small claim". Whoever says either statement is true is either a liar or doesn't know the facts or both

- In an e-mail sent by him to the Information Commissioner Graham Noyce of the U.K. Government's Department for Business, Innovation and Skills said about me "I assume time wasting of this kind is not unusual. Do you keep a list of vexatious litigants?" Not only does this constitute a threat it happens to be another lie, since the time-wasting occurred elsewhere, as it did in other cases about which I complained to the ICO

- As mentioned earlier, in another case where I sought official information from the Ministry of Justice Roger Davies of that Department told me on 24 November 2010 "In your particular case, the Admin [meaning Administrative] Court Judgment was never transcribed and the judgment was not paced [which I assume should read placed] on Bailii [who {which should surely say "which"} the Court of Appeal uses as their service provider for the purpose of publishing judgments online}. [My brackets] Since this was gobbledygook to me I asked Davies to explain what he was on about, which he refused to do, as did his bosses, who referred me to the old reliable, the ICO, who predictably did nothing before I pulled the plug, following the issue of his Decision Notice whitewashing the actions of the U.K. Attorney General. You might think, as I did at the time, that if all this was yet another bureaucratic blunder it could and would have gone away. But no. This is the U.K. Government, where lies and deception are endemic. Unless, of course, the above—mentioned events actually took place behind my back and I happened to be asleep at the time. Not all that unusual in the Hole.

Nor, on the face of it, were the hands of Essex University unsoiled, at least under Thai law. Not just for privacy breaches but, like other Universities, for providing reasons for denying me enrolment which looked increasingly dubious. Essex University's website, where the smear had turned up yet again in an unexpected place and form linking us had tried to fob me off with empty, unconvincing reassurances. How did its explanations square with those supplied by the IT boffin I had consulted and in Judge Eady's judgment [incorporating the testimony of other experts] in the Google case? Had Essex University and others conspired in a cover-up, contrary to Section 432 of the Civil Code?   Whatever they said what had happened was evidence of the adverse knock-on effects of the internet smears, recognized in S.423 of the Civil Code. So, like it or not, the Universities of Essex, James Cook and New South Wales – along with other potential candidates - were still very much in the loop.

Nor, may I emphasise, am I on about one internet smear in the same location. How many viewers have enjoyed the fun and gossip from the various entries about me – and are still at it? Thanks to the vindictive hounding of the EAT and Court of Appeal the breaches of my rights continue to this day and will never be erased. [For some enlightening insights into defamation in general, see 18]. When the offences are on-going the time limit for bringing proceedings about them only starts when the offences stop [19]. Meanwhile, collectively their actions also breach Articles 10, 11 and 17 of the HRA.

Theoretically if and when the victim had proved his or her case – fat chance before a U.K. judge out to look after his own mates and rotten system, exemplified by Judge Underhill, who is typical of the breed - UK and European laws might have provided the following relief::-

As a first step, a declaration of incompatibility under Section 4 of the HRA

an injunction banning further publication of the offending material

damages and any other effective remedy to be decided by the Court

In the latter respect, Article 13 of the Convention entitles me to an "effective remedy", which despite the customary watering-down by vested interests in my case should include an award of substantial damages, since the breaches of my rights are numerous, long-standing and have had serious, irreversible consequences. Regarding an award of damages as a "last resort" – apparently the expedient policy and practice of U.K. judges – is, in my case, not only inappropriate it would simply encourage more human rights abuses. The extent of the damages should reflect the gravity of the offence, its effects and the underlying motive and purpose. [For more on the subject, see 20-22].

Making me appear to be nut-case [which disappointingly for the dirty dirt-mongers I am not, especially compared to them] is but one effect. Others include stopping me getting work and enrolling for a PhD. Does the punishment fit the crime, even if no crime was committed? Yet the same Government which enacted the Rehabilitation of Offenders Act – giving convicted criminals the rights to privacy once their convictions are spent and to sue for libel for breaching their privacy right – has encouraged unlawful judicial breaches of others' human rights for political advantage. In England, better to be a burglar, fraudster, bugger and mugger than a critic and opponent of "New Labour" policies and practices. Which is another reason why the prospect of submitting myself and any claims to the mercy of a U.K. beak is about as advisable as shooting Niagara Falls in a wicker-basket. Better do nothing than that. But doing nothing was not the answer either – not yet, at least.

I consulted the internet and a bevy of lawyers, most of whom [as elsewhere] seemed to be devoid of knowledge but not so of greed. After more fruitless effort I had two brainwaves. The first was to stop chasing around and do what I always try to do – find out for myself. Which led me back to the precious internet, where I downloaded an English translation of the Thai Constitution. From that and other internet material it was pretty clear not only that both I and my Thai partner could sue the UK Government in a Thai Court but which breaches of the Constitution had occurred. But more research was needed. One lawyer I'd visited showed me an entry in a fat book called the Thai Code. At the time I made a mental note and left it at that, because the risky and expensive route of instructing an avaricious Thai lawyer seemed the only unpleasant and unpalatable option. Back to the internet, where I spotted a blog about the Thai

Codes, in plural. One was named the Penal Code [for criminal offences], the other the Civil and Commercial Code, whose purpose was self-evident. Even better, some of these publications were produced in Thai and [on the facing page] English. If only I could get hold of these publications. Here again, the Gods were smiling on me. A Thai University not more than an hour's drive away stocked both and another publication about Court procedures. Away we drove, and back we came with the precious goods. More study and research, until I had a good idea what was possible. But only possible in theory. I badly needed legal help, which didn't come cheap even in Thailand. Meanwhile I summarized what appeared to be the relevant sections of Thai law as I saw them.

References hereunder to "Penal Code" and to "Civil Code" mean The Criminal Code and The Civil and Commercial Code of Thailand respectively. It is important to remember that the originals of these Codes are naturally written in Thai, that exact equivalents of Thai words and/or expressions may not exist in the English language [and vice-versa] and although my copies of the Thai Codes are written in both tongues by highly qualified translators they are not infallible, so occasional errors are inevitable. Nevertheless, given the sources of the manuals I have the utmost confidence in their overall reliability and accuracy [23].   Below are some of the most relevant extracts from or references to the Thai Codes and Constitution.

"The law <u>must</u> be applied <u>in all cases</u> which come within the letter or the spirit of <u>any</u> of its provisions – S.4 Civil Code [my underlinings].

Every person must, in the exercise of his right and in the performance of his obligations, act in good faith – S.5 Civil Code.   Every person is presumed to be acting in good faith – S.6 Civil Code.

Victims are <u>entitled</u> to "appropriate legal assistance from State" in <u>civil</u> actions – S.40[8] Constitution

Under the Thai Constitution victims have the right to sue whoever commits an offence in Thailand

<u>Time Limits</u>

Thai Constitution – none specified

Penal Code – 3 months allowed [from the date of the victim becoming aware of [a] the date of the offence and [b] the identity of the offender] to complain re compoundable offences   – S.96.   Regarding the internet, the offence has been continuous.

10 years to file a claim – S. 95

Civil – Ss 400 and 423 refer. 1 year or 10 years [if any criminal offences also occurred] – S.448. Re S.448, any claim for damages from a wrongful act must be made within 1 year from the day when the wrongful act and person bound to make compensation became known to the injured person [or <u>10 years</u> from when the wrongful act was committed]. So which applies? Clarification – if a criminal act is involved the longer prescriptive period applies – S.448.

Regardless of other factors pointing to the same conclusion, if, as in my case, the offence is a continuous, unbroken one it can be argued that it's a single offence enduring until it stops. Until then the time limit doesn't even start running.

<u>Offences</u>

By virtue of S.35 of the Thai Constitution <u>violations of or affecting one's privacy, family rights , dignity and reputation</u> - which closely resembles defamation - disseminated to "the public" by statement, picture or "in any manner whatsoever" are unlawful unless doing so is beneficial to the public. Unlike defamation, truth is immaterial. Publishing anything [true or false] which breaches one's privacy and/or has the effect of damaging one's family rights, dignity and reputation is unlawful unless the publisher can prove doing so benefits the public – meaning, at the very least, the Thai public.

Regardless of defamation damages are claimable for loss of income arising from any breaches of S.35 of the

Constitution, which in addition to privacy includes family rights, dignity and reputation, all of which include the right to further one's education and to work so as to pay family bills, and were lost through the effects of unlawful acts on the internet. So though desirable proving defamation is not essential.

Just how significant these rights are can be gauged from other provisions in the Constitution, including Sections 4, 6, 27 and 29.

S.4 – "The human dignity, right, liberty and equality of the people shall be protected".

S.6 – "The Constitution is the supreme law of State. The provisions of any law, rule or regulation, which are contrary to or inconsistent with this Constitution, shall be unenforceable".

S.27 – "Rights and liberties recognised by this Constitution explicitly, by implication or by decisions of the Constitutional Court shall be protected and directly binding on the National Assembly, the Council of Ministers, the Courts, the Constitutional organizations and all State organs in enacting, applying and interpreting laws".

S.29 – "The restriction of such rights and liberties as recognized by the Constitution shall not be imposed on a person except by virtue of the law specifically enacted for the purpose determined by the Constitution and only to the extent of necessity and provided that it shall not affect the essential substances of such rights and liberties". [I have omitted paragraphs 2 and 3 of this Section in the belief that they do not affect my argument, which is that if, as appears to be the case, the Constitutional rights such as that to privacy are absolute ones how can they be restricted by subordinate laws contained in the Codes? At face value they can't be, at least so far those I have in mind are concerned. In particular, how can it be argued that time limits - called "Prescription" in the Codes - apply equally to the Constitution? If they don't, why bother with defamation suits and their attendant problems and restrictions, when damage to one's reputation – which is all defamation is – is actionable under the Constitution? Whereupon the onus is on the alleged offender to prove he or she acted in a manner "beneficial to the public", which I would have thought would not be easy to achieve in many, if not most, cases. Beyond that, causing "damage" to another's reputation isn't the legal criterion. Violating or affecting a person's reputation is what matters, which opens up another can of worms and scurrying for legal textbooks.

As might be expected, apart from the Thai Constitution the Civil Code is where other answers are to be found. With the notable exception of civil defamation [S.423 refers] Section 420 was the crucial starting point, by defining "wrongful acts" in the following terms:-

"A person who, willfully or negligently, unlawfully injures the life, body, health, liberty, property or *any right* of another person, is said to commit a wrongful act and be bound to make compensation therefor" [my italics]. ["Any right must include those enshrined in the Constitution]. But on whom does the onus to prove the existence or absence of "willfully or negligently" lie? Probably in S.422 Civil Code, which says "If damage results from an infringement of a statutory provision intended for the protection of others, the person who so infringes is presumed to be in the fault". So in each and every instance the onus seems to be on the offender to prove his innocence. Where S.35 of the Constitution is concerned, the only defence available is apparently public benefit, which must be proved by the defendant. In turn this surely means that under the Thai Constitution [the Supreme law] even if the statement is true publishing it is unlawful unless doing so [in my case for over 10 years] can be proved by the U.K. Government to be beneficial to the public. If it fails under the Constitution damages are payable for loss of dignity and reputation etc and for privacy breaches. More damages can be claimed under S.420 of the Civil Code, where the defendant would have to prove it had not "willfully or negligently" committed the wrongful act.

Although what these terms mean is pretty obvious I had to turn to the Penal Code to find some legal definitions. In S.59 an alternative version of willfully, namely "intentionally" is adopted. "To commit an act intentionally is to do an act consciously and at the same time the doer desired or could have foreseen the effect of such doing", while committing an act "by negligence is to commit an offence unintentionally but without exercising such care as might be expected from a person under such condition and circumstances, and the doer could exercise such care but did not do so sufficiently." Here again this seemed an insuperable task for the U.K. Government given the evidence to the contrary. On top of that, the final paragraph of S.59 of the Penal Code says "An act shall also include any consequence brought about by the omission to do an act which must be done in order to prevent such consequence". Which might well implicate all those who knew about or should have known about the internet insertions, and chose to condone or approve them [as had Lindsay and Underhill] or turn a blind eye. Did this amount to a criminal conspiracy involving the upper echelons of The English judicial and political Establishment? If so more trouble loomed, in the shape of Sections 83 to 89 of the Penal Code. And if, as seemed certain, more than one offender was involved, according to S.432 of the Civil Code "If several persons by a joint wrongful act cause damage to another person, they are jointly bound to make compensation for the damage. The same applies if, among several joint doers of an act, the one who caused the damage cannot be ascertained. Persons who instigate or assist in a wrongful act are deemed to be joint actors. As between themselves the persons jointly bound to make compensation are liable in equal shares, unless under the circumstances, the Court otherwise decides."

<u>Defamation</u>

Under the respective Codes what is "true" and "fact" only arise in defamation suits, and then on different bases, although a defence against criminal defamation can be used in civil cases also. Somewhat peculiarly, a special criminal offence whereby "Any person insulting the other person in his presence or by publication, shall be imprisoned not over one month or fined not over one thousand Baht, or both" exists by virtue of S.393 Penal Code.

As elsewhere, in Thailand two distinct forms of defamation – usually known as libel or slander – exist. So too does criminal libel, probably reflecting the gravity Thais attach to dissemination of personalized, wounding affronts and insults, with their attendant potential loss of face. Depending on the circumstances, one, two or all three can be used in litigation.

Criminal defamation is defined in Section 326 of the Penal Code as follows:-

"Whoever falsely accuses the other person before a third person in a manner likely to impair the reputation of such other person or to expose such other person to be hated or scorned, is said to commit defamation, and shall be punished with imprisonment not exceeding one year or fined not exceeding twenty thousand Baht, or both". [When the defamation is committed via publication.....by broadcasting.........or by propagation with any other means the maximum penalties increase to two years imprisonment and a fine of two hundred thousand Baht respectively, per Section 328].

Statutory defences are available in Sections 329 and 330. In the former, all of them depend on the defendant having acted in good faith, which he or she must prove. Many people, myself included, might think that sticking smears on the worldwide internet for over a decade was acting in bad, rather than good, faith. That apart, none of the individual circumstances listed in Section 329 seemed to apply to my case. Which left Section 330, which states the following:-

"In case of defamation, if the person prosecuted for defamation can prove that the imputation made by him is true, he shall not be punished. But he shall not be allowed to prove if such imputation concerns personal matters and such proof will not be benefit [sic] to the public". So again it is clear where the legal onus of proof lies – on the defendant. And he or she must prove all three requirements – the imputation was "true", which is far from easy to prove in many circumstances, the more so in mine. If, and only if, that obstacle can be overcome can the defendant move to stages 2 and 3. Proving one and not the other means failure. In my case I intended to put the U.K. Government to the test on all three counts.

Simple to answer on the face of it, what does "true" actually mean? One man's truth is another's fabrication or invention. Or in my case what's been proved in a U.K. set-up under U.K. law counts for nought in Thailand, where not only are foreign judgments not recognized there is no such thing as a "vexatious litigant". In other words, in the U.K. it may be "true" but in Thailand it's a fiction invented by foreigners. The concept also happens to offend the word and spirit of Thai law and its Constitution. So how the U.K. could argue, let alone prove, any one of the three requirements, never mind all three, in a Thai Court would be a Herculean task. So the customary dirty tricks, covers-up and attempts to divert attention and blame – some of which had already been put into practice – could be expected.

And so to civil defamation and the Civil Code, Section 423 of which says the following:-

"A person who, contrary to the truth, asserts or circulates as a fact that which is injurious to the reputation or the credit of another or his earnings or prosperity in any other manner, shall compensate the other for any damage arising therefrom, even if he does not know of its untruth, provided he ought to know it.

A person who makes a communication, the untruth of which is unknown to him, does not thereby render himself liable to make compensation, if he or the receiver of the communication has a rightful interest in it".

Notice the dual references to the "truth" and "fact", which seem to me to be different animals, although neither would be exactly easy to prove. Unlike the truth a fact can be defined as an indisputable, scientifically proven and Universally accepted state. Anything less doesn't qualify as "fact". It may be the "truth" and a "fact" that a particular Thai is a foreigner when he or she is in England, but the opposite applies when they are in Thailand. So it may be the "truth" and "fact" that in the eyes of U.K. lawyers I'm a vexatious litigant, but woe betide anyone who says that what applies there is equally the case elsewhere. So it is neither the "truth" nor "fact" that in Thailand and other countries I can be smeared in that way with impunity, any more than branding someone a criminal in the country where he lives, when he has committed no criminal offence under the laws of that country, is not just idiotic folly it's giving the finger to those laws. Which more or less summarises the arrogant and supercilious attitude of U.K. judges, basking in the delights and enjoying the good-life of Tuscany. And, it goes without saying, looking down on the natives, just as they have for centuries in The Dump whence they came [For an interesting discourse on criminal and civil defamation law in Thailand, see 24].

Even more fascinating would be the prospect of the U.K. Government, with its veritable army of lawyers at its command, pleading ignorance of the law. No, none of them, from the Attorney-General downwards knew the first thing about Thai or any other foreign laws, nor could be expected to find out. Better still, none of them had any inkling about U.K. law on the subject either, and unlike millions of British readers of "Private Eye" and English tabloid newspapers even the legal illiterates among them had never heard of the somewhat notorious libel-king, Judge David Eady or read his and related judgments about the potential dangers of publishing abroad, where laws may be very different to those in Blighty. Come off it. Who doesn't know that by now?

Belatedly, thanks again to the oft-invaluable internet I came across another Thai law governing internet activities. Among other criminal acts the Computer Crimes Act 2007 was enacted to tackle unlawful hacking, interception, viral infection and posting of obscene and offensive material on the internet, for which severe penalties can arise, although its relevance to my circumstances was unclear, at least to me. In any case, by the time it came to my notice I'd already set the wheels in motion.

Sometime and somehow came my second brainwave, which was staring me in the face. In the Thai Constitution I had the right to file a petition, which Thais often submitted in their thousands to The King. I mulled it over, and thought doing so would get me nowhere, especially as The King was ailing and in no condition to do other than delegate the job elsewhere, where it would probably founder. But what about the Attorney-General's office? That was definitely worth a shot, especially as the Constitution guaranteed one the right to State assistance and advice – in what form and type are unstated. So I prepared and my Thai partner and I submitted our initial petition to the Thai Attorney-General, followed shortly afterwards by a second and amplified one specifying which offences had, in our view, occurred, and asking the Attorney-General to take action against the U.K. Government in a Thai Court. Despite my firm intention to leave it at that until I got a decision or it became obvious little or nothing was being done events brought on by others conspired against me, precipitating another approach and complaint to the Thai Attorney General. Copies of our two petitions dated 22 November 2010 and 16 December 2010 respectively and of my letter of 23 January 2011 are reproduced below.

PETITION AND REQUEST TO THE ATTORNEY GENERAL OF THAILAND,

MR. CHUI SING SING YSANE

Sir, please forgive us if we have inadvertently failed to address you correctly.

I, Geoffrey Arnold Wheen, am a 70 year-old retired dual citizen of the United Kingdom and New Zealand who has frequented Thailand since 2000 and is now living with my Thai partner Amporn Suwannara [I.D. card number 3 3014 00069 56 6].

We are respectfully addressing you and seeking your assistance by virtue of Section 28 of the Thai Constitution, which states, inter alia, "A person shall have the right to be enhanced, supported and assisted by the State in exercising of right under this Chapter". Undoubtedly regardless of any rights bestowed on other people this "right" applies to Amporn Suwannara as her birthright. Moreover, the use of the expression "A person" – as opposed to other qualifying criteria such as a "citizen" – which can apply to virtually anybody, implies that Geoffrey Arnold Wheen is no less protected by Thai laws and its Constitution. We are proceeding on that basis, but if we are wrong in that belief our arguments and requests still apply with regard to Amporn.

In our cause we also cite the numerous duties and responsibilities of your goodself, extracted from the internet, which include helping the general public, protection of rights and interests of the people, legal assistance, legal knowledge to the public, contact and coordination with foreign entities, involvement in criminal and civil actions, suing a judge, pursuing offenses punishable under Thai law, and protecting the interests of the State and the rights and freedoms of the people.

Our problem concerns on-going derisive entries on the internet [instigated by a judge of the UK Government at or about April 2000, no less than ten and a half years ago], where they have remained ever since.   Although they have apparently been accessible to a global audience of many billions throughout that time their existence only came to our notice earlier this year, thanks to a tip-off from a well-wisher. There is no possible justification for such conduct by a judge, Government or anybody else for a day, let alone repeatedly and incessantly round the world for approaching 4,000 days.   Dishing out this calculated and cynical humiliation to a Thai woman who at no stage was involved in these events and to our family is even more inexcusable, deplorable, scandalous and callous.

In choosing this course of action the UK Government has breached various rights in the Thai Constitution, including Section 35, Article 17 of the International Covenant on Civil and Political Rights and Section 423 of the Thai Civil and Commercial Code, and quite possibly committed criminal defamation. The internet entries cannot possibly exist to serve the interests of the Thai people, so cannot be "substantially justified" under

Thai law. They were inserted and left there in order to cause the maximum harm and damage.

That being so among other relief we are entitled to damages, including punitive and exemplary ones, for these serious, longstanding and repeated breaches of our legal rights and for cruel and unusual punishment [which we have assessed modestly at present at the equivalent of 2,900 baht per day for 2 people over a period of 10.5 years], about which the evasive UK Government has disregarded our complaints and has no legal defence regarding Amporn Suwannara and our family. Nor are we the only ones to suffer this fate. We submit, therefore, that the UK Government should be brought to account before a Court in Thailand, where we have made our home and the internet entries – which still vilify Geoffrey Wheen as a vexatious litigant – can be challenged for their veracity, propriety and proportionality under Thai law. To that end we seek and crave the invaluable assistance of your goodself, as the protector and upholder of Thailand's Constitution and laws and the rights of its people.

This petition has been drafted in English by Geoffrey Arnold Wheen. Should you require a Thai translation for your convenience and timely consideration we will be pleased to so arrange.

Thank you.

Most respectfully yours,

Signed and Dated

....

SECOND AND FINAL PETITION AND REQUEST TO THE ATTORNEY GENERAL OF THAILAND,

MR. CHUI SING SING YSANE

Sir, please forgive us if we have inadvertently failed to address you correctly.

2. We are respectfully submitting this second and final petition and seeking your assistance by virtue of Sections 28 and 59 of the Thai Constitution.

3. In amplification of our first petition concerning this matter, which was faxed to your goodself on 22 November 2010, this second petition is also filed by Geoffrey Arnold Wheen [hereinafter called "Wheen"] and Amporn Suwannara [hereinafter called "Amporn"] and concerns the actions of the Government of the United Kingdom, including its employees [hereinafter called "GUK"].

4. Wheen, who is divorced, retired and enjoys dual British and New Zealand citizenship, has

frequented Thailand since the year 2000 and now lives there with his partner Amporn, who was born in Thailand and is a Thai citizen [ID Card Number 3 3014 00069 56 6]. As such both are entitled to the rights and protections afforded in the Constitution and other laws of Thailand.

5.   Among the immediate members of their families are three children, brothers, half-brothers and parents.   Their wider family extends to approximately twenty individuals.

6. Unbeknownst to them in or about April 2000 GUK posted on the global internet derogatory information concerning Wheen. It has remained there ever since. Neither Wheen nor Amporn was aware of its presence until comparatively recently, and then only after Wheen had been put in the picture by a third party.

7.   According to information supplied by the Ministry of Justice of GUK the internet entries were authorized and approved in or about April 2000 by Judge Lindsay, the then President of the Employment Appeal Tribunal of GUK, who along with two other lay members of the same body issued documents denigrating, belittling and defaming Wheen.

8. These internet entries, which appear in several locations, not only describe Wheen as a vexatious litigant [which in the eyes of many if not most people is tantamount to declaring that the recipient of this calculated smear is an idiot if not insane, and is invariably used insultingly and pejoratively] they include orders and judgments issued by the Employment Appeal Tribunal [EAT] and the Court of Appeal of GUK, which can readily be downloaded for further distribution, purportedly supporting the allegation. The wording of these entries also creates a misleading impression of what had taken place in 2000.

9. Regardless of what preceded the decision to do so it was never incumbent on GUK to post anything on the internet, and indeed Wheen and Amporn contend that doing so breached the relevant laws of the United Kingdom, Europe, Thailand and internationally.

10. Of the alternatives available GUK chose the internet in order to cause Wheen and his friends, family and colleagues the maximum damage and humiliation, knowing full well of the massive impact and readership on the internet. It is no exaggeration to say that over a period exceeding a decade billions of internet users will have either

seen or had access to the offending entries, to do with, pass on and laugh about as they saw fit. Nor is the tactic by any means isolated, as Wheen and Amporn will prove. Collectively the incidents amount to a politically-motivated vendetta against Wheen, contravening his civil and human rights.

11. When GUK was confronted with the abuses of such rights its employees displayed more arrogant indifference, disregard and disrespect. For instance on separate occasions Wheen has complained to GUK's Attorney-General [in whose name the proceedings were initiated and the internet entries appear], its Minister of Justice and Cabinet Office, all of whom did nothing. Indeed, the Attorney-General's office attempted to dupe Wheen into believing the GUK bore no responsibility for its actions.

12. Despite his knowing full well that the proceedings against Wheen were instigated by GUK's Attorney-General, that the internet entries appear under his name and that the "others" to which he referred [see under] are or include paid employees of the Government of which he is the chief law officer when Wheen served on the Attorney-General of GUK a Notice of intention to commence legal proceedings in Thailand his office

replied dismissively as follows — "The Attorney General is not responsible for material published on the internet by others. Therefore I am afraid to say that this office is unable to assist you in this matter".

13.   Other employees of GUK went even further. When on 18 October 2010 Wheen filed a formal complaint with its Office of Judicial Complaints [an arm of the Ministry of Justice] specifying wrongdoing by Judge Lindsay and his successors, the EAT and Court of Appeal he was told the matter had been referred to Mr. Justice Underhill, the current President of the EAT, whose response was, inter alia "I am bound to say that the complaint seems to me to be wholly misconceived since it involves no question of judicial conduct; nor in any event can I see how there can be a legitimate objection to a judgment delivered publicly being publicly available on the website." Meanwhile when on 19 October 2010 Wheen complained again about the way in which his complaint had been handled his protest was ignored.

14.   Setting aside the other factors involved [such as the length of time involved, which Judge Underhill swept under the carpet] and individuals

adversely affected such is the conclusion of an individual who, like his predecessors, not least Judge Lindsay, decides that those who make worthless claims in their eyes are by definition vexatious and deserve to be castigated globally and indefinitely on the internet. In a nutshell, based on the above and other sources GUK's attitude, if not defence, seems to be that it can do what it likes, regardless of the damage, humiliation and havoc it causes not just to its target but to innocent members of his family. It knew all along that similar treatment has led to the disintegration of family units.

15. Along with his peers Judge Underhill further contends that internet entries are mere dissemination of public knowledge, so anybody who does not share his views and attitudes must be further condemned. Thus for having the audacity to criticize those responsible [which Judge Underhill says in no way resembles judicial misconduct] Wheen must be admonished merely for raising the issue.

16. That the smears only became public, worldwide knowledge was and is solely down to the fact that GUK chose to act as it did for 10.5

years and running. There is absolutely no logical or legal justification or sense for its actions.

17.   Apart from their being derogatory, spiteful, malicious, emotionally destructive and unlawful on several counts GUK could not fail to know what harmful economic effects its actions would inevitably produce.   Not only would Wheen's career prospects be severely curtailed should he wish to come out of retirement he has evidence that the internet entries were responsible in part or whole for sabotaging the realistic likelihood of his obtaining a doctorate degree in various countries.

18. In one case Wheen had to quit the doctorate course in which he had enrolled due to the bizarre and inexplicable conduct of his principal supervisor, who he was told would be replaced, but wasn't.

19.   In late 2010 Wheen tried to enroll for a doctorate with another University.   To his astonishment and dismay the heading on its internet webpage comprised yet more of the same derogatory references to Wheen.   Although the University has denied responsibility it has never explained satisfactorily how it and Wheen [a mere applicant for enrolment] came to be linked together on its website.

20.   Of those with the motive and resources to intercept Wheen's communications and acquire such knowledge GUK seems by far the most likely transgressor.   This belief is supported by more evidence of wrongdoing and obfuscation, as demonstrated in the next paragraph.

21.   On 19 September 2010 Wheen utilized the UK Freedom of Information Act to seek official information from GUK's Minister of Justice and its Attorney General.   One of his requests was for "the amount of money expended by the UK Government on intercepting, recording and hacking into communications to and from myself [Wheen] and the legal authority for doing so".   The answer from the Attorney-General's office not only contained blatantly erroneous statements and veiled threats it flatly refused to answer Wheen's request.

22.   After Wheen complained to GUK's Information Commissioner out of the blue the Attorney General then stood on his head, and after saying Wheen's request was covered by the Freedom of Information Act answered it by stating that he could neither confirm nor deny that his office holds the information.   Contrarily, the Information Commissioner continues to say the opposite, by

insisting that the Act in question does not apply to Wheen's request.

23.   The upshot is yet more confusion and unanswered questions. Why doesn't the Attorney-General of all people know the law? If Wheen's communications were not being intercepted no expenditure would have occurred, so surely the answer would be "nil", not we refuse to answer one way or the other. And if it has been going on [which would include to and from Thailand] why, and under what legal authority?

24. Since none of the above bodies, nor any others contacted by Wheen have produced satisfactory explanations for their actions, which are relevant to these complaints, perhaps they should also be required to explain themselves in a Thai Court.

25.   GUK was fully aware these incidents were occurring, and conspired with others to conceal them. Various individuals in its employ could and should have put a stop to these internet entries. Instead they deliberately chose to leave them in place, and now attempt to justify their actions after the damage has been done to the victims and their families.

26. More than anyone else, despite her being in no way responsible or involved in the events which occurred in the year 2000 Amporn has had to put up with the abuse of her rights at the hands of GUK, which knew from the outset other individuals would suffer, yet didn't care.

27. Hundreds of other victims have suffered loss and damage through the unlawful use and abuse of the internet by GUK, which we respectfully submit should be reflected in any relief granted.

Claim

By virtue of the Constitution, laws and Codes of Thailand and international law Wheen and Amporn claim relief and damages [including punitive and exemplary damages] for the wrongful and joint wrongful acts to which they have been subjected, including the excessive, continuous and longstanding breaches of their rights to privacy, losses of human dignity, reputations and family rights, abuse of their civil and human rights, civil and criminal defamation, loss of earnings and opportunity to earn financial rewards, and use of cruel and inhumane means.

In addition to other relief and award of substantial damages Wheen and Amporn also request that

GUK be ordered to take whatever steps are necessary and appropriate for the rehabilitation of the reputations of Wheen and Amporn.

Having submitted two petitions regarding this matter we will trouble you no further unless you request us to supply further information.

This petition has been drafted in English by Geoffrey Arnold Wheen. Should you require a Thai translation for your convenience and timely consideration we will be pleased to so arrange.

Thank you.

Most respectfully yours,

Signed and Dated

....

23 January 2011

Dear Attorney General

Reference Numbers 27319 and 29190

I write pursuant to the two Petitions dated 22 November 2010 and 16 December 2010, which were signed by myself and my partner, Amporn Suwannara, and faxed to your goodself on the aforementioned days respectively. I now put on record and complain about the following turn of events, which also pertain to the aforesaid Petitions.

Recently I have received from the U.K. Information Commissioner a Decision Notice purporting, inter alia, to summarize an exchange of correspondence between myself and the Office of the U.K. Attorney-General, about which paragraphs 20-23 of the Petition dated 16 December 2010 refer. Prior to his issuing this document the Information Commissioner tried to sweep statements made by the U.K. Attorney-General under the carpet on a pretext [see paragraphs 22 and 23 of the Petition dated 16 December 2010], then – after I had protested – completely distorted them and the relevant chain of events in his subsequent Decision Notice. In brief, the facts are as follows:-

On 19 September 2010 among other information I requested the following from the U..K. Attorney General and Minister of Justice : "the amount of money expended by the UK Government on intercepting, recording and hacking into communications to and from myself and the legal authority for doing so". To that request, on behalf of the Attorney General, James Ross replied by return as follows : "You are making a very serious allegation of criminal activity being perpetrated against your being. If you have evidence of such activity taking place, then you will need to inform your local police authority for investigation". Despite my categorically telling him he was wrong Ross repeated his ridiculous and defamatory statements on 21 September

2010, wherein he averred firstly that my request fell outside the Freedom of Information Act, and "you are making very serious allegations that your communications are being hacked into, this is a criminal offense and should be reported to the correct body, in this instance your local police authority".

When I requested an internal review of his decision and comments [which is invariably conducted by another, more senior member of the same Government Department] which was addressed to his immediate boss, Peter Fish [a lawyer] per advertised procedures - Ross himself told me on 22 September 2010 a review was "not possible" and repeated the libel by stating "You are claiming that a criminal offence is or has taken place against your person, as you know this would be a matter for the police to investigate, and I have informed you of such" Since my request was addressed to Fish it can be assumed he too was aware of what was going on and thus subscribed to the three defamatory statements made by his subordinate Ross. Moreover, even if the Attorney General himself, Dominic Grieve, was deliberately kept in the dark and knew nothing – which I very much doubt – he and the U.K. Government carry the ultimate responsibility.

One need only ask one question about these libels. Were they written in the knowledge, or ignorance, of the U.K. law authorizing such interceptions, which was later trotted out by the Attorney General to justify his refusals to answer my question? If, as the evidence clearly suggests, Ross did not know what he was talking about until the penny finally dropped or he was told what the law permitting interceptions actually said [which I knew all along] taken as a whole his answers are nevertheless erroneous, inconsistent, contradictory, threatening and defamatory. Coming from the Department in whose name the vexatious litigant proceedings were brought against me and insertions about them still appear on the internet over a decade later makes me and others wonder what its advice about the Iraq war was worth. The chain of events also supports the view that in September 2010 the warrant referred to below did not exist, and if it does so today was issued subsequently in order to further intimidate and threaten myself and my family and in retaliation for our having filed the Petitions in question.

On 23 September 2010 I had complained to the U.K. Information Commissioner. By a strange coincidence and at an almost identical moment in time on 26 November 2010 I received two e-mails. One from the Information Commissioner closing his file, the other from James Ross, who without being asked or prompted by me changed his tack, referred me to the relevant Act [see below] and refused to supply any information under the Freedom of Information legislation. He has since done the same under the Data Protection Act, thanks to the urging of the supposedly "independent" Information Commissioner, who just happens to work for their joint employer, the U.K. Government. As does MI5 [see later].

Consequently I have advised the Information Commissioner that in my view the contents of his Decision Notice are both inaccurate and defamatory, and if he pursues his intention to publish it or an amended version on the internet he will face the consequences. But don't take my word about this latest turn of events. The only objective way to determine whether or not the Attorney-General and Information Commissioner have colluded to whitewash what was said and done and to fabricate an official record of those events is to subject them to a fair and independent trial and/or to publish them all on the internet, whereupon any reader can be the judge.

Not only is this the latest attempt by the U.K. Government to shift blame from itself onto the shoulders of its victims, by reading between the lines the message conveyed to any objective and independent reader of this Decision Notice is a legitimate warrant has been issued against me under the UK Regulation of Investigatory Powers Act 2000, legally authorizing interception of my communications. From that two more issues arise. Even if that is true [about which I have grave doubts, given past events and information] such a warrant may still have been issued recently, in retaliation against my having filed the two Petitions, about which, regardless of having acquired such knowledge from your Office or not, it will be aware from its own interception of my faxes and other communications. Before I go any further, lest you are in any doubt about the volume of, and sinister motives underlying such activity please do not imagine that interception of communications does not, and cannot, occur without a warrant, even by Governments whose purported purpose is to uphold and enforce the law and protect citizens against unlawful snooping. On the contrary, U.K. internet sources have reported that widespread, systematic interceptions of communications occur legally and illegally, with or without warrants, in that country. The latest scurrilous and scandalous example, which is unfolding daily, is enveloping the "News of the World" weekly newspaper, which has a readership of multi-millions.

Next, even if it exists, how can such a warrant, issued under U.K. law, possibly apply in Thailand without the consent of the Thai authorities, about which, so far as I am aware, there is absolutely no evidence? So if any U.K. warrant has no relevance or legal validity in Thailand intercepting my communications, including between ourselves, should be stopped immediately, if necessary via an injunction, and the perpetrators prosecuted in a Thai Court. Thirdly, on what grounds can the issue of such a warrant be justified and authorized? None whatever, so far as I am concerned. Yet the ICO and other U.K. Government documents refer to the need for "secrecy" about potential "crimes". Presumably committed by me, under the

Regulation of Investigatory Powers Act 2000, which is widely and commonly associated with actual and potential terrorist activities.

Whatever else the U.K. Government is trying to achieve by its underhanded, if not unlawful, smear tactics — standard practice in its case, especially when it has a case to answer involving blameless victims like my partner and family who, like me, they are trying to threaten, hound and intimidate because we have had the audacity to challenge their abuse of our legal and human rights for over a decade — I am not going to be branded a terrorist, terrorist suspect, potential criminal or anything else just because the U.K. Government chooses to exercise its powers to abuse the rights of individuals for no good or lawful reason. In my book merely implying in a document [or other means] which has been transmitted to me and seen by others in Thailand [never mind hackers] via the internet that a warrant is in force which has been issued under the above-mentioned Act is so serious and offensive a calumny that its very existence, purpose, justification and why it was issued in the first place and by whom must be proved in a Thai Court, especially as it is grossly defamatory and appears to be blatant, criminal retaliation. Even if — which would be par for the course — the U.K. Government and Attorney-General try to wriggle out of it they should be required to explain and justify statements they have made to my detriment, of which their recent combined whitewash is the latest example. Considering that their jurisdiction ends in the U.K. – whence I happily departed for good long ago - if they have a scrap of evidence implicating me in terrorist or any other criminal activities in Thailand, the U.K. or anywhere else they can produce it and prove it. In other words, "put up or shut up".

For the record and complaint purposes, apart from the ICO document two other breaches of my privacy rights have recently occurred at the hands of U.K. Government employees, while others have transmitted libelous comments about me, again via the internet. And after eliciting an application fee, personal details regarding my passport, address etc. and bank account [superficially for identification purposes] MI5, the U.K. Security Service, told me it had posted a letter to me on 6 December, which has never arrived. Could that be another fraudulent lie, especially as requests for a copy of its supposed letter to be e-mailed to me have been systematically ignored by it and other U.K. Government bodies?

With respect, I submit there is more than enough, and increasing, evidence and justification to bring legal proceedings against the U.K. Government in Thailand, about which I am conscious of the time limits [prescription] involved. On 28 December 2010 my partner spoke to Jenny of your Office, and was advised a decision might be forthcoming within the next month, i.e. by the end of this month. That being so my partner and I would appreciate your decisions regarding this and our Petitions [one of which - reference number 27739 - concerns my house in Isaan] at the earliest opportunity.

Meanwhile unless it is legal in Thailand I request that any and all interceptions of my and my family's communications be stopped forthwith, if necessary via an Injunction and Court proceedings. Here again, if the U.K. Government has any defence it can produce it in open Court before a judge, where I can put my case about this latest sordid episode.

Thank you.

Most respectfully yours,

Signed

....

APPENDIX ONE

Internet Entry dated 22 January 2011

fraud
actions. Because if you look at the consumer **fraud** statutes, they require in ...
www.manhattan-institute.org/html/mics9b.htm - 84k - รูปภาพ

Hornby Bike Lane Consultation--A PROVEN Sham--Vision Vancouver Cir ...
Oct 6, 2010 ... So, once again, let me show you why **Geoff** Meggs is the biggest liar on city
..... **Wheel** in on your Raleigh, or if not, by trolley, ... I'll be sure to
block the bike lane every time I leave my Hornby St residence just ... to
continue to point our **FRAUD** of his ways and that of YOUR movement ...
alexgfapktanik.com/2010/10/06/hornby-bike-lane-consultation-a-proven-sham-vision-vancouver-cir-geoff-meggs-lies-again/ - 262k - หน้าที่อยู่ในแคช

The Mudflats | The Lies of Sarah Palin: A Mudflats Exclusive ...
May 17, 2010 ... I'll take any bets. I gotta pay for my kids' college educations. ..... She's the
hamster , they are the **wheel** They need each other to function. ..... Even
hearing her latest iterations of the telling expose her lying fraud ways. ...
Thanks for the interview AKM & **Geoff**! I pre-ordered the book ...
www.themudflats.net/2010/05/17/the-lies-of-sarah-palin-a-mudflats-exclusive-interview-with-geoffrey-dunn/ - 888k - หน้าที่อยู่ในแคช

PlayTV Canada is a **Scam** « Mike Battista's Blog
Nov 2, 2009 ... I got a call from Play TV Canada today saying I'll be getting my cheque in the
..., when you called in they actually had the sound of a casino **wheel** ,.. hey
GEOFF ...that puzzle question was on today dec.12/09 at 1:00 am ...
mikebattista.com/2009/11/02/playtv-canada-is-a-scam/ - 482k - หน้าที่อยู่ในแคช

VEXATIOUS LITIGANT - ATTORNEY GENERAL v **WHEEN** (COURT OF APPEAL)
GEOFFREY ARNOLD **WHEEN** Respondent/Appellant. ....
.... and the
court accepted that Mr Barker had been seriously ill at the time, ... where it
was said that the judgment was vitiated by the **fraud** of other parties, ...
www.vexatiouslitigant.org/vex_lit_at_gen_wheen_appeal_c.html - 32k - หน้าที่อยู่ในแคช

หน้าแสดงผล   ก่อนหน้า   1 2 3 4 5 6 7 8 9 10 11 12   ถัดไป

geoffrey wheen is a fraud

FOOTNOTES

<u>Note</u> : references to "Downloaded" mean from the internet

<u>Introduction</u>

1 – More than three million migrants under Labour by Tom Whitehead, Home Affairs Editor, The Telegraph. Dated and downloaded on 22 February 2011

2 – What Australian Universities Don't Want You to Know – archsoc.com. Downloaded on 16 October 2010

<u>Chapter One</u>

1 – "Plausible Denial" by Mark Lane. First published by Thunder's Mouth Press, U.S.A. in 1991

2 – "Behind Closed Doors" by Laurence Rees. First published by B.B.C. Books in 2008

3 – "Rush to Judgment" by Mark Lane. Published by Thunder's Mouth Press, U.S.A. in 1992

4 – Judicial accountability and independence, Judiciary of England and Wales. Downloaded on 3 January 2011 [as were footnotes 5 to 9 below]

5 – The justice system and the constitution

6 – Independence

7 – Judicial appointments

8 – The principles of judicial accountability

9 – Judicial conduct

10 – The Judicial Branch of Arizona, Maricopa County, Superior Court, Self-Service Center, Glossary. Downloaded on 11 August 2010

11 – Peter Goldsmith, Baron Goldsmith – Wikipedia. Downloaded on 7 October 2010

12 – Obituary regarding Lord Bingham of Cornhill – Telegraph. Downloaded on 3 October 2010

13 – U.K. Attorney General's memorandum to Prime Minister dated 30 July 2002. Published on internet

14 – U.K. Attorney General's draft advice regarding Iraq War handed to Prime Minister on 14 January 2003, ibid

15 – Lord Goldsmith's Advice on March 7, 2003 – skyNEWSHD. Downloaded on 7 October 2010 [as were footnoted 16 to 19 below]

16 – Full text : Iraq legal advice – guardian.co.uk.

17 – John Kampfner. The law chief who bowed to Blair – first appeared in the New Statesman

18 – The Attorney General's advice on the Iraq war – The Independent

19 – How Goldsmith changed advice on legality of war

20 - Goldsmith admits to changing view over Iraq advice by BBC News. Downloaded on 19 October 2010

21 – How we were duped over Iraq – www.safecom.org, ibid

22 – Extract from memorandum of Bush/Blair meeting on 5-7 April 2002

23 – Jeremy Bamber – Wikipedia. Downloaded 2 February 2011

24 – Lockerbie : The Flight from Justice by Paul Foot. A Special Report from "Private Eye"

25 – A. J. P. Taylor – Wikipedia. Downloaded 15 February 2011

26 – Judiciary of England and Wales. Downloaded on 3 January 2011

Chapter Two

1 – A History of vexatious litigant statutes in the UK – www.martinfrost.ws. Downloaded 6 December 2010

2 – Sir Robert Mark – Telegraph. Downloaded 3 October 2010

3 – Human Rights – U.K. Treasury Solicitor, July 2010

Chapter Three

1 – Metropolitan International Schools Limited [t/a Skillstrain and/or Train2Game] and [1] Designtechica Corporation [t/a Digital Trends] [2] Google UK Limited [3] Google Inc. [2009] EWHC 1765 [QB]

2 – Sweet verdict for tourists – Private Eye magazine Edition number 1271

3 – Crispin Blunt leaves wife as he 'comes to terms with being gay' – The Telegraph. Downloaded on 18 December 2010

4 – Tilleke and Gibbins article. FAQs : Dispute Resolution/Litigation. Downloaded 30 December 2010

5 – Rylands v Fletcher [1868] LR 3 hl 330 [HL]. LAWSTUDENTFORUM. Downloaded on 22 December 2010

6 – How can I access official information? – ico publication. Downloaded on 30 September 2010

7 – Interception of Communications – Security Service MI5 publication. Downloaded on 25 September 2010

8 – Why am I such a threat to national security? by Peter Hitchens, Mail on Sunday. Downloaded on 26 September 2010

9 – Police set to step up hacking of home PCs by David Leppard, The Sunday Times, January 4 2009. Downloaded on 2 January 2011

10 – Regulation of Investigatory Powers Act 2000 – guardian.co.uk. Downloaded on 16 January 2011

11 – Reputation law : differences between the English and US approach in libel and privacy by Jenny Afia and Jon Oakley, Schillings, 16 October 2009. Downloaded on 17 October 2010

Chapter Four

1 – Privacy and Human Rights : An International Survey of Privacy Laws and Practice by Privacy International. Downloaded on 22 December 2010

2 – Privacy by Wikipedia, the free encyclopedia. Downloaded on 22 December 2010

3 – 200 people suspect they have been hacked by Tom Moseley and Oliver Wright, The Independent 10 December 2010. Downloaded on 10 December 2010

4 – MI5 by Wikipedia. Downloaded on 2 January 2011

5 – Privacy rights and protection : foreign values in modern Thai context by Ethics and Information Technology 1 March 2005. Downloaded on 22 December 2010

6 – Universal Declaration of Human Rights by United Nations Department of Public Information, NY. Downloaded on 30 September 2010

7 – International Covenant on Civil and Political Rights by Wikipedia. Downloaded on 12 January 2011

8 – Your Rights : The Liberty Guide to Human Rights. Article 8 – the right to respect for private and family life, home and correspondence. Downloaded on 30 September 2010

9 – A Guide to the Human Rights Act 1998

10 – Data Protection Act 1998 by Wikipedia. Downloaded on 16 September 2010

11 – Security phone tappers still get numbers wrong by Richard Norton-Taylor, The Guardian 24 July 2004, ibid

12 – How to stitch up a terror suspect by Nick Cohen, The Observer 12 January 2003. Downloaded on 26 September 2010

13 – Bugging, burgling agents may now bribe too by David Leigh, The Guardian 2 June 2003, ibid

14 – MI5 Bugged families of soldiers at death base, Sunday Express 26 January 2003. Downloaded on 26 September 2010

15 – Rehabilitation of Offenders Act 1974 by Wikipedia. Downloaded on 7 October 2010

16 – Article 8 ECHR by anon

17 – Article 8 : Right to respect for private and family life by Environmental Law Centre, UK. Downloaded on 19 October 2010

18 – Defamation by Wikipedia. Downloaded on 22 December 2010

19 – Exclusions : Fraud upon the court, ibid

20 – Damages Under The Human Rights Act 1998, Report Law Com No 266 / Scot Law Com 180

21 – Damages Under The Human Rights Act by Richard Clayton QC 1 December 2003

22 – Is There any Money in it? Public Law Damages by David Hart May 2005. Downloaded on 17 October 2010

23 – The Criminal Code Update [No.23] B.E.2551

The Civil and Commercial Code Update [No.19] B.E.2551

Authored by numerous professional Thai lawyers. Translated by Asst. Professor Dr. Preecha Kanetnog, Department of Foreign Languages, MCU 2008. Published by Soutpaisallaw Press

24 – Defamation and Thai law by Tilleke and Gibbins, Bangkok. Bangkok Press article - TeakDoor.com. Also Criminal defamation of character : the Thai regime. Downloaded on 30 October 2010

25 – How to Sue a Judge by David C. Grossack. Included in article Pro Se Chicago's Weblog 6 December 2008, Linda Shelton. Downloaded on 17 October 2010

26 – Sex offenders to get right of appeal against lifetime registration by the Press Association and guardian.co.uk. Downloaded on 16 February 2011